Development of Buddhist Ethics

Development of Buddhist Ethics

G.S.P. Misra

Munshiram Manoharlal
Publishers Pvt. Ltd.

Published and printed by Munshiram Manoharlal Publishers Pvt. Ltd.,
Post Box 5715, 54 Rani Jhansi Road, New Delhi-110055.

यतो वाचो निवर्तन्ते
Where Words Fail

Contents

Preface viii

Abbreviations xi

CHAPTER I
Early Historical and Doctrinal Background 1

CHAPTER II
The Buddhist Doctrine of Karman and the Concept of Action 31

CHAPTER III
Psychological Analysis and Moral Life 54

CHAPTER IV
Ethical Ideals 70

CHAPTER V
Compassion and Perfection 118

CHAPTER VI
Beyond Good and Evil 142

Appendix 155

Bibliography 171

Index 181

Preface

'Religion is a doing and doing what is moral'. In Buddhism, there is such a great emphasis on moral doing that it is very often designated as an 'ethical religion' (*śīlaparaka dharma*). As an institutionalized religion, Buddhism derives from the vision of Buddha, the historical Śākya-muni. This vision was at once mystical in content and rational in its expression. Starting from the spiritual realization of suffering as a universal phenomenon, Buddha, out of his great compassion (*mahā-karuṇā*), was moved to teach the Way which would lead others to the eradication of suffering (*duḥkha-nirodha-gāminī-pratipadā*). The Way symbolizes a spiritual journey on the part of the seeker who has to undertake it in gradual courses, constantly aspiring for higher perfection and exerting for it, till wisdom (*Prajñā*) dawns on him and the goal is achieved. In a way, thus, Buddhist ethics stands for the means of perfection which Buddha taught to the suffering humanity.

Belonging primarily to the *Śramaṇic* genre, Buddhism is ascetic in its general tenor. However, with the institutionalization of the spiritual vision of Buddha and the transformation of his teachings in a popular faith, Buddhism was bound to become very comprehensive in its scope, showing concern not only for the monks and nuns who had abandoned the worldly society to form a separate spiritual communion but also the lay people who found it hard to sever their social bonds but cherished faith in the teachings of Buddha and aspired to lead a life which conformed to the general ideals of conduct prescribed by him. Buddhist ethics, thus, should be studied as representing a total scheme of culture in which form it has greatly influenced the social life and thought of the people in the various lands of its adoption. In the Indian context, no one can miss its vital contribution in the shaping of the general cultural orientation, finding its expression in the diverse activities and institutions of the people.

Buddhist ethics marks a definite variance from the earlier Vedic *Weltanshauung* and sought to introduce a number of new elements in the ethical thought and formulations which existed prior to its advent. The activistic and optimistic outlook of the Vedic Aryans missed, generally, the *Duḥkha* aspect of the *Śramaṇic Weltanshauung* which constitutes the starting point of Buddhism. As such, the morality of heart is generally found missing in them and there is not so much emphasis in their ethical framework on such moral virtues as peacefulness (*śānti*) and compassion (*karuṇā*) as in Buddhism ; on the other hand, they have great appreciation for such virtues as strength, liberality, friendliness, truth, sincerity and cooperativeness which served a positive purpose in the making of a good and happy social life. In the Vedic thought, moral law is conceived as natural law. There is glory of the moral law but the glory of the moral person or the definite image of an ideal person is generally missing. Buddhist ethics puts forth moral idealism as a dominant kind of idealism. Contrasted with the earlier Vedie Brahmanical ethics, Buddhist ethics is more universal and more feminine.

Indian thought believes that any vision of Truth has both unchangeable and changeable elements in it—the fundamentals do not change but the peripheral and outer forms undergo change and are subject to new understanding and interpretations arising to meet the needs of changed times and circumstances. It is such a belief in *sādhana-bheda* and *yuga-bheda* that saved the various later and changed forms and expressions of the original teachings of Buddha from being labelled as distortions of the Master's vision and led to the postulation of three *dharma-cakra—parvartanas* by him.

The present work seeks to study Buddhist ethics as a developmental process not only in terms of inner dynamics inherent in its doctrinal and ethical formulations but also in terms of its response to various historical compulsions and the ensuing willingness on the part of its followers to introduce in its general framework novelties of forms and expressions. It is hoped that such an approach would lead to a greater appreciation of Buddhist ethics both as an emergent of a unique spiritual vision and a social force. The work is divided in six chapters which cover the entire range of Buddhistic development in India. As Buddhism does not rely on any conventional authority and tries to give to ethics a psychological basis it concerned itself in a very marked manner with a deep study of mind and its operations; the *Abhidhamma* books, particularly, manifest this activity as their major concern. Chapter III of the work is devoted to this aspect. An Appendix at the end is included to provide an understanding of the scientific and logical attitude and the methodology that is evidenced in the early Buddhist texts.

After the publication of my earlier work *The Age of Vinaya* (Messrs Munshiram Manoharlal, New Delhi) in 1972, I have been working on this theme in phases. The theme was suggested to me by my revered *guru* Prof. G.C. Pande. Always seeking inspiration from him, I am also indebted to Professor Pande for his kindness in going through the manuscript of the work and enriching it by his corrections and suggestions. With a profound sense of gratitude I also remember late Dr. I.B. Horner, ex-President, Pali Text Society, London, who took great interest in all my pursuit pertaining to Buddhistic studies and guided me from time to time through her scholarly letters. I take this opportunity to register my feelings of great appreciation and thankfulness to Miss Rekha Daswani, my student and colleague, who helped me in many ways in the final stage of the work. I am also thankful to Mrs. Pratibha Jain my friend and colleague, for the help she rendered me in the finalization of the manuscript. My thanks are also due to Mr. V.K. Ratnani for his painstaking and genuinely sincere job in preparing a neat and near flawless type-script.

The Appendix entitled 'Logical and Scientific Method in Early Buddhist Texts' was first published in the *JRAS*, 1968 ; I am thankful to Mr. E.V. Gibson, Secretary, Royal Asiatic Society, London for his kind permission to use the same in the present work. I am also thankful to the authorities of the Indian Council of Historical Research for financial help in the form of a travel-and-contingency grant. I am thankful to Mr. Devendra Jain of Messrs Munshiram Manoharlal Publishers, for his ready response to publish this work and his helpful cooperation towards its early publication.

Department of History G.S.P. Misra
& Indian Culture,
University of Rajasthan,
Jaipur
20 April 1984

Abbreviations

ABORI	:	Annals of the Bhandarkar Oriental Research Institute
Ait. Br.	:	Aitareya Brāhmaṇa
Aṣṭ. Pr.	:	Aṣṭasāhasrikā-Prajñāpāramitā
AV	:	Atharvaveda
Bbhū.	:	Bodhisattvabhūmi
BDVI	:	Bauddha Dharma ke Vikāsa kā Itihāsa by Govind Chandra Pande
Bodhic.	:	Bodhicaryāvatāra
Bodhisattva Doctrine	:	The Bodhisattva Doctrine in Buddhist Sanskrit Literature by Har Dayal
Bṛ. Up.	:	Bṛhadāraṇyaka Upaniṣad
BST.	:	Buddhist Sanskrit Texts
Ch. Up.	:	Chāndogya Upaniṣad
Cv.	:	Cullavagga
Dial.	:	Dialogues of the Buddha
DN	:	Dīgha Nikāya
EBM	:	Early Buddhist Monachism by S. Dutt
EMB	:	Early Monastic Buddhism by N. Dutt
ERE	:	Encyclopaedia of Religion and Ethics ed. James Hastings
Gradual Sayings	:	The Book of the Gradual Sayings
JAOS	:	Journal of the American Oriental Society
JBRS	:	Journal of the Bihar Research Society
JRAS	:	Journal of the Royal Asiatic Society
Kindred Saying	:	The Book of the Kindred Sayings
Middle Length Sayings	:	The Book of the Middle Length Sayings
MN	:	Majjhima Nikāya
MSL	:	Mahāyāna-Sūtrālaṅkāra
MV	:	Mahāvagga

Mvy.	:	Mahāvyutpatti
Pāc.	:	Pācittiya
Pār.	:	Pārājika
Ṛ V.	:	Ṛgveda
Sad. Puṇḍ.	:	Saddharma-Puṇḍarīka
Śat. Br.	:	Śatapatha Brāhmaṇa
Śat. Pr.	:	Śatasāhasrikā-Prajñāpāramitā
SBB.	:	Sacred Books of the Buddhists
SBE.	:	Sacred Books of the East
Śikṣā.	:	Śikṣāsamuccaya
SN	:	Saṁyutta Nikāya
Studies	:	Studies in the Origins of Buddhism by Govind Chandra Pande
Taitt. Br.	:	Taittirīya Brāhmaṇa
Taitt. Up.	:	Taittirīya Upaniṣad
Up.	:	Upaniṣad

CHAPTER 1

Early Historical and Doctrinal Background

In its classical form, Indian culture affirms a philosophy of life which purports to realise a happy fusion of activism (*pravṛtti*) and quietism (*nivṛtti*). These two tendencies have a basis in two distinctive systems of metaphysics which approach and view human existence from different angles. While the one takes this world as the best of the worlds that could be conceived and, therefore, considers worldly objects of pleasure to be properly pursued and enjoyed, the other is so much struck by pain and suffering invariably associated with worldly existence that it feels compelled to consider withdrawal from the world and worldly objects as the only way of relief. In the former, diverse social institutions, observance of customs and social norms are naturally relevant in so far as they serve as means to make this world a better place to live and to make life happy and comfortable; in the latter, on the contrary, all these become, essentially, factors which bind man to suffering and a final release from which is possible only through an understanding of their transitory nature and the cultivation of a feeling of quietude. From the former would derive the notion of social obligations which all the members of society would be called upon to fulfil; the latter, impelled by its deep-rooted dissatisfaction with the world, would give birth to a tendency of other-worldliness and a sort of pessimism. It is not that one attitude prevails to a complete exclusion of the other, but a disproportionate dominance of one over the other is possible in an individual or society.[1]

The mature genius of the Indian mind sought to provide its people with a meaning-system in which both these attitudes could be assimilated and accorded a proper place in the life of an individual or

[1]In a specific context—that of quest for Truth—the two attitudes have received a sound philosophical treatment in Govind Chandra Pande, *Mūlya Mīmāṁsā*, pp. 245-48.

society. The maintenance of proper balance was considered essential for a happy growth and development of the two. It has been exemplified in the *Gītā* which, in order to strike such a balance, seeks to redefine action and renunciation. True renunciation is not complete withdrawal from the world and worldly actions, but is action done without selfish motives or any attachment with its result, and with perfect equanimity of mind.[1] Such a notion of action and renunciation is already anticipated in the very first verse of the *Īśa Upaniṣad*[2] from which the *Gītā* has probably taken the cue. The inclusion of *Saṁnyāsa*—though it is the last—in the conceptual scheme of human life[3] is another instance of how a blending of action and renunciation was sought by the Indian mind in the life of an individual. The underlying philosophy behind the *Āśrama* scheme was the realisation that after a person has lived in the world as an active member of the society, fulfilling his manifold obligations to his family and society at large and undergoing all the experience of pain and pleasure involved in the worldly living, he must be prepared to retire, to withdraw from the worldly objects, leaving place for others, which would also provide him an opportunity for self-perfection and for the attainment of the final goal of life, viz., salvation (*Mokṣa*).

The Śramaṇa Tradition

Such an undertaking was embarked upon by the Indian mind in the

[1]See *Gītā*, 3.19: *Tasmādasaktaḥ satataṁ kāryaṁ karma samāchara; Asakto hyācaran karma paramāpnoti pūruṣaḥ.*

ibid., 18. 9: *Kāryamityeva yatkarma niyataṁ kriyate' rjuna, Saṅgaṁ tyaktvā phalaṁ caiva sa tyāgaḥ sāttviko mataḥ.*

[2]*Īśāvāsyamidaṁ sarvaṁ yatkiñci jagatyāṁ jagat, Tena tyaktena bhuñjīthāḥ mā gṛdhaḥ kasyasviddhanam.*

[3]That the fourth *Āśrama* of *saṁnyāsa* was originally alien to the Aryan Brāhmaṇical society and was assimilated in it as an institution much later is attested by the fact that in the beginning the Brāhmaṇical attitude was hostile to it. See S. Dutt, *EBM*, pp. 46-52; G.C Pande, *Studies*, pp. 322-26. Kane, *History of the Dharmaśāstras*, II, pt. I, p. 418 has pointed out that "The word does not occur in the *Saṁhitās* or *Brāhmaṇas*". It is to be further noted that in the *Dharmasūtras* the nomenclature and the order of mention of the four *Āśramas* have not yet been settled. *Āpastamba* (II.9.21:1) mentions them as *Gārhasthyam, Ācāryakulam, Maunam* and *Vānaprasthyam, Gautam* (I.3.2.) as *Brahmacārī, Gṛhastha, Bhikṣu* and *Vaikhānasa*, and *Vasiṣṭha* (VII. 1-2) as *Brahmacārī, Gṛhastha, Vānaprastha* and *Parivrājaka*. This irregularity shows the unsettled form of the *Āśrama* institution. See G.S.P. Misra, *The Age of Vinaya*, p. 107.

background of its specific experiences in historical times. The early Buddhist and Jain canonical texts do not only champion the idea of withdrawal and renunciation but present it as a concrete reality which fascinated the people and impelled them to cut off their worldly ties and lead the life of homeless anchorites.[1] The general social and religious milieu of the sixth century BC appears to have been characterized by an abundance of such religious seekers who were peripatetics and strove after salvation through renunciation of the world. They are generally called *bhikṣhu* (Pāli *bhikkhu*) or *Śramaṇa* (Pāli *samaṇa*), the latter term probably denoting those among them who were considered spiritually more advanced.[2] In the Buddhist and Jain texts, the appelation *Śramaṇa* is used for Buddha and Mahāvīra; apart from them, many more religious teachers are mentioned in them who, like these two, had renounced the world, founded their own distinctive sects and exercised leadership over a band of disciples. The ascetic upsurge characterizes the religious movement of this period which may be designated as *Śramaṇa* movement in view of the ideology which prevailed as the dominating phenomenon. Though divided among themselves in matters of views, code of conduct, etc., the *Śramaṇas* agreed on certain fundamentals which were in striking contrast with the Vedic Brahmanical beliefs. They denounced the worldly society as a place of bondage. Contrary to the Brahmanical belief, which considered the *Vedas* as repository of eternal truths and so the supreme authority in all matters, they rejected the Vedic authority: they did not believe in any God or gods who had created this world, and accorded no sanctity to the social framework as conceived and theorized by the Brahmanical thinkers. The compound *Śramaṇa-Brāhmaṇa*, frequently juxtaposed together in the Buddhist and Jaina texts and also in the edicts of Aśoka, thus, points to two sets of thought—currents which prevailed in the society. From the

[1]For detail about general ascetic activity and the various ascetic sects of the time see Misra, *The Age of Vinaya*, Ch. II.

[2]It is obviously such a distinction between the Śramaṇa and other ascetics that is indicated when the 'Kassapasīhanāda-sutta' in the *Dīgha Nikāya* (*SBB*, Series I, p. 232), putting forth the higher ideal of religious life, says: "From that time, O Kassapa, is that the Bhikkhu is called Samaṇa, a Brāhmaṇa". Similarly, in the 'Mahāparinibbāna-sutta', *DN* (Nal. ed.), II, pp. 116-17 Buddha says that there is no Samaṇa in a Dhamma wherein the 'Noble Eightfold Path' does not exist. See S. Dutt, *op. cit.*, pp. 31-32.

references, it is evident that both these ideologies had strong roots in the society and the laymen had a general feeling of reverence for both. In matters of beliefs and practices, however, their opposition to each other was quite conspicuous, a fact attested by a later reference found in the *Mahābhāṣya* of Patañjali where the eternal opposition between them is likened to the one as exists between a serpent and a mongoose.

The *Śramaṇa* ideology, thus, had a distinctive character. It is also proven fact that its appearance in the times of Buddha and Mahāvīra was not the result of any sudden explosion of an ideology; it had rather a long historical tradition and assumed dominance at that period when a number of historical factors converged to create a favourable situation. It is probably not without reason that Buddha said that he was not teaching something new but an old religion (*porāṇa dhamma*). The Jaina tradition, which speaks of twentythree teachers (*Tīrthaṅkaras*) prior to Mahāvīra, is confirmed by the researches of Jacobi who established beyond doubt the historicity of the twenty-third *Tīrthaṅkara, Pārśvanātha.*[1] Even the historicity of the first *Tīrthaṅkara*, Ṛṣabhadeva, has been argued for.[2] The *Keśī-Sūkta* of the *Ṛgveda-saṁhitā*, which has seven *mantras* in it, refers to a class of people called *Munis*; they are described having long hair, wearing coloured (*pītavasana*) or dirty (*mala*) garments, inspired by *Muni*-nature (*Mauneyena*) and flying in the air (*vātaraśanā*).[3] At another place in the *Ṛgveda*, the shaking of trees is likened to the 'shaking' (probably a result of ecstacy) of *Muni.*[4] Dwelling on these and many other references in the Vedic literature to the *Munis* and *Yatis*, scholars have suggested that they were the precursors of the ascetics and peripatetic wanderers mentioned in the Buddhist, Jaina as well as Brāhmaṇical texts.[5] The terms '*Muni*' and '*Yati*' definitely denote such people in later texts. In the Vedic literature, thus, the two terms appear to have been used for the wandering ascetics living beyond the pale of strictly Brahmanical tradition. In view of the uncertainty that prevails over the issue of the decipherment of the Indus Valley script, it is difficult to go beyond this, but the possibility of this

[1]See Jacobi's *Introduction to Jaina Sūtras*, II, pp. XI-XII.

[2]H.L. Jain, *Bhāratīya Saṁskriti Men Jaina Dharma Kā Yogadāna*, pp. 10-18.

[3]*ṚV.*, X. 136.

[4]ibid., VII. 56.8.

[5]Keith and Macdonell, *Vedic Index*, II, p. 164; Haran Chandra Chakladar, *Aryan Occupation of Eastern India*, p. 22; G.C. Pande, *Studies*, pp. 258-59.

tradition being as old as the Indus Valley civilization is very strong.[1]

It was not possible for these two ideologies to coexist as water-tight compartments. The mingling of the two started very early to give birth to a composite philosophical outlook which is so clearly evinced in the *Upaniṣads.* The Vedic Brahmanical tradition was eager to absorb and integrate in itself the ideas which-though originally alien to this tradition—had a dominant appeal to the people or appeared sound intellectually and rationally. The *Upaniṣads* contain discussions on a number of such problems and issues which do not appear to have stemmed from original Vedic tradition; they rather appear as adaptations, sometimes even hesitant and secondary in character. The scholars are inclined to take many *Upaniṣadic* ideas as such adaptations the origins of which would have to be traced to the non-Vedic and pre-Vedic thought-complea.[2] The idea of *Saṁsāra* and the theory of *Karman* and transmigration may be taken as such examples. Concluding his account of these doctrines in the *Upaniṣads,* Professor G.C. Pande writes: "It is thus impossible to see a linear and simple evolution from the Brahmanic views regarding afterlife to the theory of transmigration found at places in the *Upaniṣads.* We are left to the hypothesis of an influence ab extra, . . . The Brahmanas with their ideas of death as a rebirth, their fervent quest for immortality coupled with the incipient fear of dying again or suffering through hunger in a world won by sacrifice, and the hope of a timeless world beyond the sun had induced no doubt a certain receptivity in the Vedic mind for the doctrine of *Saṁsāra.* The sources of this doctrine must have been the *Munis* and *Śramaṇas* already alluded to, who harked back to pre-Vedic times."[3]

[1]See Marshall, *Mohenjodaro and Ancient Indus Civilization,* I, p. 49 and Chanda, *Memoirs of the Archaeological Survey of India,* no. 41, pp. 28-30 who take the Śramaṇa to be the descendent of the pre-Vedic *Yogī.* G.C. Pande, *op. cit.,* p, 285. Also, Kamata Prasad Jain, 'Mohenjodaro Antiquities and Jainism,' *The Proceedings of the Indian History Congress,* Bombay, 1947, pp. 115-16; the same author in *Jaina Antiquary,* 14, pp. 1-7. Cf. R.N. Dandekar, *Some Aspects of the History of Hinduism,* p. 27.

[2]See Pande, *Studies,* pp. 280 ff; his *Śramaṇa Tradition,* pp. 4 ff; also R.N. Dandekar, *op. cit.,* p. 77; La Vallée Pousson, *L'Inde jusquau 300 avant J.C.,* pp. 282 ff.

[3]*Studies,* p. 285.

The introduction of these new ideas in the thought-complex of the Vedic people was bound to bring about radical change in their general outlook toward life and worldly existence. The true nature of the world and worldly objects was being understood along different lines and human aspirations were, thus, to be redefined in the light of this new orientation. Coupled with these, the material changes in the social complex, too, accounted for alteration in the general philosophy of life as well as the ethical and moral considerations of the people. The emergence of medicancy and ultimately its synthesis with the traditional *Weltanschauung* represented a veritable revolution in the social and intellectual development of India.

The Vedic Background and Experiences

By the time Buddha founded his religious sect, the so-called Vedic phase of Indian civilization had reached its full circle. But, it had been a long journey ranging roughly over thousand years during which the diverse ideas and institutions had undergone many changes and developments. It is only against the background of the general social, religious and moral experience which had already accumulated to constitute a distinctive cultural ethos that the true significance of the emergence of Buddhism and its contribution to Indian cultural tradition in general and Indian ethics and moral outlook in particular can be seen in proper perspective. Buddhism, though it primarily belongs to the Śramaṇic genre, was the historical child of a tradition which had got its form as a result of a synthesis of two distinct life-views; in order to understand it, therefore, one has to consider this background. The *Upaniṣads*, for example, echo and anticipate many such metaphysical and ethical issues connected with general social situation, which Buddha, later, felt compelled to take up in a detailed and elaborate manner and come out with his own distinctive conclusions regarding them.

In a way, the Vedic age begins with a primitive simplicity. The Vedic Aryans, who first appear to be settled in the north-west of the country and only gradually advanced to the east and towards the south, belonged in the beginning to a society essentially pastoral but at the same time familiar with agriculture also. They lived in villages which lay scattered in the midst of thick forests. Later, they became predominantly agricultural and, by the end of the period, town life had begun to rise. In this later Vedic age, we hear of several cities such as Āsandīvat, Kāmpilya, Kauśāmbī and Kāśī. Crafts and industries had become quite extensive and diversified.[1] Trade and commerce too had developed considerably. We find mention of the *Śreṣṭhin* at several places, and it has been suggested that the development of the trade-guilds date back to this period.[2] Society and thought came to be much more complex than in the earlier period.

The change from the early Vedic age to the later Vedic age is clearly exemplified by a comparison between the geographical horizon found in the *Ṛgveda* and what we come across in the later Vedic literature. In the early Vedic age we hear of settlements on the banks of the river Kubhā, Suvāstu, Krumu and Gomatī in Afghanistan, and in the region watered by the Indus and its tributaries in the Punjab. In the east the Aryan settlements extended only as far as the Yamunā and the Gaṅgā. The chief centre of early Vedic civilization was the area between the rivers Sarasvatī and Dṛṣadvatī, the former river mentioned as the foremost among all rivers.[3] The considerable eastward and southward expansion of the Aryans by the later Vedic age is apparent from the fact that now we hear of such regions and peoples as Magadha, Aṅga and Āndhra. The chief centre of the Vedic civilization now appears to have shifted to the east in the Kuru-Pañcāla region.

Old Aryan society was tribal in character. Its highest unit of organization was called *Jana:* among them we hear of the Purus, the Anus, the Turvasas, the Bharatas, the Kurus, etc. At the head of the *Jana* stood the king who was assisted by the priest. Although kingship gradually became hereditary, it was, in its origins, popular and elective. It is possible that the institution of kingship was much more firmly established among the pre-Aryans and that the Vedic people were influenced by them in this as in many other respects.[4] King was the "protector of the people" (*gopā janasya*) and in wars

[1]For a very comprehensive list see *Vājasaneyī Saṁhitā*, Ch. 30; *Taitt. Br.* 3.4.

[2]Jogiraj Basu, *India of the Age of the Brāhmaṇas*, p. 73.

[3]It has been called '*nadītamā*' (*ṚV.* 2.41.16) and '*sindhumātā*' (ibid., 7.36.6). There is one full hymn of the *Ṛgveda* (6.61) in its praise.

[4]See *Ait.Br.*, 1.1.14 which relates how the gods were defeated by the demons and they, reflecting over the cause of their defeat, discovered it in the absence of leadership among them. This led the gods to elect a king who then led them to victory.

against the enemies provided leadership. At this time, very few officials are mentioned to aid him in administration and regular taxation had not appeared as yet. Gradually, the kings tended to be hereditary and the office of kingship became more stable and powerful. The early Vedic *Jana*-states were replaced in the later Vedic age by territorial states called *Janapadas*. By performing such sacrifices as the *Rājsūya* and *Aśvamedha*, the king obtained a divine and superhuman sanction for his office and power.[1] The establishment of trrritorial states gave birth to expansionist tendencies and the kings were now naturally impelled to increase their area of power by subjugating the weaker ones. The use of epithets like '*ekarāṭ*,' '*samrāṭ*' for the kings in the *Brāhmaṇas* clearly suggests that efforts in this direction were being made by some of them.[2]

In the early period, the rulers, along with their kinsmen, called *Kṣatriyas*, and the priests constituted special classes in the society and were distinguished from the mass of the people-the *Viś*, who met the economic needs of the society. Later, the mass of the people came to be divided into two broad classes, viz., the Vaiśyas and the Śūdras. The first reference to the four-fold division of the society into Brāhmaṇa, Kṣatriya, Vaiśya and Śūdra is found in the 'Puruṣa Sūkta' of the *Ṛgveda*[3] where the four classes are conceived as having originated from the four limbs of the divine Primordial Person. It is implied that society is like a person and its constituent classes like limbs performing different functions. From the *Ṛgvedic* references it is abundantly clear that in the early period the *Varṇas* were 'open classes' without any feeling of high or low attached to them. The *Varṇa* and occupation were as yet not homogeneous and we hear of different members of the same family pursuing different occupations or the sons developing expertise in occupation other than pursued by their fathers.[4]

This pristine character of the society, however, gave way to a more rigid social system in the later Vedic age. So far as the first

[1] *Śat. Br.*, 5.1.3.4; 5.1.4.2; 5.2.2.14; *Taitt. Sam.*, 1.8.16.

[2] The *Śat. Br.*, (5.2.1.13), for example, says that '*rājya*' is inferior and '*sāmrājya*' is superior and that a king obtains the position of '*samrāṭ*' by performing the Vājapeya sacrifice.

[3] *ṚV.*, 10.90.

[5] See N.K. Dutt, *The Origin and Growth of Caste in India*, pp. 64ff, 68ff. P.H. Prabhu, *Hindu Social Organization*, pp. 286-87· also S. Cromwell Crawford, *Hindu Ethical Ideas*, p. 23.

two classes are concerned, it was generally agreed that the Brāhmaṇas stand in a peculiar relationship to the kings. If the latter were the will of the executive power of the body-politic, the former represented its intellectual aspect. The Brāhmaṇas and the Kṣatriyas were considered complementary and coordinate. In the later Vedic literature the Brāhmaṇas and Kṣatriyas have an obvious precedence over the Vaiśyas. Though some passages in the later Vedic literature suggest that the comparative superiority of the Brāhmaṇas over the rulers or the vice versa was a matter of debate,[1] there does not appear to have taken place any serious struggle between the two for social supremacy. The Brāhmaṇas never claimed the right to exercise political authority; nor did the Kṣatriyas wish to become priests. In the sphere of higher or esoteric learning, however, a certain challenge to priestly ritualism is noticeable, and this challenge came from the Kṣatriyas as well as the Brāhmaṇas. The ultimate source of this challenge lay in the *Śramaṇas*, but some enlightened kings also appear as teachers of esoteric learning. The fact cannot be amplified as a general social conflict between the Brāhmaṇas and the Kṣatriyas.[2] It is noteworthy that if the priest Uddālaka Āruṇi and his son Śvetaketu learn from the king Pravāhaṇa Jaivali of Pañcāla,[3] the royal sage Janaka of Videha was equally eager to learn from the Brāhmaṇa and priest Yājñavalkya.[4] The Śūdras emerged as a distinct class and were ranked lower than the other three, viz., the Brāhmaṇas, the Kṣatriyas and the Vaiśyas. Many features of the later day rigid caste system came to be introduced in the social fabric which was to sap gradually the natural process of vitality in the society. Various rules were laid down to show the segregation of the four classes[5] and the Śūdras were deprived of some religious

[1]See *Vājasaneyī Saṁhitā*, 21.21, *Śat. Br.*, 1.2.3.3; 4.1.4.6;12.7.3.12 for the superiority of the Brahmaṇa, and *Kāṭhaka Soṁhitā*, 28.5 and *Ait. Br.*, 7.29.4 for the superiority of the king over the Brāhmaṇa.

[2]Some scholars see in the social religious movement of the sixth century BC, a class affiliation and Kṣatriya leadership against the Brāhmaṇas. Rhys Davids, *Buddhist India*, pp. 138-43; *Vedic Age*, pp. 468-69.

For the refutation of this contention See Misra, *The Age of Vinaya*, pp. 35-36.

[3]*Bṛ. Up.*, 6.2.1-3, *Ch. Up.*, 5.3.1-6.

[4]*Bṛ. Up.*, 3.1.

[5]*Śat. Br.*, 1.1.4.12; 13.8.3.11; 2.1.3.4; 5.3.2.11.

and social privileges which the others enjoyed.[1] There is, however, no ground to believe that the distinction between the twice-born and the Śūdras is based simply on a distinction between the Aryans and the non-Aryans.[2] Even if any racial distinction might have existed in the earlier period, it appears to have faded out completely by the later Vedic age. It is important to note that the *Bṛhadāraṇyaka Upaniṣad*[3] prescribes an orthodox Vedic magic for obtaining a son having a dark complexion and red eyes; it may be contrasted with the reference of Patañjali to the characteristic of a Brāhmaṇa as of fair complexion and with blonde hair.[4] It is, thus, clear that by the time the Śūdras emerge as a distinct class there did not exist any pure Aryan race. The lower status assigned to the Śūdras can, however, be explained by the fact that the majority of them were received from among the economically and culturally more primitive tribes which were perhaps largely pre-Aryan; economically depressed and culturally backward Aryans too were assigned the same status. The later day caste-system, in fact, cannot be explained as the result of any one single factor; tribe, occupation, skilled labour, inter-marriages, all contributed to it. The low status of the Śūdras, however, remains a patent fact in the later Vedic age.

From the point of view of their religion the early Vedic people may be designated as *devavādin* and *yajñavādin*. They believed in a number of divinities who had a close relationship with the cult of sacrifice through which the devotees could propitiate them and have an access to them. Gods are invisible powers, beneficent and luminous, indwelling the phenomena of nature and human life. Themselves superpersonal, they are capable of responding in a personal manner to suitable worship. Sacrifice was the main instrument of

[1] *Śat. Br.* 6.4.4.9; 3.1.1.10; *Pañcaviṁśa Br.*, 6.1.11. According to R.K. Mookerji, *Ancient Indian Education*, p. 53, the Śūdras too were eligible to study the Vedas; R.S. Sharma (*Śūdras in Ancient India*, pp. 67-68) believes that *Upanayana saṁskāra* was performed by the Śūdras also. Contra, Vijai Bahadur Rao, *Uttara-Vaidika Samāja evaṁ Saṁskriti*, p. 114.

[2] On the origin of the Śūdras see generally R.P. Chanda, *Indo-Aryan Races*; The History and Culture of the Indian People, I, *The Vedic Age*; R.S. Sharma, *Śūdras in Ancient India*; Vijai Bahadur Rao, *Uttara-Vaidika Samāja evaṁ Saṁskriti*.

[3] *Bṛ. Up.*, 6.4.16.

[4] *Mahābhāṣya* 2.2.6: *Gauraḥ śucyācāraḥ kapilaḥ piṅgalakeśa ityenānapyabhyantarān brāhmaṇya guṇān kurvanti.*

religious worship. It has been called the 'eulogy of the gods';[1] it makes them strong.[2] The Brāhmaṇas composed hymns to the gods and by officiating at the sacrifices acted as intermediaries between men and the gods. As the technicians of sacrifice the Brāhmaṇas naturally held the highest esteem in Vedic society. Besides, they were also the priests, prophets, theologians and pailosophers of the day, and gradually came to monopolize the profession of teaching. When, gradually, by the later Vedic age, the sacrifices became highly professional and the correct pronunciation of the prayers and the proper performance of the sacrifices came to over-emphasised,[3] as the specialists of the sacrifice the importance of the Brāhmaṇas naturally increased. In the *Brāhmaṇas* sacrifice becomes too much magical in character. It becomes a sort of machinery through which the sacrificer could get any desire fulfilled. Even this did not matter if the performing priest was an ill-reputed man, which implies that ethical consideration was assigned no importance in this respect.[4]

The early Vedic religion envisaged good life as a cooperation between men and gods. The gods are closely connected with the concept of *Ṛta*-an objective-norm which was the basis of all order, cosmic as well as moral. It is because of *Ṛta* that the rivers flow and the moon and stars follow their ordered course.[5] The gods are called the upholders of Law, and Varuṇa is the 'protector of Law' (*Ṛtasya gopā*) *par excellence*. *Ṛta* is closely associated with Truth (*satya*) and to say that the concept of *Ṛta* does not have 'any express ethical implication'[6] is not correct. In many verses of the *Ṛgveda*, *Ṛta* and *satya* occur together.[7] In the *Upaniṣad,* the association of *Ṛta* and *satya* is clearly stated; and Vidyāraṇya, the commentator of the *Ṛgveda*, has explained *Ṛta* as 'the mental perception and realisation of truth' (*mānasaṁ yathārthasaṁakalpanam*).[8] "The

[1]See K. Balasubrahmania Iyer, *Hindu Ideals*, p. 24.

[2]*Ṛv*. 1.181.1: *Ayaṁ vo yajño akṛta praśastiṁ.*

[3]ibid., 2.2.1: *Yajñena verdhata jātavedasaṁ*; 3.32.12: *Yajño hi na Indra vardhano'bhūta.*

[4]Any error might produce grave results. For committing such an error the priest Bhāllaveya fell down from the chariot and broke his arm, *Śat. Br.*, 1.7. 3.13; the priest Āsāḍhi Sausromateya even died, *Śat. Br.*, 6.2.1.37.

[5]See Crawford, op. cit., pp. 27-28. [6]*Ṛv*. I. 23.5.

[7]See Surma Dasgupta, *Development of Moral Philosophy in India*, p. 8.

[8]*Ṛv*. 9.113.2: *ṛtavākena satyena śradhayā tapasā sutaḥ*; 9.113.4: *ṛtaṁ vadan-nṛtadyumna svyam vadan satyakarman*; 10.85.1: *satyenottabhitā bhūmiḥ sūrye-ṇottabhitā dyauḥ, ṛtenādityāstiṣṭhanti divi somo adhiśritaḥ.*

human will must seek to follow this ultimate law which is discoverable from *Satya* or Truth."[1] There is an indissoluble connection between human and divine laws. 'Morality is an expression of divine law; sin is opposition to that law. The sinner is one who is out of harmony with the higher spiritual environment, which encompasses and controls the world.'[2] *Ṛta* stands both for Rite and Right.

The *mantras* of the *Ṛgveda* point to the Vedic Aryans as being an activistic and optimistic people who wanted to have all that was good and pleasant in life. But, such aspirations were to be in accordance with the law. Happiness is connected with virtue and, therefore, Vedic morality should not be interpreted as purely hedonistic or utilitarian in character.[3] A distinction was made between virtuous men and vicious men. Gods keep on eye on the deeds of men and nobody can escape from them;[4] they punish those who sin.[5]

The ethical framework of a people is in many ways conditioned and shaped by social conditions and environment.[6] The tribal and rural character of the early Vedic society tied the individual very closely to the community. Faced with the common problem of fighting against the enemies--both the indigenous people as well other Aryan *janas*--and clearing out forests for the acquisition of new land for agriculture, the early Aryans were bound to lay great stress on the unity of all. The general tenor of morality, therefore, was communal rather than individual in character. As A.C. Bose has observed, "we find a systematic attempt to build up *saṃ-hṛidaya* (or sahṛidaya), literally, con-cord, i.e., the union of hearts, and *saṃ-jñānaṃ*, unity through common understanding, at all social levels."[7] It is not to say that the individual sins were not recognised[8] but there is definitely a greater stress on collective morality.[9] Due

[1]G.C. Pande, *Śramaṇa Tradition*, p. 28.

[2]E.W. Hopkins, *Ethics of India*, p. 44.

[3]S.G. Sathaya, *Moral Choice and Early Hindu Thought*, p. 9.

[4]*Ṛv.*, 4.4.3; 6.67.5; 7.61.3; 7.87.3; 9.73.4. etc.

[5]*Av.*, 1.10. 1-4; 4.16.7; ibid., 1.25.3: *takman* or fever is spoken as the son of Varuṇa.

[6]See John Dewey and James H. Tufts, *Ethics*, pp. 379-80.

[7]A.C. Bose, *Hymns from the Vedas*, p. 14.

[8]*Ṛv.* 2.28.5; 2.29.1; 5.3.12; 7.86.3 etc.

[9]ibid., 1.179.5; 2.17.14; 4.3.5; 5.3.7 and 5.3.12. See S.N. Shukla, 'Concept of Morality in the Avesta and the Ṛgveda,' *Indian Antiquary* (Third Series), III, nos. 1-4, 1969 (Prof. R.N. Dandekar Felicitation Volume), pp. 139-40.

to a number of social, economic, political and intellectual factors, however, communal feeling gradually gave way to individualism and the tenor of morality too tended to be individualistic.

We have already discussed the peculiar position of the *Upaniṣads* which abundantly show the cross-currents of two originally different and contrasting philosophical and metaphysical attitudes. Their aim is to delve deep into the mystery of the cosmos and reach the ultimate truth which they ultimately found to be monistic in nature. The idea had its roots in the *Ṛgveda* itself[1] but in them it gets matured and consolidated. *Brahman* and *Ātman* are the words used for the ultimate Reality which is at once transcendental and immanent.[2] It is from this that all in the world is derived,[3] and one must make all efforts to know it.[4] However, knowing it means realising it, experiencing it directly; it amounts to complete universalization of one's ego transcending all selfish feelings. Reality is not discernible by logic or intellect, it is ineffable.[5]

But why, after all, is it so necessary to know the Reality? The answer to this question given in the *Upaniṣads* is a pointer to the change that had crept in regarding the general attitude towards life and the worldly objects. There is now a consciousness of the fleeting nature of existence[6] which is, therefore, of little worth.[7] The little is contrasted with *Bhūman* or the ultimate and the former is condemned because of its perishable nature.[8] A distinction is now made between the pleasurable (*preyas*) and the good that transcends the pleasurable and painful (*śreyas*),[9] implying a new spiritual concept. The aim of life is not to obtain pleasure here in this world

[1]To be seen in such expressions as '*tadekaṁ*' and '*ekaṁ sad viprāḥ bahudhā vadanti*,' etc. or in the concept of '*Puruṣa*'.

[2]*Kaṭha. Up*., 2.2.15; *Bṛ. Up*., 4.3.6; *Muṇḍaka Up*., 2.1.4 for its transcendental character; *Bṛ. Up*., 3-7; ibid., 2.5.15; *Śvetāśvatara Up*., 3.13 for its immanent character.

[3]See *Taitt. Up*., 2.1.5 which gives the theory of evolution from *Brahma* through its five sheaths (*kośas*).

[4]*Muṇḍaka Up*., 2.2.5: *tamevaikaṁ jānatha . . . anyā vaco vimuñcatha.*

[5]*Kaṭha. Up*., 1.2.9: *naiṣā tarkeṇa matirāpaneyā*; *Taitt. Up*., 2.9.1: *yato vāco nivartante aprāpya manasā saha.*

[6]*Kaṭha. Up*., 1.26: *śvobhāvā martyasya*; *sarvaṁ jīvitamalpaṁ eva.*

[7]*Ch. Up*. 7.24.1: *Yadalpaṁ tan martyam.*

[8]ibid.

[9]*Kaṭha.*, 2.2.

or in heaven but to become immortal. In the *Bṛhadāraṇyaka Upaniṣad*, Maitreyī says to her husband, Yājñavalkya, that she is not interested in anything which does not make her immortal (*yena ahaṁ na amṛtā syāṁ kim ahaṁ tena kuryām*).[1] The knowledge of *Brahman* is the source of immortality;[2] for this one has to leave the desires for the worldly pleasures and renounce them. "This attitude, however, is only partially and fitfully expressed in the *Upaniṣads*. It is Buddhism and later Advaita Vedānta that were to express it most eloquently."[3]

The Ethos of the Vedic Ethics

In the light of the above discussion, we can now make an attempt to summarise the Vedic view of morality and the salient points of its ethical framework. In the *Vedas* there are two directions of moral ideas : (i) Ritualism (*karma*) and (ii) a sort of intellectualism (*jñāna*). Conceiving the world as full of desirable objects which were to be pursued and enjoyed, the activistic and optimistic outlook of the Vedic Aryans—or the early Vedic Aryans—missed the *Duḥkha* aspect of Śramaṇic *Weltanschauung*, which is so much emphasised in Buddhism, for example. Such an activistic and optimistic outlook went a long way to influence their ethical attitude and their notion of moral virtues. Generally, the morality of the heart is found missing in them and there is not that emphasis on such moral virtues as peacefulness (*śānti*) and compassion (*karuṇā: anukampā*) which appear as cardinal virtues in Buddhism. The virtues praised are strength, liberality, friendliness, truth, sincerity and cooperativeness, which are positively conducive to a good and purposeful social life. Moral law is conceived as natural law or cosmic law. Though there is not an indifference towards morality and moral virtues are praised and upheld, but moral idealism as a dominant kind of idealism is generally missing. There is no image of an ideal person who could be contrasted from others for his exalted moral qualities; *glory of the moral law is to be found but not the glory of the moral person*. This thing is definitely present in the Epics. In the *Vedas* the element of moral struggle is missing. The problem of war and peace is a great problem in Buddhism and even a

[1] *Bṛ. Up.*, 2.4.3.
[2] *Muṇḍaka Up.* 2.2.5: *amṛtasya setuḥ*; *Śvetāśvatara Up.*, 3.8: *tam eva viditvā. atimṛtyum eti nānyaḥ panthā vidyate ayanāya.*
[3] Pande, *Studies*, p. 290.

king is ordained to abide by the principle of *ahiṁsā*. In the *Vedas* there is no doubt about war or propriety of victory over the enemies. The Vedic people are activistic and optimistic people and therefore Vedic morality is *pravṛtti* morality. As we will see later, by contrast Buddhist morality is more subjective, more universal and more feminine.

The Age of Buddha: Ethico-Spiritual Legacy of the Upaniṣads

We have seen above that the Vedic age, although a single period from the point of view of its literary sources, represents nevertheless a long and varied stretch of cultural history. By the time it came to completion, many new trends had already set in which were bound to exercise manyfold repercussions on the general complexion of life and thought. Much has been written on the socio-economic and religio-philosophical environment that existed at the time when Buddha taught his doctrine,[1] and it would be unnecessary to dwell here on that aspect. From all accounts it was an age of great changes—a 'Time of Troubles' as Toynbee has called it[2]—and one would naturally be tempted to see a certain *Zusammenhang* between them and the religious movement of the sixth century BC of which Buddha was one of the leaders. We have already discussed that Śramaṇism, of which Buddhism was one offshoot, existed as a distinct—though not so dominant—ideology from an earlier period. These changes, therefore, should be treated not as causes for this widespread movement but rather as factors which served its claim for wide popularity.

The old tribal structure of the society now tended to break up under the influence of growing urbanism and the emergence of strong monarchies. These two features were further responsible in the growth of the idea of individualism which characterizes this period in a very marked manner.[3] Some scholars have sought to see a class affiliation in the religious movement led by Buddha and Mahāvīra.[4] The thesis

[1]See generally Rhys Davids, *Buddhist India*; Pande, *Studies*, ch. IX, and *BDVI*, ch. I; Misra, *The Age of Vinaya*; Narendra Wagle, *Society at the Time of the Buddha*; Trevor Ling, *The Buddha*, chs. 3-5; R.S. Sharma, 'Material Background of the Origins of Buddhism', *Das Kapital Centenary Volume*.

[2]*A Study of History*, III, p. 270.

[3]See Trevor Ling, *The Buddha*, pp. 72-77. Also Romila Thapar, *Ancient Indian Social History*, p. 51.

[4]See, for example, Rhys, Davids, *Buddhist India*, pp. 138-43; *Vedic Age*, pp. 468-69; R.S. Sharma, loc. cit.; Thapar, *Ancient Indian Social History*, pp. 49-50.

is, however, not sustainable. There was no occasion for any serious struggle between the Brāhmaṇas and the Kṣatriyas.[1] Buddha had among his disciples a sizable number of Brāhmaṇas; very early in his missionary activity Buddha was successful in converting the three Jaṭila teachers,[2] who had large bands of followers, to his fold and one of them, Mahākassapa, was responsible for convening the first Buddhist Council after his demise; Sāriputta and Moggalāna, the other two important disciples, were also Brāhmaṇas. Among the 'Gaṇadharas' of Mahāvīra many came from the Brāhmiṇ caste. In the Buddhist texts there are many references to Brāhmaṇa house-holders inviting the Śramaṇas on food which is inconceivable in an atmosphere of hostility. In fact, the religious movement of the sixth century BC may be best described as Śramaṇic movement which was classless and casteless. Its appeal moved across all social divisions and attracted to it men from all the sections of the society.

Buddha was the heir of a long and rich cultural tradition which had already assumed a universalistic temper. By reconciling the various antinomies it had recognised the wholeness of life and had developed a mystical outlook. The earlier distinction of Aryan or non-Aryan as a social or cultural distinction had become irrelevant and the term '*Ārya*' had rather become a metaphysical connotation. When Buddha contrasted the '*Ārya*' from the '*pṛthagjana*' he meant by these terms the men who possessed a particular metaphysical insight and those who lacked it. Through the conception of primordial '*Puruṣa*' the *Ṛgvedic* seer had already laid the foundation of the conception of monistic reality; the expression 'That One' (*tadekam*) of the *Ṛgveda* anticipates the later day *Upaniṣadic* conception of *Brahman* or *Ātman*. The idea of a universal ethics is clearly noticeable in the *mantras* of the *Ṛgveda*; *ṛta* is contrasted from *anṛta* and so are the moral men from those who do not observe the law (*avrata*). Sin and punishment, virtue and reward are recognised as two distinct sets, and all human actions and results belong to the one or the other. The *Upaniṣads* take this universalistic temper further. They spoke of one reality as the source of all that exists, which implied oneness of life; this reality was to be realised through the universalisation of one's ego which implied renouncing the narrow outlook about one's self and transcending all the dualities of

[1]See above.

[2]The 'Jaṭilas' were Brāhmaṇa ascetics. See G.C. Pande, *BDVI*, pp. 27-28.

worldly existence. In preference to '*preyas*' one was to choose '*śreyas*' and leaving the '*alpam*' (the little or the transitory objects of the world) aspire for the '*Bhūman*' ('the Vast' or the ultimate Truth). That man is not only a body-mind-complex but something much more and a spiritual entity had been duly recognised. The desire for a spiritual quest had already got sharpened which can be clearly seen in the *Upaniṣadic* quest for immortality. Not to accumulate wealth or other pleasurable objects of the world but to become immortal was the goal of life. It is this spiritual hankering that prompted Naciketā to refuse all the bounties of supposedly happy life such as longevity, cattle, horses, sons and grandsons, fine women etc., granted to him by Yama[1] and Maitreyī to exclaim to her husband Yājñavalkya—who wanted to retire as an ascetic after dividing his wealth between his two wives—what would she do with a thing which did not lead to immortality (*yena ahaṁ na amṛtā syāṁ kim ahaṁ tena kuryām*).[2] Death is used as a synonym of desire[3] which binds man to the particular; it is the sin of attachment. Death means this sin and it has to be killed or conquered (*pāpmānaṁ mṛtyum apahatya*).[4] Immortality, thus, is the end of all desires (*kāmasyāptim*).[5] A distinction had come to be made between scriptural or bookish knowledge, which is called 'lower' (*apara*), and spiritual or transcendental knowledge (*para*); while the study of the four Vedas along with its accessory texts is said to be falling under the former category, the latter is said to be the one which leads to the attainment of the 'Imperishable' (*akṣara*).[6] Nārada lamented to Sanatkumāra, whom he had approached for instruction, that though he had learnt the various sciences—he recites a long list of them—what he had acquired was only bookish knowledge and not the knowledge of his essential self (*mantravideva asmi na ātmavid*); and only he who had the knowledge

[1]*Kaṭha Up.*, 1.23-29.

[2]*Bṛ. Up.*, 2.4.3.

[3]ibid., 1.2.1.: *aśanāyā hi mṛtyuḥ*. i.e., 'hunger is death'. This hunger is nothing but synonym of desire. See Govinda Gopala Mukhopadhyaya, *Studies in the Upaniṣads*, p. 30.

[4]ibid., 1.3.11.

[5]*Kaṭha Up.*, 2.11.

[6]*Muṇḍaka. Up.*, 1.1.4.5; *Dve vidye veditavye . . . parā caivāparā ca . . . Tatrāparā Ṛgvedo Yajurvedaḥ Sāmavedo'tharvavedaḥ śikṣā kalpo vyākaraṇam nirukto chanda jyotiṣāmiti, Atha parā yayā tadakṣaramadhigamyate.*

of his essential self could cross over all sorrow (*tarati śokam ātma-vid.*)[1] The *Upaniṣads* have prescribed a number of practices through the observance of which this attainment is possible and many of them, in modified forms or with slightly changed connotations, found their way in the spiritual path laid down by Buddha and other contemporary teachers of his age. With this spiritual quest were linked a number of other metaphysical issues, some of which had been anticipated earlier but not taken up with great seriousness; references to them are also accidental and approach sometimes casual. The doctrines of *Karman*, body-soul duality and their inter-relationship, the theory of transmigration are such instances. These had become so important in Buddha's own time that all the religious teachers of his age felt moved to discuss and debate them. How to become immortal or, in other words, how to end misery and sorrow, appears as the most fundamental philosophical and metaphysical problem of the age. It was a sort of obsession which haunted the sensitive and enlightened minds, and urged them to take up the ascetic's garb. Whereas the general people lived by their popular beliefs and faith in a number of divinities, and the orthodox Brahmanical view emphasised the overall importance of house-holder's life recommending retirement from active life only after the fulfilment of various social obligations, there were many who thought the state of homelessness the only suitable way through which the goal could be pursued in right earnestness.

Buddha was one of them. Born as Siddhārtha Gautama in the Śāk-yan republic, he lived a householder's life till the age of twenty-nine, when he decided to renounce the worldly life and became a recluse with a view to obtaining the Truth. The event of his leaving home is noted in the Buddhist texts as 'Mahābhiniṣkramaṇa' or 'Great Renunciation.' Though the popular account ascribes his decision of renouncing the worldly life to his first sight of old age, sickness, death and an ascetic, an account of the Pāli texts depicts him as a child of reflective nature who felt inclined to brood over the subjects of old age, sickness and death and, as a result of such a reflection, saw no pride in youth, good health or the worldly life of luxury. Conforming to the general practice of the age, he took up religious apprenticeship with some of the renowned teachers of the age. He was, however, not satisfied with the teachings of any

[1] *Ch. Up.*, 7.1. 2-3.

one of them. Nevertheless, it is plausible to suppose that he might have imbibed many ideas from their teachings. He continued his effort and took up to austere penance but that too failed to bring about the desired result. Finally, it occurred to his mind that he used to practise *jhāna* (*dhyāna*=meditation) in his childhood[1] and he decided to know the truth through it; sat under a tree—later to be known as the Bodhi—tree of the 'Tree of Enlightenment' at Uruvelā (modern Bodh-Gaya in Bihar) with the firm resolve to leave the seat only after having realised his aim. It is here that the Truth flashed in his mind and he became a Buddha, an 'Enlightened' person. He had now seen the *Dhamma*, had found the key to the eradication of suffering and pain. After some hesitation, he took up the career of a teacher, gave his first sermon at Isipattana (modern Sarnath near Varanasi)—the event is known as *Dhammacakkapavattana*[2] or the 'Rolling of the Wheel of Law—, founded the Saṅgha, i.e. organised a band of disciples who believed in his teachings, moved along with his followers thereafter from place to place converting people from all sections of the society to his fold. He died at a ripe age at Kusīnārā (modern Kushinagar in District Deoria of Uttar Pradesh), the event being known in the Buddhist texts as 'Mahāparinirvāṇa' or the 'Great Decease.'[3]

The Vision of Buddha

What was the content and nature of the *Dhamma* the realisation of which made Siddhārtha Gautama 'All Enlightened' (*Sammā-*

[1]"*Tassa mayhaṁ etadahosi. Abhijānāmi kho panāhaṁ pitu Sakkassa hammante sītāya jambucchāyāya nisinno vivicceva kāmehi pe paṭhamajjhānaṁ upasampajja viharatā, siyā nu kho eso maggo bodhāyati. Tassa mayhaṁ—satānusāri viññāṇam ahosi. Eso'va maggo bodhāyati*" (*MN.*, I, 247).

[2]Senart has suggested that the original word was *Dharmatakka* or *Dharmatarka* (suggesting a discourse on *Dhamma*) which was later transformed into *Dhammacakka* or *Dharmacakra* with a view to making this event conform well with the poetic imagery of Buddhism as a vehicle which could carry all men to the other shore. See M. Senart, 'Le Manuscript Kharoṣṭhī du Dhammapada' in *Journal Asiatique*, 1897; see also B.C. Law, 'Buddha's First Discourse' in *Indological Studies*, II, p. 3.

[3]On the biography of Buddha see, E.J. Thomes, *The Life of Buddha;* E.J. Brewster, *The Life of Gotama, The Buddha*; E. Senart, *Essai sur la legende de Buddha*; Christmas Hymphreys, *Buddhism*; Paul Carus, *The Gospel of Buddha*; A.K. Coomaraswamy, *Buddha and the Gospel of Buddhism*; C.A.F. Rhys Davids, *Gotama The Man;* Alexander Csoma Koras, *The Life and Teachings of Buddha.*

sambuddha) and liberated (*vimutta*)? It was, no doubt, as Buddha himself is reported to have considered on reflection, hard to realise, most subtle and accessible only to the wise;[1] his initial hesitancy to teach his doctrine to the people derived from the realisation of the subtlety of the *Dhamma*. According to the account of Enlightenment, Buddha's vision of *Dhamma*, which should be taken as a synoptical vision of the Truth, consisted in the mental perception of *Paṭiccasamuppāda* in the direct order and then in the indirect order.[2] The former tended to explain the origin of Suffering through a causally connected series of events and their conditions; the latter, as a logical corollary, went on to show how by removing the antecedent causes one by one suffering would come to an end in the final analysis, thus, leading to *Nibbāna*. The doctrine of *Paṭiccasamuppāda* is enumerated in many ways in the texts, sometimes in the form of a clean-cut formula consisting of twelve links, sometimes only in the form of a statement pointing out an invariant relationship between cause and its effect. There is, however, no doubt that the teaching went to Buddha himself and, from the beginning, was considered the sum-total of his teaching. This is clear from an account of the *Vinaya* relating the conversation between Sāriputta, who was not yet ordained, and Assaji. When asked by Sāriputta what did Buddha teach, Assaji said that he had been admitted in the order very recently and had not yet known the *dhamma-vinaya* fully, but in the nutshell (*saṁkhittena*) he could define it thus: '*ye dhammā hetuppabhavā tesaṁ hetuṁ Tathāgato āha. Tesaṁ ca yo nirodho evaṁ vādī Mahāsamaṇo.*'[3] Modern scholars have expressed diverse opinions regarding the exact significance of the doctrine of *Paṭiccasamuppāda*.[4]

[1]*MV.*, p. 6: *Adhigato kho mayāyaṁ dhammo gambhīro, duddaso, duranubodho santo paṇīto atakkāvacaro nipuṇo paṇḍitavedanīyo.*

[2]ibid., p. 1.

[3]ibid., p. 39.

[4]According to Keith, 'the chain of causation is essentially an explanation of misery' and it does not denote causation in nature, Keith, *Buddhist Philosophy*, p. 112; Rhys Davids, on the contrary, considers it to be principle of natural causality in all phenomena, *Dial*, II, pp. 42ff. Mrs. Rhys Davids, *Gotama The Man*, pp. 77-78, too, takes the formula as an expression of 'law' exactly in the sense in which '*ṛta*' or '*vrata*' were used in earlier times but which had, however, come into disuse because the gods with whom they were associated had lost their bearings on human mind. According to Oldenberg, the bipertite formula of the 'causal Nexus of Being' was drawn up 'to supplement, or rather streng-

It is evident that the doctrine contains within it numerous metaphysical and philosophical implications the illustrations and amplifications of which go to constitute the total body of the tenet which is known as Buddhism. The doctrine of *Paṭiccasamuppāda* explains the origin of *Dukkha* and its causation, and by implication the nature of *Saṁsāra* and the way of escape from it which is *Nibbāna*, the *summum bonum*.

In Buddha's explanation of the world, thus, there is no place for a first beginning or a personal creator. In the 'Brahmajāla-sutta,' Buddha has rejected opinions (*diṭṭhis*) about *pubbanta* and *aparanta* and, instead, has preached a form of *Paṭiccasamuppāda*[1] which tends to characterise the world as "without maker, without known beginning, continuously to exist by nature of concatenation of cause and effect."[2] The world is, thus, a procession which moves ahead in cause-and-effect series following a necessary order and it would keep going on till the individual understands its true nature and, by freeing himself from worldly grasping (*taṇhā*=*tṛṣṇā*) and ignorance (*avijjā*), gets plunge into *Nibbāna*.

'All things are suffering (*sabbe saṅkhārā dukkhā*), 'all things are impermanent' (*sabbe saṅkhārā aniccā*) and 'all elements of a being are devoid of any self' (*sabbe dhammā anattā*) are the three characteristics (*tilakkhaṇa*) which, according to Buddhism, characterize the whole phenomenal existence. The idea of the fleeting nature of the worldly objects, occasionally and casually mentioned in the *Upaniṣads*, finds a place of prominence in Buddhist thought. The world and all the objects of the world are in a state of constant change. How can one hope to be happy in such a world? Schopenhauer is putting forth the Buddhist viewpoint when he writes, "In a world

then the tenets regarding the origin of suffering and its cessation', *Buddha*, pp. 226-227. Coomaraswamy, *Hinduism and Buddhism*, p. 80 note 225, says that "it is the grasp of the very fact that we are mechanisms, causally determined . . . that points out the way of escape."

Keeping in mind the point that Buddha's realisation of the Truth consisted of *Paṭiccasamuppāda* and *Nibbāna*, G.C. Pande says: "Since Nibbāna is apparently the final principle or experience, Paṭiccasamuppāda may be designated as the principle of non-ultimate experience and what corresponds to it; in short, as the principle of phenomentality, of the nature of things transcended in Nibbāna." *Studies*, p. 414.

[1]'Brahmijāla-sutta' in the *Dīgha Nikāya*.

[2]S. Radhakrishnan, *History of Indian Philosophy*, I, p. 374.

where all is unstable, and naught even endure, but is swept onwards at once in the hurrying whirlpool of change . . . in such a world, happiness is inconceivable."[1] Things which appear pleasurable too, because of inherent impermanence and evanescence, only bring about pain after their exhaustion;[2] that moment of rapture is, thus, a short-living phenomenon "a perishing series" which eludes satisfaction one is looking for. The fleeting nature of mind, which does not stick to any one object for long and craves for something else after one desire is satisfied, makes the situation still more undesirable. In the following passage, F.H. Bradley speaks like a Buddhist: "Pleasures, we saw, were a perishing series. This one comes, and the intense self-feeling proclaims satisfaction. It is gone, and we are not satisfied. It was not that one, then, but this one now; and this one now is gone. It was not that one, then, but another and another; but another and another do not give us what we want; we are still left eager and confident, till the flash of feeling dies down, and when that is gone nothing is left. We are where we began, so far as getting happiness goes; and we have not found ourselves, and we are not satisfied."[3] Thus, what looks pleasure is only 'a baited hook for fools'; it only enchains.[4]

Since all things, animate or inanimate, are caused (*pratītyasamutpanna*) and conditioned (*saṁskṛta*), they lack any substantiality of their own. The four great elements, viz., earth, water, fire and air constitute the basis of all material life. Each thing is only a combination of various elements (*dharmas*) which are interrelated with each other and are in a state of unceassing origination and destruction. An individual too is only a combination, a putting together or a compound (*saṁghāta*) of some material and mental qualities. The two qualities together are known as *nāma-rūpa*, the former denoting the mental and the latter the material elements;

[1]Schopenhauer, *Studies in Pessimism*, p. 35.

[2]In Buddhism, it is called *Pariṇāmadukkhatā* or *Dukkhapariṇāmata* i.e., suffering in the form of result.

[3]F.H. Bradley, *Ethical Studies*, p. 96.

[4]*Sutta-Nipāta*, 'Khaggavisāṇasutta', verse 62. The English rendering by Lord Chelmers in *The Harvard Oriental Series*, 37, p. 16:

'Go forth alone! Be sure
pleasure's a chain, brief bliss,
short rapture, long-drawn woe,
a baited hook for fools'. *Kindred Saying*, I, p. 55.

in an expanded form they are known as the '*five skandhas*' in which *rūpa* (form or body) stands for the material aspect while *vedanā* (sensation), *saṁjñā* (the reaction of the mind to the sense stimuli), *saṁskāra* (mental process) and *vijñāna* (consciousness) denote the mental aspect of an individual personality. None of these components is stable, each is ever-changing, the change being too fast and subtle to be easily perceptible. Buddha analysed human personality in terms of conglomeration of the five *skandhas* and denied in each of them any selfhood (*netaṁ maṁ nesohamasmi na meso attā*).[1] This is known as the Buddhist doctrine of *Anattā*.[2]

Men, however, not knowing the true nature of their own self and the worldly objects, crave for the latter, to be always left dissatisfied and frustrated. In ignorance they continue weaving for themselves the net of suffering and pain. Buddhism emphasises the all pervasive character of *Dukkha* which spares nothing in the phenomenal realm; human existence is just another name for suffering, as Buddha says in his first sermon.[3] The world is like a house burning on

[1]See *MV.*, pp. 16.17.

[2]Whether Buddha denied self altogether has been an issue of debate among scholars. Some scholars, for example Stcherbatsky, *The Central Conception of Buddhism*,, p. 59 and T.W. Rhys Davids, *Buddhism*, pp. 95-99, maintain that Buddha denied the existence of soul and that it had no validity in his system of thought. Some others have called him an agnostic, Keith, *Buddhist Philosophy*, pp. 39-46; Poussin in *ERE.*, I under 'Agnosticism; for refutation of Keith's view see Radhakrishnan, *Indian Philosophy*, I, pp. 679-80. Mrs. Rhys Davids, on the other hand, has taken great pains to prove that Buddha was a believer in *Attā* and to drive her point home has given a number of Pāli parallels already used in the *Upaniṣads*, *The Birth of Indian Psychology*, pp. 206-14. Coomaraswamy too says, "... Bref, il est ā fait certain que dire que le Bouddha (ni ait un Dieu, ni ait un Āme, ni ait L' Eternité) est faux". *La Pensé de Gotama, le Bouddha*, p. 53.

In the 'Anattapariyāya' discourse quoted above in the text Buddha has only denied self in the phenomenal realm and not self altogether. When he was directly asked about the questions like the existence of *Ātman* or the state of Tathāgata after his death, he is reported to have adopted complete silence, e.g., *SN.*, IV, pp. 281-82. Obviously, he thought that the problem stood beyond the sphere of word and thought. The *Upaniṣads* also held the same attitude.

[3]Delivering his first sermon to the five disciples (the event is known as *Dhammacakkapavattana*) in the form of the four-fold formula of the Aryan Truths (*Cattāri ariyasaccāni*) Buddha has enumerated *Dukkha* in the words: '... Birth is dukkha, old age is dukkha, disease is dukkha, death is dukkha, coming in contact with the undesired ones is dukkha, separation from the dear one is

fire.[1] *Dukkha* constitutes the most important point in the teaching of Buddha so much so that he said that 'it is just sorrow and the ceasing of sorrow that I proclaim.'[2] Suffering has however a long history in every individual case. The experience of pain, which everyone is bound to undergo as a creature of the world, is not imposed on him *ab extra* but is his own creation, the necessary result of his past deeds. Buddhism conceived human existence as a series of many lives connected with each other by the *karmic* forces of the individual. Man is responsible for what he is and he is also the maker of his future. The path leading to continuing bondage and the path of liberation are both there before him and he may choose anyone of them. We would have the occasion to discuss the doctrine in detail later, but we refer to it here merely to point out that Buddha's notion of *Dukkha* should not be understood merely as unrest or commotion resulting from the phenomenal experience[3] but as something much deeper. As Coomaraswami has said, "Dukkha is to be understood both as symptom and as disease."[4] It would also be wrong to say that the word *dukkha* used in the Buddhist texts points merely to the ills of body and mind and lacks the conception of ill in the spiritual realm.[5] G.C. Pande has rightly observed, "When he came to summarise his view in former terminology and declared "*saṅkhittena pañcupādānakkhandhā dukkhā*," he did not mean merely to speak of a discontent of body and mind, but rather of discontent with body and mind, and this latter is the form of all spiritual discontent."[6]

Desire or craving for sense-pleasures (*taṇhā or tṛṣṇā*) is the immediate cause of suffering. Desires can never be quenched through

dukkha, not getting of what is desired is dukkha, in short, the five 'upādānakkhandhas' are dukkha. See *Mv*. 'Dhammacakkapavattanasutta'.

[1]The imagery is very popular in the Buddhist texts. See 'Āditta-pariyāya' in the *Mv.*; *Kindred Sayings*, I, p. 42; *Sutta-Nipāta*, verse 592; *Psalms of the Sisters*, verse 200.

[2]*Kindred Sayings*, III, p. 101.

[3]See, for example, Stcherbatsky, *op. cit.*, p. 41. Explaining his concept of *Nirvāṇa* he writes, ". . . The Absolute (*Nirvāṇa*) is inanimate, even if it is something. It is sometimes, especially in popular literature, characterised as bliss, but this bliss consists in the cessation of unrest (*dukkha*)". ibid., p. 45.

[4]*Buddha and the Gospel of Buddhism*, p. 83.

[5]Mrs. Rhys Davids, *What Was the Original Gospel?*, pp. 56-57.

[6]Pande, *Studies*, p. 403.

the fulfilment of desires as mind is quick enough to cling to a new object and the objects themselves are of transitory character to last only for a short time. All desires are, therefore, undesirable; they are like 'flames of fire' (*aṅgārakāsūpamā kāmā*)[1] which burns, like 'spears and javelins' which 'pierce and vend the mortal frames of us.'[2] They are to be abandoned; 'like elephant in battle charging' one has to 'break through desire for joys of sense.'[3] In the root of all desires, however, lies Ignorance (*Avijjā*), failure to see the true nature of the things and one's own self. It is the first link (*nidāna*) in the twelve-fold formula of *Paṭiccasamuppāda*. It is to be displaced by correct understanding (*sammā diṭṭhi*).

When one has overcome all desires, such inveterate tendencies of mind as attachment, malice, hatred, envy, illusion are automatically annihilated and one comes to possess complete equanimity of mind. One has now attained the *summum bonum*, *Nibbāna*, and become Worthy, an *Arhat*.[4] It is a state of mind which has no burning passions, nothing to grieve over, no object to be attached to, and none to come in clash with. *Nirodha* is no doubt a very important aspect of *Nibbāna*. Poussin has observed, "Parmi les aspects (*ākāra*) du *Nirvāṇa*, le plus important est l'aspect de destruction (*nirodha*). Par le fait *Nirvāṇa*=*nirodha*; le *Nirvāṇa* est la treiséme véritié, (ca qui est vraiment la destruction dué désir et de la douleur)."[5] Mind is now in a state of complete peacefulness (*śānti*) having transcended all dualities. *Nibbāna* is, however, also conceived positively; it is the state of perfect bliss (*Nibbānaṁ paramaṁ sukhaṁ*) and coincides with perfect wisdom (*paññā*=*prajñā*).[6] It is closely related with

[1] *Cv.*, p. 56; *Pac.*, p. 181. This undesirable character is further stressed by likening them to skeleton, meat-piece, grass, dream, borrowed ornaments, fruit of tree, sword edge, spear-point, and serpenthood, ibid.

[2] *Psalms of the Sisters*, verse 58.

[3] *Psalms of the Brothers*, verse 1105, p. 373.

[4] See *Mv.*, p. 6, p. 7 and p. 8 where *Nibbāna* is defined in these words: '*sabbasaṅ khārasamatho sabbūpadhipatinissago taṇṇhakkhay virāgo nirodho nibbānaṁ.*' As E. Conze has observed, even *Nirvāṇa* is desired only so far as it has not been attained but the moment it is attained the desire for it also ceases. *Buddhist Thought in India*, p. 67.

[5] Poussin, *Nirvāṇa*, p. 158.

[6] *Prajñā* is supreme wisdom which arises from contemplation and quietude (*Samādhi, Samatha*). It is a series of successive stages which in the end becomes absolute, spotless and calm, see Gopinath Kaviraj, 'The Doctrine of Pratibhā in Indian Philosophy', *ABORI*, 5, 1924, p. 122.

Paṭiccasamuppāda; whereas the latterpoints to the essence of phenomena, its changeability, conditioned character and inherent painfulness, *Nibbāna* points to that which lies beyond that, the changeless (*ajātaṁ, ajaraṁ, amaraṁ*), the unconditioned (*asaṅkhata*), the transphenomenal (*appapañca* or *nippapañca*), the perfect happiness (*paramaṁ sukhaṁ*).[1] Defining the relationship between *Paṭiccasamuppāda* and *Nibbāna* and the sea-change that the attainment of the latter brings about in the seeker, E. Conze has to say the following:

"A new organ of vision known as the 'wisdom-eye' completely transforms the Yogin's outlook. Nirvāṇa, having become more real to him, than anything else, now can act as his 'objective support', not in the sense that he can make statements about it, but in the sense that it increasingly motivates his conduct. What is assumed here is that there are two objectively existing and mutually exclusive poles—the everchanging five skandhas and the everlasting Nirvāṇa which results from their cessation. When the one ceases, the other takes over. Deathless Nirvāṇa is in fact conceived as a kind of force which 'bends faithless dharmas to itself' by means of the condition known as 'the decisive influence of the object'. Nirvāṇa, the ineffective, cannot, of course, exert any effect. All that is asserted is that the mind of the Yogin increasingly stresses the idea of Nirvāṇa to the exlusion of everything else."[2]

The human effort and exertion necessary for the attainment of this goal was conceived by Buddha by the figure of a Way.[3] The Pāli canonical texts use two terms *paṭipadā* and *magga*—to denote the way, which are sometimes used side by side.[4] According to Mrs. Rhys Davids, *magga* was the original term which Buddha preferred

[1]For the various aspects of *Nibbāna* see Pande, *Studies*, pp. 472-82.

[2]E. Conze, *Buddhist Thought in India*, p. 58.

[3]A.C. Bouquet rightly observes that the Way-figure is a characteristic feature of oriental religious thought as a whole–in contrast with the Western view about religion wherein the conception is that of a fixed relationship between the human self and some non-human entity, the Sacred, the Supernatural, the Self-existent, the Absolute, or simply, 'God'–which is so powerful as to affect even communist Russia which, true to its semi-Oriental ancestry, though rejects theism but talks about a dialectical process, which is again a 'Way'. A.C. Bouquet, *Comparative Religion*, pp. 15-16.

[4]For example, *Mv.*, p. 13: *Idaṁ kho pana, bbikkhave, dukkhanirodhagāminīpaṭipadā ariyasaccaṁ-ayameva ariyo aṭṭhangiko maggo.*

and used to signify the progress or marching ahead towards the goal.[1] The term *paṭipadā*, however, is more explanatory and appears to suggest that in Buddha's conception the goal could not be attained to through any big leap; the way signified a gradual moving ahead, 'step by step' as a passage in the *Saṁyutta Nikāya* says.[2] Buddha conceived the way as the 'Middle Way' (*majihimā paṭipadā*) which, as he saw it, consists in the avoidance of two extremities, the extremity of self-indulgence (*kāmasukha*) and that of self-mortification (*attakilamatha*); according to him, both these extremities are ignoble and devoid of any gain.[3] The 'Middle Way' is the same as the Eightfold Path (*aṭṭhaṅgiko maggo*). True to its claim of being analytical in approach (*vibhajjavādī*), Buddhism analyses the Path too as consisting of eight components, viz., *sammā diṭṭhi* (Right view), *sammā saṅkappa* (Right Determination), *sammā vāca* (Right speech), *sammā kammanta* (Right Action), *sammā ājīva* (Right Livelihood), *sammā vāyāma* (Right Ethics), *sammā sati* (Right Mindfulness) and *sammā samādhi* (Right concentration). "The eight-fold way may be regarded as the practical ethics of Buddhism for the purpose of building up the human character and improving it, but at the same time it is the way of the holy religion for attaining the highest enlightenment—Buddhahood."[4] In all probability, however, Buddha had originally taught only the Way-figure in the form of the Middle Way, and only later it got formulized into eightfold way.[5]

Importance and Nature of Morality

It has been rightly said that 'religion is essentially a doing and doing what is moral'.[6] Buddha too conceived religious life as virtuous life which the seeker has to undertake for the realisation of the goal. Though in the state of realisation there is transcendence of even virtue as of evil, till it has not been achieved virtue has to constitute a firm support of the seeker in his spiritual exertion. Virtue is the mother of the Eightfold way which in Buddhism constitutes the straight way to *Nirvāṇa;* virtue, a passage in the *Saṁyutta Nikāya*

[1]See *Gotama The Man*, p. 41.
[2]*Kindred Sayings*, I, p. 246.
[3]*Book of the Discipline*, Part 4 (*Mahāvagga*), p. 15.
[4]Junjiro Takakusu, *Essentials of Buddhist Philosophy*, p. 20.
[5]Pande, *Studies*, pp. 517-18; Misra, *The Age of Vinaya*, p. 76.
[6]F.H. Bradley, op. cit., p. 314.

says, is the fore-runner, the harbinger of the arising of the noble Eightfold Way.[1] A passage in the *Aṅguttara Nikāya* clearly says that the possibilities of release lack a basis if a person is immoral.[2] A monk who is perfect in virtue, has his sense faculties well-guarded, is moderate in eating and even watchful in the observance of the *dhamma*—such a monk is in the vicinity of *Nirvāṇa*.[3] The following utterance in the *Milindapañho* has highlighted virtue thus:

Virtue is the base on which the man who is wise,
Can train his heart and make his wisdom grow,
Thus shall the strenuous bhikkhu undeceived,
Unravel all the tangled skein of life.[4]

Gnosis is the goal of spiritual journey and desire accompanied with a sincere effort for the acquisition of a pure moral conduct is the starting point in this journey. The Buddhist triplet of *Śīla*, *saṁādhi* and *Prajñā* points to the three hallmarks of the spiritual journey which starts from purity of conduct (*Śīla*) and, *via* perfect equanimity of mind through concentration (*Samādhi*), ends in the attainment of transcendental Wisdom or Intuition (*Prajñā*). All the three are closely linked up with each other. Conduct and Intuition are inseparably united; they form an essential pair, each performing its specific part with the help of the other.[5] "Morality", remarks M. Anesaki, "is merely a means to perfection . . . it is an integral part of the perfection, and hence of the epithets of Buddha-'abounding in wisdom and goodness' ".[6] Moral habit and wisdom are spoken of as essential elements in the personality of Buddha.[7]

Morality of the act is inseparably united with the morality of the intention.[8] Recognising it too well Buddhism too has conceived

[1]*Kindred Sayings*, V, p. 27.

[2]*Gradual Sayings*, V, p. 5.

[3]ibid., p. 45.

[4]*Question of King Milinda*, I, (*SBE*., XXXV), p. 53.

[5]'Soṇadaṇḍa Sutta' in *The Dīgha Nikāya* (Nalanda ed.), p. 106.

[6]M. Anesaki in *ERE* ('Ethics and Morality' Buddhist), V, p. 448.

[7]*Middle Length Sayings*, 'Saṅgāravasutta', vol. II, p. 399: "But do not you, dear learned friend, know this Lord's moral habit and wisdom? If, dear learned friend, were to know this Lord's moral habit and wisdom, you, dear learned friend, would not consider that this Lord should be abused and reviled."

[8]See Westermarck, *Origin and Development of Moral Ideas*, I, p. 205. He says that moral judgements do not really relate to the event but to the intention of the doer. Quoting Sidgwick and Stuart Mill in this regard he writes, "Even

morality not only in terms of disciplining of the physical action but also as disciplining of the mind which, in fact, is the source of all conscious action. One wills, and then acts. The *Aṅguttara Nikāya* says: "Determinate thought is action. When one determines, one acts by word, deed and thought."[1] Mind is ever restless. Like a monkey on tree, which leaves one branch only to catch the other, mind keeps on jumping from one sense-object to the other, ever arousing fresh desires and creating fresh occasions for frustration, disillusionments and sufferings. It has to be brought under control, and it is a tough task.[2] It requires constant vigilance on the part of the seeker so that it is not swayed away by the powerful attraction of the sense-objects. This is called *indriya-bhāvanā*.[3]

Conception of the Way includes a number of spiritual and ascetic practices[4] the specificities of which are pointed out by the application of different terms and particular assignments to them. *Sati* or mindfulness, one of the constituents of the Eightfold way, is an exercise in mind-control throngh contemplation on the nature of body and feeling, on the one hand, but also on mind and mind states.[5] It, thus, denotes a faculty which is distinct from and superior to mind. The four *sammapadhānas* consist of *saṁvara* and *pahāṇa*, which serve respectively as a check to any further influx of *akusala dhammas* and means to repel out the already existing ones, and of *bhāvanā* and *anurakkhaṇa*, which are to be employed for inculcation and intensi-

Stuart Mill who draws so sharp a distinction between the morality of the act and the moral worth of the agent, admits that 'the morality of the action depends entirely upon the intention'."

[1]*Gradual Sayings*, III, p. 294; see also *Kindred Sayings*, II, p. 46. Nāgārjuna expresses the same when he (*Madhyamaka*, ch. 17) says–*cetanā cetayitvā ca karmoktaṁ paramarṣiṇā*'. Vasubandhu, *Abhidharmakośa*, 4.1, lays down the definition as '*cetanā—cetayitvākaraṇa*'.

[2]Arjuna, the spiritual seeker in the *Gītā*, points to this difficulty when he laments to Kṛṣṇa: *Cañcalaṁ hi manaḥ Kṛṣṇa pramāthi balvaddṛḍham, Tasyāhaṁ nigrahaṁ manye vāyoriva suduṣkaram.*

("Kṛṣṇa, the mind is very unsteady, turbulent, tenacious and powerful; therefore, I consider it as difficult to control as the wind"). *Gītā*, VI, 34.

[3]For elaboration, see *The Age of Vinaya*, pp. 94-95.

[4]A passage in the *Pārājika*, p. 116, lays down a definition: '*Maggabhāvanā ti cattāro satipaṭṭhānā, cattāro sammapadhānā cattāro iddhupādā, pañcindriyāṇi, pañcabalāni sattā bojjhaṅgā, ariyo aṭṭhaṅgiko maggo*.' In the *Cullavagga*, p. 357, these are called jewels (*ratanāni*) which are found in the *Dhammavinaya*.

[5]*Kindred Sayings*, IV, pp. 119-20.

fication of *Kusala dhammas.*[1] By far the most important of such practices were *jhāna* and *samādhi.* Buddha himself had realised the Truth through *jhāna* or meditation, and *samādhi* constitutes the last step in the *Aṭṭhangika-magga.* In order to curb the dallying nature of mind, it was to be withdrawn from the undesirable sense-objects and concentrated on some fixed desirable object[2] so that the ripples of mental tendencies are completely calmed down and the arising of Wisdom becomes possible. In the words of Mrs. Rhys Davids, "The musing was apparently considered to be a preparatory practice favourable to the inception of psychic experience."[3] In respect of *jhāna*, the same scholar has further pointed out that it is not meditation as in it feeling as well as thought both remain suspended.[4] Commenting on the mystical and the psychic nature of the *jhānic* practice, Professor G.C. Pande writes: "What resulted was not a state akin to sleep or coma, but rather of the mind stilled or hushed before leaping into a far-reaching intuition. The theory was that in the depth of the still and even consciousness reality mirrored itself as in the unruffled waters."[5]

The above is, in short, Buddha's vision of *Dhamma* which he finally condescended to teach the humanity for the eradication of all ills and sufferings. Buddha, however, considered himself only a 'good friend' (*Kalyāṇamitra*). He can only tell the way for the benefit of the spiritual seekers. If they have the intensity of desire and make sincere efforts, they can reach the goal and realise the Truth themselves by treading on it. The *Dhamma* of Buddha was practical and dynamic, it was was also mystical. True to its mystical form, it presented an intermixture of religion and ethics as an inseparable pair, the latter being not an end in itself but a means leading to a higher stage which was a state of complete transcendence. Buddha's original teaching of his *Dhamma* must have been synoptical but it had latent potentialities of further interpretations and elaborations which got manifested in the succeeding stages of the development of Buddhism.

[1]See *Gradual Sayings*, II, pp. 15-16; ibid., pp. 83-84.

[2]See 'Kusalacittekaggatā-samādhi' in *Visuddhimagga.*

[3]*Birth of Indian Psychology*, p. 333.

[4]Mrs. Rhys Davids, *Sakya*, p. 166.

[5]Pande, *Studies*, p. 535.

CHAPTER 2

The Buddhist Doctrine of Karman and the Concept of Action

"[In the Vedic view] The sacrifice is the basic principle of creation, representing a mutual bond between gods and men. It stands for a cycle of ritual giving and receiving. In contrast to this, Śramaṇism cut man lose from the sense of dependence on the gods. . .It replaced the gods by the force of *Karman.* What man receives he does not owe to the favour or frowns of any god but to his own past action and efforts." And further,

"Vedic ethics is based on theistic belief. It is the gods who uphold the moral order and punish its transgression and they have the authority to remit or waive punishment in their graciousness in response to human prayer and worship. In contrast, man is wholly dependent on himself in Śramanism: '*tumaṁ eva tumaṁ mittā kiṁ bahiyā mittamicchasi*', '*attā attano nātho ko hi nātho paro siyā*' '*attadīpā viharatha attasaraṇā anaññasaraṇā*', '*Kammassakā sattā kammadāyādā*'. The force of *Karman* is inexorable and impersonal. The law of moral retribution is eternal and works by itself without requiring any support from the gods who are themselves subject to it."[1]

In these words has Professor Pande sought to bring out the fundamental difference between the Vedic-Brahmanical and Śramaṇic moral outlook. Rejection of gods and sacrifice by Śramaṇism naturally tended to raise the status of the individual, pointing out that he was not subject to any power exterior to himself and was complete master of his own destiny. So, whatever a man is, along with his pleasant or painful experiences here, it is not because of any other force or entity but a result of his own doing, and his future position too depends entirely on his own actions. This view makes him a full-fledged moral agent responsible for whatever he does through deeds,

[1]G.C. Pande, *Śramaṇa Tradition-Its History and Contribution to Indian Culture*, pp. 31-32.

speech or thought. The implied belief is in the continuity and effectiveness of a force which a moral act produces. Every moral action produces, along with the immediate perceptible result, potential energies which linger on in the form of an invisible force till its fruition is accomplished at some suitable time in future. The aforesaid process is technically called *Karman*, though literally the term means only 'action' or prescribed duties.[1] The doctrine also links the present human existence with other existences, past as well as future. The doctrine of *Karman*, is necessarily and closely associated with the belief in transmigration, the cycle of birth and rebirth.

It is obvious that the belief in such a principle–a self evolving force without any dependence on gods or sacrifice–could hardly find a place in the priestly and ritualistic religion of the Vedic times. "If the moral quality of an action solely and irrevocably determines the future, man becomes the captain of his destiny; the priest and sacrifice, then, cease to be indispensable".[2] It penetrated into the Vedic Brahmanical circle through the latter's contact with Śramaṇic ideology and emerges in some developed form for the first time in the *Upaniśadic* texts. Its not too popular and alien character, however, is attested by the cautious approach of Yājñavalkya while he dis-

[1]In *Īśa Upaniṣad*, 2: '*Kurvanneveha karmāṇi jijiviṣecchataṁ samāḥ*' ('Let a man aspire to live for hundred years, doing his duties'). The term is used here in the sense of duty one is required to perform as a member of society. In the *Brāhmaṇas* the term is, however, used also in the technical sense of ritualistic action, see *Sat. Br.*, II, 833.

[2]Pande, *Studies*, p. 287. Some scholars have, however, sought to trace the roots of the doctrine of *Karman* in the framework of Vedic thought itself. According to Dasgupta, the magical belief in the potency of sacrifices to produce the desired results developed into the doctrine of *Karman*. He writes, "The law of *karman* was thus rooted in the Indian mind from the earliest days in the tribal belief in the efficacy of magical operations, incantations and the like, and it was only extended at a later stage into the ethical field." *Indian Idealism*, p. 3.

R.D. Ranade, *A Constructive Survey of Upanisadic Philosophy*, sees the beginning of the theory of karman in '*prithivīñca dharmaṇā*' of the *Ṛgveda*, X.16.3.

John Mckenzie, *Hindu Ethics*, p. 15 has this to say, "...though the *karman* doctrine is not yet formulated, its ethical principles are already in evidence. Thus suffering is recognised as the fruit of previous sin, and when a good man dies he goes to the next world carrying his merit with him."

cusses this idea with Ārtabhāga. He says to him: 'Give me your hand, my dear Ārtabhāga. We two alone shall know of this, we must not speak of it in public' (*āhara saumya hastam Ārtabhāga āvāmeva etasya vediṣyāvo na navetsajana iti*).[1] However, in the time of Buddha all the religious sects and schools felt themselves moved to debate this idea seriously. While there appears to be a general agreement with regard to the acceptance of the doctrine, the different sects entertained diverse opinions on many important issues connected with it, such as the nature of *Karman*, its relationship and inter-action with the soul (*Jiva*), the way it works out itself, and so on.[2]

Before we set out to examine the doctrine in the Buddhist perspective, it would be pertinent to scrutinize the Jaina and the Ājīvaka views on it for such a scrutiny would put the views of Buddha into much clearer focus.

The Jainas were great exponents of the doctrine of *Karman*. They called themselves *Karmavādin* and *Kriyāvādin* and were sharply opposed to *Akarmavādins* and *Akriyāvādins* or those who denied *Karman* and did not admit that the action of the soul is transmitted to the future moments.[3] The use of the terms '*Karman*' and '*Kriyā*' side by side appears to suggest that the Jainas considered the former as the binding factor which polluted the original nature of the soul whereas the latter term denoted the human initiative through which the bondage could be sundered and the soul restored to its original nature.[4] According to the Jainas, an individual is a total production

[1]*Br. Up.*, 3.2.13.

[2]Pūraṇa Kassapa, Makkhaliputta Gosāla, Ajita Kesakambala, Pakudha Kaccāyana, Sañjaya Belaṭṭhaputta, and Nigaṇṭhanātaputta are other prominent philosophers of the age who are mentioned in the Buddhist texts. Gosāla and Nigaṇṭhanātaputta or Mahavira had founded the Ājīvaka sect and the Jaina sect respectively. For detailed discussion on the views of these teachers see Barua, *Pre-Buddhist Indian Philosophy*; Schrader, *Über den Stand der Indischen Philosophie Zur Zeit Mahāviras ünd Buddhas;* Pande, *Studies;* Jayatilleke, *Early Buddhist Theory of Knowledge*, ch. II and III; Misra, *The Age of Vinaya*, ch. II. On the Ājīvakas particularly see A.L. Basham, *History and Doctrine of the Ājīvakas;* Hoernle, 'Ājīvakas' in *ERE*, I.

[3]See *Jaina Sutras*, II, pp. 316-317.

[4]According to B. C. Law, *Indological Studies*, II, p. 285, there is no difference between 'Kriyāvāda' and 'Karmavāda' and both denote the doctrine of action.

Contd.

of his own deeds and also the sole arbiter of his future. "Individually a man is born, individually he dies, individually he falls (from this state of existence), individually he rises (to another). His passion, consciousness, intellect, perception, and impressions belong to the individual exclusively."[1] Fruits of *Karman* are not sharable by any one, the doer himself has to taste them. "Neither his kinsmen, nor his friends, nor his sons, nor his relations will share his suffering, he alone has to bear it; for the Karman follows the doer."[2] The Jaina view takes the nature of *Karman* to be material[3] and believes that every deed would irrevocably entail its result without any consideration of whether intellect or consciousness was applied to it or not.[4] *Jīva's* association with *Karman* is the root-cause of its suffering and it could win its liberation by hindering the absorption of new *Karman*

Contra, Misra, *The Age of Vinaya*, p. 55; also Pande, 'The Role of the Idea of Kriyavāda in Jaina Logic', *Jijñāsa*, I, July-October 1974, I. 3 & 4, p. 1.

Attention may be drawn to an interesting passage in the *Mahāvagga*, p. 248. When Sīha approaches Nigaṇṭhanātaputta (Mahāvīra) for permission to go to see Buddha, he retorts why Sīha, a believer in *Kiriyavāda* wanted to see Buddha who preached *akiriyavāda-kiṁ pana tvaṁ, Sīha, kiriyavādo samaṇo akiriyavādaṁ samaṇaṁ Gotamaṁ upasaṅkamissasi*. Here Nigaṇṭhanātaputta calls Buddha '*akriyāvādin*' but not *akarmavādin*. Buddha too was a staunch believer in *karman* and sharply differed from *akriyāvādin* philosophers of his age such as Makkhali Gosāla, Pūraṇa Kassapa and Pakudha Kaccāyana.

[1]*Jaina Sutras*, II, p. 349.

[2]ibid, p. 59; also ibid., p. 301.

[3]M. Hiriyanna, *Outlines of Indian Philosophy*, p. 168 write, "It is conceived here as being material and permeating the jīvas through and through and weighing them down to the mundane level."

The Jaina philosophers put forth the following argument to prove the material nature of *Karman*. They argue that an effect having a material form must follow from a material cause. All the real objects of the universe are constituted by atoms. As the atoms are considered material, therefore the causes of the objects too should be considered material. If somebody were to counter by saying that experiences like pleasure, pain, enjoyment and suffering are purely mental and their causes too should be mental or not-material, they hold that all these experiences are not independent of corporeal causes. These experiences are always associated with some material object; 'there is no experience of pleasure etc., in association with a non-material entity, just as in connection with the ether'. They, thus, maintain that 'at the back of these experiences there are natural causes' and that is *karma*. See S. Gopalan, *Outlines of Jainism*, pp. 166-167.

See also Glasenapp, *Doctrine of Karman in Jaina Philosophy*.

[4]*Jaina Sutras*, II, pp. 399ff.

(it is called *saṁvara*) and elimination of the *Karman* already accumulated (the process is called *nijjarā*).[1] For this the Jainas prescribe artificial physical means which even involves deliberate subjection of the body to torture.

The Ājīvaka philosopher, Makkhali Gosāla, believed in the principle of *Karman* but advocated the philosophy of *akriyāvāda* or absolute determinism. A passage in the 'Sāmaññaphala Suttanta' of the *Dīgha Nikāya* puts forth his views on the subject thus:

natthi hetu. . .natthi paccayo sattānaṁ saṅkilesāya, ahetū apaccayā sattā saṅkilessanti/natthi hetu natthi paccayo sattānaṁ visuddhiyā/ahetū apaccayā sattā visujjhanti/natthi attakāre natthi parakāre natthi purisakāre natthi balaṁ natthi viriyaṁ natthi purisatthāmo natthi purisaparakkamo/savve sattā savve pāṇā savve bhūtā savve jīva avasā abalā aviriyā niyati—saṅgati-bhāvap ariṇatā chasvevābhijātisu sukhadukkhaṁ paṭisaṁvedenti.

"There is. . .no cause, either ultimate or remote, for the depravity of beings; they become deprived without reason and without cause. There is no cause, either proximate or remote, for the rectitude of beings: they become pure without reason and without cause. The attainment of any given condition, of any character, does not depend either on one's own acts, or on the acts of another, or on human effort. There is no such thing as power or energy, or human strength or human vigour. All animals, all creatures. . .all beings. . .all souls are without force and power and energy of their own. They are bent this way and that by their fate, by the necessary conditions of the class to which they belong, by their individual nature; and it is according to their position in one or other of the six classes that they experience ease or pain."[2] Thus, according to him, everything is fixed and man is absolutely 'destitute of force, power or energy'. He is a total creation of his destiny and he has no choice in its making or unmaking. *Karman* is conceived in the form of a potential energy which empties itself in course of time through repeated

[1]*Jaina Sutras*, II, p. 167: "By turning from the world he will strive to do no bad actions, and will eliminate his already acquired *Karman* by its destruction; then he will cross the forest of the fourfold Saṁsāra". As has been remarked, "The 'release' of the soul from the negative influence of *karma* is the *sine qua non* for liberation or *moksa*, the ultimate goal in life to be achieved." S. Gopalan, *Outlines of Jainism*, p. 164.

[2]*DN.*, I, p. 47: *Dial*, I, p. 71.

birth and death. "*Seyyathāpi suttagule khitte nibbeṭhiyamanameva phaleti evameva bāle ca paṇḍite ca sandhāvitvā saṁsaritva dukkhans-santaṁ karissanti.*" "Just as when a ball of string is cast forth it will spread out just as far, and no farther, than it can unwind, just fools and wise alike, wandering in transmigration for the alloted term, shall then, and only then, make out end of pain."[1] The process of *Karman* will observe its determined course and no human effort can succeed in making immature *Karman* mature or putting an end to mature *Karman*. As the passage further reads: '*Tattha natthi imināhaṁ sīlena va tapasā vā brahmacariyeṇa vā aparipakkaṁ vā kammaṁ paripācessami paripakkaṁ vā kammaṁ phussa vyanti karissāmi hevaṁ natthi*: "Though the wise should hope: 'By this virtue or this performance of duty, or this penance, or this righteousness will I make the karma (I have inherited) that is not yet mature —though the fool should hope, by the same means, to get gradually rid of karma that has matured—neither of them can do it."[2]

Thus, whereas the Jainas held that the *jīva* was bound by his actions but could come out of this bondage with the help of certain measures, the *Ājīvakas* advocated the ultimacy of the power of *karman* which could by no means be checked from bearing its results. Pūraṇa Kassapa and Pakudha Kaccāyana, two other renowned thinkers of the age, looked at the principle from a different angle. Did human actions pollute soul ? In answer to this question the former held that any ethical distinction between two actions was patently absurd and believed that no sin or virtue was involved in any action.[3] Pakudha Kaccāyana held the same view. He believed in seven ultimate substances which existed in emptiness (*vivara*)-"Thus interaction between the four types of matter, *sukha*, *dukkha* and *jīva* was impossible, and hence such action as involved interaction, for in-

[1]*DN.*, I, p. 47: *Dial.* p., 73.
[2]*DN.*, I, p. 47: *Dial.* p., 72.
[3]*Dial.*, pp. 69-70.
Karoto...kārāyato chindato chedāpayato pacato pācāpayato socayato socāpayato kilamato kilamāpayato phandato phandāpayato pāṇamati pātāpayato... paradāraṁ gacchato musā bhaṇato karoto na karīyati pāpam. Khurapariyantena ce pi cakkena yo imassa paṭhaviyā pāṇe ekaṁ maṁsakhalam ekaṁ maṁsapuññaṁ kareyya, natthi tatonidānaṁ pāpaṁ, natthi pāpassa āgamo...Dānena damena saṁyamena saccavajjena natthi puñña, natthi puññassa āgamo. DN., I, pp. 45-46.

stance, killing another, was also impossible."[1] Soul was thus not at all affected by good or evil.

Buddha believed in the doctrine of *karman* and its corollary, the doctrine of transmigration. According to an account in the *Majjhima Nikāya,* it constituted the second (*dutiyā vijjā*) of the three items of knowledge which led him to the realisation of *Bodhi*. It reads: 'Then with the mind composed, quite purified, quite clarified, without blemish, without defilement, grown soft and workable, fixed, immovable, I directed my mind to the knowledge of the passing hence the arising of beings. With the purified *deva*-vision surpassing that of men I see beings as they pass hence or come to be; I comprehend that beings are mean, excellent, comely, ugly, well-going, ill-going, according to the consequences of their deeds...This was the second knowledge attained by me in the middle watch of the night.."[2] The principle envisaged the inevitability of experiencing the results of one's past actions. A passage in the *Aṅguttara Nikāya* reads: "Monks, there are these two faults (*vajjāni*). What two ? That which has result in this very life and that which has its result in some future life."[3] Through this principle Buddha also explained the inequality which exists in the world around us. In the *Cūlakammavibhaṅga Sutta* is given the account of a conversation which took place between a Brahmin youth and Buddha. The former put to him why among human beings some have a short life-span while others live long, some come across many difficulties while others come across not many difficulties. Some are sickly while others are healthy, some have ugly look while others are handsome, some have little influence while others are influential, some are poor while others are rich, some belong to lower social status while others belong to a higher social status, some are devoid of wisdom while others possess wisdom.

[1]Pande, *Studies*, p. 348.

Ime satta kāyā akaṭā akaṭavidhā animmitā animmātā vañjhā kūṭaṭṭhā esikaṭṭhāyiṭṭhitā. Te na iñjanti, na vipariṇāmenti, na aññamaññaṁ vyābādhenti, nālaṁ aññamaññassa sukkāya vā dukkhāya vā sukhadukkhāyā vā. Tattha natthi hantā vā ghātetā vā sotā vā sāvetā vā viññātā vā viññāpeta vā. Yo pi tiṇhena satthena sīsam chindati, na koci kiñci jīvitā voropeti; sattannaṁtveva kāyanamantareṇa vivaramanupatatī, ti. DN, I, p. 49; for the rendering see *Dial.*, I, p. 74.

[2]*Middle Length Sayings* I, pp. 28-29.

[3]*Gradual Sayings*, I, p. 42.

In answer to this query Buddha says that: "Deeds are one's own. . . beings are heirs to deeds, deeds are matrix, deeds are kin, deeds are arbiters" (*Kammassakā sattā kammadāyādā kammayoni kammabandhū kammapaṭisaraṇā*) and that it is *kamma* which divides the beings (*kammaṁ satte vibhajjati*).[1]

One should not fall into the misconception of taking the Buddhist doctrine of *Karman* as mere rational speculation trying to explain the existing inequalities among human beings. Prof. K.N. Jayatilleka, after discussing the above Sutta in all its details, concludes his account in the following words: "But it would be mistaken to consider the passage in the above Sutta as presupposing a rational ethical argument with a concealed ethical premise. It is true as Ānanda has said of the Buddha that "so far as anything can be attained by reasoning (takka), thou has ascertained it" (Yāvatakaṁ takkāya pattabbaṁ anupattaṁ tayā S.I. 56) but the doctrine of karma is not put forward in Buddhism as a product of mere speculative reasoning (takka). . .The Buddha's statement even in this Sutta are based on clairvoyant observation and reasoning and not on mere rational speculation."[2] On many occasions, Buddha is recorded to have said: "With clairvoyant vision, purified, I see beings passing away in one state and reappearing in another state".[3] Such a vision was not confined to a Buddha only; it could be attained by others also.[4]

Karman is the connecting link between this life and the former life of an individual. *Saṁsāra* means the succession of births and deaths, births and deaths may be likened to intermediary stations in a long journey before the train reaches one to the place of destination which in this case is *Nibbāna* or the realisation of the ultimate truth. Thus, a new birth is not a starting from scratch; it has a past history which has a conditioning value. It is known as heredity. There are three factors which ought to combine for a new birth: the third factor is the 'being to be reborn' (*gandhabba*). "Where, monks, these

[1]'Cūlakammavibhanga Sutta', *MN.*, III, p. 280. The passage is oft-repeated in the *Nikāyas*, see *The Gradual Sayings*, III, pp. 60, 137, 249. *Middle Length Sayings*, III, p. 249.

[2]K.N. Jayatilleke, *The Message of the Buddha*, pp. 142-143.

[3]*Middle Length Sayings*, I, pp. 28, 45, 95, etc.; *Kindred Sayings*, II, p. 87; *Gradual Sayings*, I, pp. 148, 150, 234, etc.

[4]See *Gradual Sayings*, I, pp. 20, 22; *Kindred Sayings*, I, p. 249.

are found in combination, there a seed of life is planted. Thus, if a father and mother come together, but it is not the mother's period and the 'being to be born' is not present, then no seed of life is planted. Or, if the father and mother come together and it is the mother's period but the 'being to be born' is not present, then again no seed of life is planted. But when, monks, the father and mother come together and it is the mother's period and the 'being to be born' is also present, then, by the combined agency of these three, a seed of life is planted".[1] O.H. de Wijesekera has suggested that the '*gandhabba*' is the 'saṁsāric being in the intermediate stage between death and birth'.[2] It may, however, be noted that the view of an intermediate stage (*antarābhāva*) was entertained mainly by the Sarvāstivādins and not the Theravadins.[3] In the context of the *Abhidhamma*, '*gandhabba*' is substituted by '*patisandhiviññāṇa*' or the 'rebirth-linking consciousness' through which one life is connected to another.[4]

Karman as Moral Causation

Compared with the Vedic eschatological thinking, the Buddhist notion of *Karman* shows a remarkable difference. Even in the *Vedas* the belief in man carrying on his merit or demerit to the next world after death existed.[5] But it was invariably linked with the cult of sacrilficial ritualism. In Buddhism, the idea no longer depended on ritualism;[6] the emphasis was now shifted to the principle of moral determination. On the one hand, Buddha rejected the notion of a 'first beginning' of the world and with it the notion of a first cause, either God or any of the elements spoken of in such term in the *Upaniṣads*.[7] On the other hand, he did away with another theory

[1]*Middle Length Saying*, 'Mahātaṇhāsankhaya Sutta', I, p. 265f.

[2]O.H. de Wizesekera, 'Vedic Gandharva and Pali Gandhabba' *Ceylon University Review*, III, no. 1, April 1945.

[3]See *L' Abhidharmakośa de Vasubandhu*, p. 32.

[4]See P.T.S. *Dictionary*, s.v.; see also O.H. de A. Wijesekera, 'The Concept of Viññāṇa in the Theravāda Buddhism', *JAOS*, 84, no. 3, July-September 1964, p. 225; H. Saddhatissa, 'Concept of Rebirth in Buddhism', *Mahabodhi*, 77, no. 4-5 (Vaishakha Number), p. 137, fn 1.

[5]See E. W. Hopkins, *Ethics of India*, p. 8.

[6]Hopkins in *JRAS*, 1906, p. 583: 'Karma struck hard against the old belief in sacrifice, penance and repentance as destroyers of sin."

[7]For the rejection of such cosmological theories see 'Mūlapariyāya Sutta' of the *MN*.

which believed in the fortuitous origin of things in the world (*Yadrcchāvāda*). In the Buddhist texts, the latter theory is called *adhiccasasamuppāda.* Jayatilleke thinks that this term was coined by the Buddhists "to contrast this theory with the Buddhist theory of paṭicca-samuppanna or 'causal conditioning'".[1] As we have seen earlier, *Paṭiccasamuppāda* is a theory of causal origination which, by asserting that everything is related to something else, takes the world as a procession in which every intentional action serves a functional purpose and leads to a moral consequence. Apparently, every action leads to the experience of pleasure or pain, the new experience leading to another action which then results into a new experience, and in this way the process goes on. Deliverance from it is obtained only when, by realising the impermanent nature of the objects of desire, one becomes free from desire. So long as desire exists the chain of action-experience-action keeps on going with absolutely no possibility of obstruction or check due to the intervention of any external factor. In Buddhism, thus, morality and causality are unified at the psychic level. Will is both ethical as well as causal.

The Human Action and Moral Standard

The future of an individual, thus, depends on his deeds. His present condition of bondage is no doubt the result of his past deeds but by his own deeds he can also achieve deliverance from this bondage. Buddha exhorts his followers to be moral in their conduct which, according to him, is the first necessary condition for the realisation of the goal. The most frequent classification of action in the *Nīkāyas* is into *kusala* (good), *akusala* (bad) and *avyākata* (indifferent). These three lead one to *sukha, dukkha* and neither-*sukha*-nor-*dukkha* respectively. Another frequent classification, using the colour analogy, puts forth a fourfold division of action according to its nature and the result it leads to.[2] Sometimes,

[1] 'The Buddhist Theory of Causality' in *Mahabodhi*, 77, no. 1, January, 1969, p. 3.

[2] *MN.*, II, p. 63: '*Cattārimāni, Puṇṇa, kammāni...Atthi, Puṇṇa, kammaṁ kaṇhaṁ kaṇhavipākaṁ...sukkaṁ sukkavipākaṁ...kaṇhasukkaṁ kaṇhasukkavipākaṁ akaṇhaṁ asukkaṁ akaṇhaasukkavipākaṁ, kammakkhayāya saṁvattati.* Also *Gradual Sayings*, II, p. 238. *Dial.*, III, p. 221.

it is categorised as good and bad only.[1] If we apply the common-sensical view, the most obvious measuring-yard for the judgement of an action would be the result (*vipāka*) it brings about. This is the notion of action which one might notice in the utilitarian formula "in so far as it asserts that conduct is good or bad only in proportion as it tends to promote the well-being of human society on the whole."[2] The above classifications take into account both the action and the result the accrues from it; action and result are taken as mutually connected entities. But, action, apart from the immediate aspect, has the ultimate aspect. Act of drinking a sweet poisonous drink may produce the immediate result of a pleasant taste but in its ultimate result it is harmful to the person. *Vipāka* is, thus, not the immediate result of an action; it is the ultimate result. If I forcibly snatch money from someone, the immediate feeling in me may be of pleasure; but it alone cannot put this action in the category of good for it ultimately causes an accumulation of sin by way of commitment of *hiṁsā* toward the other person. If the action is to be judged from the viewpoint of its consequence, it is the moral and spiritual consequence which is important.

But, since action precedes *vipāka* and the latter is not within the comprehension of all before it has been actually realized, it cannot be taken as a practical criterion to judge an action. To solve this problem of moral standard, the Brahmins recommended '*vidhi*' i.e., the prescriptions stated in the *Vedas* which, according to their belief, are *apaureṣeya* or 'not laid down by a human being' (i.e. revealed). As Buddha had no faith in an all-powerful God and the validity of the *Vedas*, he had to recommend some other criterion which could be in accordance with his

[1]*Middle Length Sayings*, II, p. 375, III, p. 117 etc.

[2]Hastings Rashdall, *The Theory of Good and Evil*, p. 91. Jeremy Bentham defines the principle of utility as follows: "By the principle of utility is meant that principle which approves or disapproves of every action whatsoever, according to the tendency which appears to have to augment or diminish the happiness of the party whose interest is in question: or, what is the same thing in other words, to promote or to oppose that happiness. I say of every action whatsoever; and therefore not only of every action of a private individual, but of every measure of government". *An Introduction to the Principles of Morals and Legislation* (1823) in Harold H. Titus and Morris T. Keeton, *The Range of Ethics*, p. 108.

rational ideas about cosmology. He discarded the mechanical notion of action and considered it primarily psychological; he believed that *Karma* is volition as expressed in action.[1] Accordingly, he laid stress on the purity of motive. An unintentional act-even if it causes an apparently undesirable and sinful result-would bring no sin to the doer as in it the accompaniment of consciousness was missing. If somebody throws a stone at the mango-fruit on the tree and it accidently hits a person resulting into his death, he cannot be considered a moral offender because his physical action of throwing the stone had not originated from an intention to kill that person. The doctrine is in conformity with the general human psychology. If, for instance, someone tramples my foot but immediately apologises for his mistake and I am convinced that it was an unintended act, my anger vanishes and no desire of retaliation is left in me. Why is it so? Bain answers as follows: "Aware that absolute inviolability is impossible in this world, and that we are all exposed by turns to accidental injuries from our fellows we have our minds disciplined to let unintended evil go by without satisfaction of inflicting some counter evil upon the offender.[2] In like manner, a deed done in all good faith cannot be called immoral even though it might cause suffering to someone for the time being. Buddhism agrees with the view that 'the rightness of our intentions should be our moral preoccupation; a rightly motivated act is morally right. . .'[3] In fact, it is this notion, which considers intention to be the plank of moral judgement over an action, that justifies the profession of a doctor, According to Buddhism, even a *Tathāgata* can commit a deed which is apparently a deed of *hiṁsā*, but, as he has always a good motive, he does not suffer any moral pollution on that account. 'The Tathāgatha . . . wounds people but to their good, he casts people down but to their profit, he kills people but to their advantage. Just as mothers and fathers. . . hurt their children and even knock them down, thinking the while of their good; so by whatever method an increase in the virtue of living things can be brought about, by that method does he contri-

[1]See above.

[2]Bain, *Emotions and the Will*, p. 185 quoted in Westermarck, op.cit., p. 315.

[3]Clarence Irwing Lewis, *The Ground and the Nature of the Right* in Titus and Keetan, *The Range of Ethics*, p. 44.

bute to their good.'[1] The *Aṅguttara Nikāya* explains it with the help of the example of a baby and its nurse; if the baby puts a piece of stick or stone in mouth, the nurse would take it out even if it might cause pain to the child.[2] Such an action could not be called sinful for it has sprung from a feeling of love, seeking the child's welfare. Buddha disagreed with the Jaina belief that the nature of *Karman* is material, and, consequently, that every action, irrespective of the good or bad intention of the agent, enwraps the soul. Buddha, it has been rightly observed, had in this respect more affinities with the Brahmanical discipline than with the Jaina and the Ajivaka creeds.[3]

It would be well to make here a brief comparison between two diametrically opposed systems of ethical thought, viz., *Intuitionism* and *Ideal Utilitarianism*, and then to see the Buddhist position in this regard. The former is identified with the Kantian system of ethics. Whereas the Utilitarian takes the stand that the moral character of a person must be judged by the consequences which arise from his actions, the Intuitionist contends that will is the only significant moral factor. 'For the Ideal Utilitarian, murder is immoral because of the baneful consequences of killing; for the Intuitionist, murder is immoral because it stems from an ill will'.[4] In the light of our discussion above, Buddha would obviously belong to the Intuitionist school of ethical thought.

Buddha lays down another practical criterion to guide an individual with regard to his actions towards others. One should act likening others to oneself-*attānaṁ upamaṁ katvā;*[5] thus acting there would be no room for selfish motives. Acting on the analogy of one's own self, one would naturally refrain from indulging in such acts as might give pain to others. While proceeding to act in a particular way, one must pause to think how he would himself feel if someone acts similarly with regard to him.

[1] *The Questions of King Milinda*, I, (*SBE*, XXXV), pp. 164-65.

[2] *Gradual Sayings*, III, pp. 4-5.

[3] Satkari Mokerji, 'Influence of Buddhism on Indian Thought and Culture', *JBRS* (Buddha Jayanti Special Issue), 1956, p. 161.

[4] See William S. Sahakian, *Systems of Ethics and Value Theory*, p. 45.

[5] *Dhammapada*, verse 129.

Detached Action : Kamma-Nirodha

Motives propelled by *rāga* (attachment), *dosa* (malice) and *moha* (delusion) constitute *akusala karmas* (wrong actions) while those propelled by their oppposites-*arāga, adosa* and *amoha*-constitute *kusala karmas* (right actions). *Kusala* and *akusala* both are divisions of *sahetuka karma* (action with desire) and, in essence, both contain the element of craving which would not allow the wheel of birth and rebirth to come to an end. In the final analysis, all actions are to be put to cessation. It is interesting to note that in one passage of the *Saṁyutta Nikāya* the '*aṭṭhangika magga*' (Eightfold Path) usually called '*dukkhanirodhagāminī paṭipadā* (way leading to the cessation of suffering), is illustrated as '*Kammanirodhogāminī paṭipadā* (way leading to the ceasing of action).[1] Buddha speaks of happiness involved in non-action (*nekkhamma-sukham; nekkhamma=naiṣkarmya*) which he further says, is an integral part of the Right Way (*Sammā paṭipadā*).[2] *Kamma* and *dukkha* are thus taken as synonymous. *Kamma-nirodha* or *nekkhamma*, however, does not mean renouncing all actions; that is impossible. On the other hand, one has to rather overcome all desires and act without being attached to the objects of the world. It is attachment, positive or negative, that binds man. In the spiritual exercise of the *Brahmavihāras*, after the seeker has perfected in the practice of friendliness, compassion and sympathy towards all beings, he is finally enjoined to practise the inculcation of the feeling of indifference (*upekkhā*). A perfect man or Arhat has no desires to base on any of the worldly objects, and, consequently, there are no results of actions for him.

[1] Kammanirodha Sutta', *SN.*, pp. 120-121-*Katamā ca, bhikkhave, kammanirodhagāminī paṭipadā? Ayameva ariyo aṭṭhangika maggo, seyyathīdaṁ-sammā diṭṭhi, sammā saṅkappo...ayam vuccati, bhikkhave, kammanirodhagāminī paṭipadā: Kindred Sayings*, p. 85.

[2]See *MN.*, III, p. 175...*Tavānanda, Tathāgato vivekaninneneva cittena vivekoponena vivekapabbhāreṇa vūpakaṭṭhena; nekkhammābhiratena byantībhūtena sabbaso āsavaṭṭhanīyehi dhammehi aññadatthu uyyojanapaṭisaṁyuttaṁ yeva kathaṁ kattā hoti.*

ibid, p. 319: 'Araṇṇavibhaṅga Sutta': *Tatra, bhikkhave, yamidaṁ kāmasukhaṁ mīḷhasukhaṁ potthujjanasukhāṁ anariyasukhaṁ, sadukkho eso dhammo saupaghāto saupāyāso sapariḷāho: micchā paṭipadā. Tasmā eso dhammo saraṇo. Tatra, bhikkhave, yamidaṁ nekkhammasukhaṁ pavivekasukhaṁ saupasāyasukhaṁ sambodhisukhaṁ adukkho eso dhammo anupaghāto anupāyāso aparilāho: sammā paṭipadā. Tasmā eso dhammo araṇo.*

Despite its negative phrasing, non-attachment entails numerous positive virtues which accounts for its significant place in the prominent religions of the world. Egoism constitutes the fulcrum of all attachment, for it is 'ego' coming in conflict with 'non-ego' that causes the notion of 'I' and 'you', 'mine' and 'yours', etc. Consequently, one begins to cling to worldly objects as exclusively one's own, denying them entirely to others. For the destruction of egoism the *Gītā* lays stress on subjective purification as well as God-realisation. The latter is a theistic means to make one see a Supreme Power in each and every being and make one feel that one is an inseparable part of it. It is clearly stated that God resides in all the beings and he who comprehends this makes no discrimination at all. Such a wise person looks on all as one and on the analogy of his own self looks upon the pleasure and pain of all with similar eye.[1] One is commanded to restrain one's restless and fidgety mind from all the allurements of the world and shift it to God[2] with the assurance that His devotee will not perish.[3] This tendency of mind would lead to the merger of the individual's will in the divine will. Devotion to God would increase in the same proportion as attachment to the sense-objects would decrease.

This theistic method for the inculcation of non-attachment has affinities with the Christian concept which attaches in its framework of ethics a significant place to devotion to God. Jesus' will to make all feel that 'they have sinned and come short of the glory of God,'[4] implies essentially a gospel of attachment to God and, conversely, non-attachment to worldly things. The Christian doctrine of common sinfulness and firm belief in the imminent Kingdom of God,[5] suggests detachment from worldly objects and shift of mind to God, for it is the good and godly only that may be admitted to it. The supreme object of desire and craving becomes the will to live in nearness to God. It is, though paradoxical it may sound, preaching *niṣkāma*

[1] *Gītā.*, VI, 31-32.
[2] ibid., VI, 26.
[3] ibid., IX, 31.
[4] See Earnest Troeltsch, *The Social Teaching of the Christian Churches*, I, p. 72; also ibid., p. 54.
[5] George Foot Moore, *History of Religions*, II, pp. 115-16; Sherman Johnson, *Jesus in His Own Times*, pp. 115-17; Troeltsch, loc. cit., p. 51.

karma (action without desire) by the way of *sakāma karma* (action with desire).

The notion of a supreme God had no place in the doctrine of Buddha. Buddhist theory of non-attachment is, therefore, free from any influence of a theistic cosmological framework. It is a product of rational thinking based upon the conviction of universal suffering and an effort towards its eradication. It arrives, nevertheless, at the same conclusion by traversing a different path, the path of self-purification. It is not surprising to see the Buddhist texts elucidating the theory sometimes in almost the same language, using phraseologies which have at times astonishing parallels in the *Gītā*[1] '*Uncontaminated*' (*anūpalitto*) is one of the many epithets used for the Buddha,[2] i.e., he is not stained by the affairs of the world as alotus leaf is not wetted by the water it floats upon. We read in the *Sutta-Nipāta* about a perfect man as one 'who does not aim at gifts nor resents their lack; he has abated all the cravings and allurements lose all powers upon him.'[3] The perfect man is uncontaminated not only by evil or vice but also by good or virtue. Perfection knows no dualism. It is a disposition of mind in which good and evil both become equally undesirable,[4] when one becomes like ocean

[1]For a detailed account of such parallels and similarities of expression see G.S.P. Misra, 'Non-attachment in the Buddhist Texts and the *Gītā* in *Quest*, 45, Spring, 1965, pp. 48-51. I am inclined to believe that the *Gītā* is indebted to Buddhism -and the repertory of Śramaṇism as a whole—from which it borrowed and made necessary modifications. For a general comparative study of ethical ideas as found in the *Gītā* and Buddhism see K.N. Jayatilleke, 'Some Aspects of Gītā and Buddhist Ethics', *University of Ceylon Review*, XII, 1955, pp. 135-51.

[2]*Mv*., p. 11: *Sabbābhibhū sabbavidūhamasmi sabbesu dhammesu anūpalitto..*; also, *Kindred Sayings*, III, p. 118; *Sutta-Nipāta*, 71.

[3]*Sutta-Nipāta*, 854-*Lābhakāmā na sikkhati, alābhe na ca kuppati, aviruddho ca taṇhāya rase ca nānugijjhaṭi. Kindred Sayings*, I, p. 78: 'Whoso hath left the world...neither feels pleasure, nor is sad at heart'. Compare *Gītā*, II. 56: '*Duḥkhasu anudvignamanāḥ sukheṣu vigataspṛhaḥ; Gītā*, II, 48: *Siddhyasiddhyoḥ samo bhūtvā samatvaṁ yoga ucyate*. This disposition of mind may be described as '*sarvadharmasvabhāvasamatāvipañcitaṁ nāma samādhi*', *Gilgit MSS*, II, p. 15.

[4]*Sutta-Nipāta*, 790: 'Uncontaminated whether by virtue or vice, self-cast away, for such there is no more action needed there.' Also ibid., 520 where a true Śramaṇa is defined as follows:

'*Samitāvipahāya puṇṇapāpaṁ, virajo ñatvā imaṁ paramaṁ ca lokaṁ Jātimaraṇe upativatto*, '*samaṇo*' *tāhi pavuccte tathattā*.'

wherein rivers of enjoyments merge without disturbing its placidity and equilibrium. The good is good only in so far as it helps in reaching the other shore; what is the sense and wisdom in bearing its burden when the destination is reached? Righteousness, according to the Buddhists, is an empirical and subjective category. As S.K. Maitra has observed, 'it is vasana, disposition of the chitta or mental continuum–a continuum which is annulled in the transcendental state.'[1] In the Buddhist texts this idea of transcendence of *dhamma* in the final stage finds enunciation by way of the parable of Raft.[2]

Karman, Doctrines of Anattā and Aniccatā, and the problem of Moral Responsibility.

Having once assumed *Karman* to be all powerful and its results unavoidable, the cultivation of mind from the standpoint of determinism would be very natural. But, if everything in the world is to be taken as preordained, there would remain no place for morality, and responsibility would mean nothing but an illusion. For, 'if there be no such originator, if the person possesses no real freedom, then retaliation, revenge, punishment are not only morally assailable, but are simply senseless, purely imaginary phenomena'.[3] The importance

[1]S.K. Maitra, *The Ethics of the Hindus*, p. 80.

[2]*MN.*, 'Alagaddūpama Sutta,' I, p. 180:...*evameva kho, bhikkhave, kullūpamo mayā dhammo desito nittharaṇatthāya, no gahaṇatthāya. Kullūpamaṁ vo, bhikkhave, dhammaṁ desitaṁ ajānantehi dhammāpi vo pahātabbā pagena adhammā,*

In the *Sutta-Nipāta*, 21 Buddha says that with the help of a well-wrought Raft he has crossed over the Flood and that he needed no further rafts:

'Buddhā hi bhisi susaṅkhatā
Tiṇṇo pāragato vineyya oghaṁ.
Attho bhisiyā na vijjati.'

This superfluousness of Law after the attainment of enlightenment has been emphasized also by some Western thinkers. St. Augustine's "Let him no longer use the law as a means of arrival when he has arrived" and Meister Ekhart's "having gotten to the other side I do not need a ship" are exact parallels of the Buddhist parable of Raft. See Coomaraswamy and Horner, *La Pansee de Gotama le Boudha*, pp. 57-58. See also Burnett Hillman Streeter, *The Buddha, and the Christ*, p. 176-'Of course, if by the "Moral Law" you mean the Ten Commandments, it is transcended. "Honour thy father and thy mother", and such like rules become merely irrelevant when one thinks of God...'

[3]*Nicolai Hartmann, Ethics*, III, p. 72. See Aristotle, *Nichomachean Ethics*, *Contd.*

of will in relation to one's feeling is known to the Vedic hymnodists. When the Vedic singer apologises-"It is not our own will, Varuṇa, that leads us astray, but some seduction-wine, anger, dice and our folly",[1] he is obviously making an excuse, that he should not be held responsible for his actions as it was without the application of his will that the deed was committed. The *Upaniṣads* show a clear awakening to the relation between desire, will, action and the effect of action.[2]

Determinism is often mistaken to be a complete human subjection to destiny, a slavery to some force which rules out completely the freedom of will. As we have seen earlier, this was the case with the Ājīvakas who refused the reality of anything which could correspond to the term 'human exertion'; man has no choice in the making or unmaking of his future. This misapprehension of the meaning of determinism is manifest also in the modern pre-Kantian philosophical thought; Fichte, until he became acquainted with Kant's philosophy, felt determinism to be an 'outrage upon man', a slavery.[3] It is upon this mental background that Kant's doctrine appealed to him as a doctrine of deliverance.

On the issue of the freedom of will and the freedom to act, Buddha's standpoint is sharply opposed to that of the Ājīvakas. He called Makkhali, the Ajivaka teacher, a 'man-trap': 'Just as, monks, at a river-mouth, one sets a fish-trap, to the discomfort, suffering, distress and destruction of many fish, even so Makkhali, the infatuated man, was born into the world, methinks, to be a man-trap, for the discomfort, suffering, distress and destruction of many beings.'[4] A preacher of deliverance as he was, the absurdity and incompatability of principle of inaction or fatalism with the rest of his teaching

A commentary by H.H. Joachim, p. 95-A classification of action is made. Man, Aristotle says, is not responsible in all cases; F.H. Bradley, *Ethical Studies*, pp. 5-7 gives a list of factors which go to make ordinary mind feel responsible for his deeds. One of them is the belief that whatever he did was not under some stress or force.

[1]*Ṛv.*, V. 7.86.6.

[2]Ranade, *A constructive Survey of Upanisadic Philosophy*, p. 313.

[3]Nicolai Hartmann, op. cit., p. 56.

[4]*Gradual Sayings*, I, p. 20, p. 30, p. 265.

is obvious. The precedence of 'volition' to action[1] in the formation of *Karma* and the significant position of Right Intention (*Sammā Saṅkappa*) assigned in the Eightfold Path is a sufficient proof of Buddha's keenness to lay an emphatic stress on the will-power of man. So many ways for its cultivation have been suggested and throughout his ethical teaching, though 'subject to the law of karman, conscious action is equivalent to spontaneous action'.[2] To Buddha, inaction is most abominable. He himself struggled for the attainment of the goal and taught the same to his followers. His doctrine is a doctrine of struggle and resistance—struggle against the forces which cause suffering, a conscious resistance against object pleasures of senses; it is an exertion, a struggle toward the attainment of the *summum bonum*. Buddha solemnly declares that he has made the *Norm* manifest and every clansman, who has left the world, should cultivate a strong will:

"Verily, let skin and sinews and bones wilt in my body, let flesh and blood dry up, yet shall there be upkeep of energy, till I have won that which by man's strength, by man's energy, by man's progress may be won."[3]

It is a mistaken view that freedom and determinism are absolutely contradictory concepts. Freedom does not mean to be free from everything for 'to be free from everything is to be free from nothing'.[4] Freedom loses all its meaning when there is no limitation on it. There is no sense in such thinking as 'had the circumstances been such and such, I could have acted thus'. Man living in India, for example,

[1]See Westermerck, op. cit., p. 323. He says that the fact that the deeds of man are generally preceded by volition is so obvious that it cannot escape even the simplest mind. It is on account of this that man attributes every event to will.

[2]Charles Eliot, *Hinduism and Buddhism*, I, Introduction, p. lxxviii.

[3]*Middle Length Saying*, pp. 24, 481; *Gradual Sayings*, I, p. 45. Monks are instructed not to decline to contest but to struggle on, saying to themselves the above formula of self-cultivation.

One comes across a beautiful description of Buddha's strong determination at the time of his final bid for the attainment of *bodhi* in *Lalita-vistara*, p. 210.

Ihā ane śuṣyatu me śarīraṁ
Tvagasthimsāṁaṁ pralayaṁ ca yātu
Aprāpya bodhiṁ bahukalpadurlabhāṁ
Naivāsanātkāyamataścaliṣyate.

[4]F.H. Bradley, op. cit., p. 56.

should judge and enact the possibilities of his actions in terms of the circumstances in which he finds himself placed and not in terms of what he could have been and done had he been positioned in America or France. It is circumstances that provide the will with the object and the concrete possibilities of direction for its striving and exertion. The supposed incompatible position of freedom and determinism is a superficial one: action implies a simultaneous application of determinism and indeterminism. Freedom is needed only for purposes of action. Action becomes an action in the true sense when the element of freedom enters, but it also assumes some degree of determinism. This is clear from common experience. The effect of our action is not strictly predictable; sometimes, an action, though based on past experiences, does not necessarily bring about the expected result.[1] And, here we must admit determinism. When Buddha condemned Makkhali Gosāla, he had in his view both Gosala's adherence to strict determinism and, on that account, the denial of any action worth the name in entirety. The law of causation, no doubt, affirms that effects by no kind of external agency can be annulled, but at the same time, it does not deny an addition to it. 'Freedom is not a Minus from determinism. It is a Plus.'[2]

Accordingly, Buddha did not find his doctrine of free will in contradistinction to his notion of determinism involved in the chain of causation. The causation theory, it has been well observed, is not a fixed theory[3] in the sense that according to Buddhism every stage is a cause as well as an effect. "There is a cause in the effect and effect in the cause'. When it is an effect it is predestined by past deeds but otherwise it is a self- determinant entity.

Karman determines, on the one hand, character (*saṁskāra*) and, on the other, experiences (*bhoga*), pleasant or painful. But, *Karman* itself is an emergent resulting from the interaction of will-power, character and circumstances. Character (*saṁskāra*) signifies characteristics conditioned by past deeds, circumstances the outside world; and the will-power the inner energy. These factors constitute one's personality and will has got an equally important place. With the

[1]See C.T. Ducasse, *Determinism, Freedom and Responsibility*. A Symposium on Determinism and Freedom in the Age of Modern Science, p. 154.

[2]Nicolai Hartmann, op. cit., p. 55.

[3]J. Takakusu, *Essentials of Buddhist Philosophy*, p. 28.

help of this faculty man can bring about a change in the circumstances he has been put in. The fact should not be overlooked that it is not only past deeds that condition what man is: *Kamma* is recognised as one of the many factors that work at a time, and it has been said that those who hold *kamma* alone to be the cause of the present condition of the individual are going against reason and common experience.[1]

Another point which need be discussed in this context is with regard to the recognition of identity between the doer and experiencer of an act 'for responsibility ceases where identity of character ceases'.[2] The apparent incongruity between a notion of moral responsibility and the Buddhist doctrine of *Anattā* (no-self) is a superficial one. Buddha's clear enunciation that "Karma" is one's own...' etc., goes to suggest that an individual is a pure product of his deeds and it is in his own hands to allow his miseries to continue or to stop it. Buddha believed all the phenomenal objects to be not-self and devoid of permanence, resulting in consequential denial of sameness in the same individual at two consecutive moments. But, he believed in the principle of continuity and that, though there is an absolute absence of sameness, there is similarity. The individual of a particular

[1]*SN.*, III, pp. 204-205. Eight causes of pain and pleasure are enumerated here; they are: *pitta, semha, vāta, sannipāta, utu, visama, upakkama, kamma-vipāka*.

The *Gītā* refers to the Sāmkhaya system which considers five factors to be necessary in the formation of *karma*. These are: the body, the doer or the *Jīvātmā*, various organs, divergent activities and, the last, *destiny*, see ch. XVIII, 13, 14, 15; the *Gītā* XVIII, 18 says that the doer, the action, and the organ of action-these are the threefold constituents of *karma* (*trividhaḥ karmasaṁgrahaḥ*.) Indian thinkers distinguish three kinds of *karma*: *sañcita*, *prārabdha*, and *āgāmi*. *Sañcita* is all the accumulated *karma* of the past responsible for the individuals' characters, tendencies, inclinations, etc. *Prārabdha* conditions our present body and *āgāmi* is the coming *karma* which includes also that which is being gathered at present. The three have been explained with the help of an analogy of a bow-man with a quiver on his back. He has already shot one arrow from the quiver, with another he is taking aim at a target. Now, the arrows in his quiver on the back signify *sañcita karma*, the arrow he has sent forth signifies *prārabdha karma*, and the one he is still to shoot is *āgāmi karma*. Of these he has every control over the *sañcita* and *āgāmi* and has lost control over the *prārabdha*. Man is, thus, free to reform his character and make himself happy. T.M.P. Mahadevan, *Outline of Hinduism*, pp. 60-61.

[2]L.T. Hobhouse, *Morals in Evolution*, p. 504.

moment cannot be independent of the one immediately preceding it in as much as the one is caused and conditioned by the other. The *Milindapañho* gives several examples[1] to explain it, one of which is that of a girl in her childhood and when she is grown up. The father of the girl cannot refuse to give her to her husband on the ground that she is not the same girl as she was on the occasion of her marriage some few years back. She is, no doubt, not the same girl but definitely not a different one.

Buddha preached the doctrine of *Anattā* on two levels-empirical and metaphysical. Buddhism does not believe in the metaphysical reality of man but at the same time it does not deny his empirical reality. When he laid down disciplinary rules for the monks or exhorted his followers to practise *samādhi* and such other spiritual means for the destruction of desire and attainment of *Nirvāṇa,* he certainly meant that there is an agent who acts and experiences the results of his deeds: otherwise, what deed, by whom and for whom? But, we find ourselves on a paradoxical ground when he admonishes monks to concentrate on the non-existence of any permanent nature in a thing. The cultivation of mind in this direction refers to a different plane, the metaphysical one, which consists of true understanding of the world and the self and the consequent destruction of ego as a prerequisite for the realisation of *Nirvāṇa.* Before the attainment of this stage of mental elevation, however, the identity of agency in the doer and the experiencer of a deed cannot be gainsaid.

Three Levels of the Doctrine of Karman[2]

In the previous pages we dealt with the doctrine of *Karman* in its relation to human action and moral standard and saw how it steers through the notion of indeterminism and determinism. Now, it has become easy and also necessary to distinguish several aspects of this law as the neglect of its multi-dimensionality has often led to many misleading conclusions. The principal aspects of the *Law of Karman* may be described as causal, moral and spiritual. The first two are generally combined in Buddhism and together belong to *Samvṛtti* or the realm of phenomenality. On the causal plane man is just an ob-

[1]*Questions of King Milinda* I, *SBE,* XXXV, pp. 64-65, 70.

[2]The philosophical standpoint expressed here derives from my teacher G.C. Pande.

ject of nature–*nissatta*, *nijjīva*–and any law of nature (*dhammatā*) holds true for him as in the case of any other object.[1] The law of *Karman* becomes, in other words, the psycho-ethical aspect of the universe. One comprehends it rationally and by its help seeks to attain mastery over nature. *Karman* is here a psychic force (*cetanā*) which may be good or evil and is responsible for the happiness and suffering of all beings. As a psycho-ethical principle, the law of *Karman* comes to acquire a regulative value for human conduct and is the source of prescription and prohibitions. The *Karmic* law on this plane lays down that a morally good volitional act brings about pleasant result whereas a morally bad volitional act would always result in misery for the doer. On the other hand, all *karman* is felt to arise from ignorance and, in a deep sense, all the experience it produces belongs to the realm of suffering. As such all *karman* ought to be finally transcended. On the one hand, the law of *karman* enables us to effect a distinction between right and wrong within the realm of phenomenality (*samvṛtti*). On the other hand, its transcendence leads one beyond the phenomenal. Those two aspects correspond to the distinction later made between *samvṛtti* and *paramārtha*. On the one hand, *karman* is at once a causal and moral factor. On the other, its transcendence is the gateway to spiritual freedom. The doctrine of *Karman* thus implies a strict moral regulation of life and disciplining of psychic forces. At the same time, the doctrine of *karman* points out that the entire life of egoistic action is one of bondage and man should seek to reach beyond the polarities of pleasure and pain, right and wrong, to spiritual freedom expressing itself in peace and compassion.

[1]For example, Newton's Law of Gravitation or the Third Law of Motion would hold true of man as well as of any other natural objects.

CHAPTER 3

Psychological Analysis and Moral Life

Need of Psychological Analysis and Logical Approach

Early Buddhism is primarily based on mendicant ideas. In it the concept of *Arhat* is dominant. An *Arhat* is a man perfected. "Under Gotama it was taught that mental development and self-mastery, of which it was believed that every monk and nun was potentially capable, would bring the aspirant into the presence of *nibbāna* and *ipso facto* to *arahatta*, the state of being an *arahan*".[1] It is apparent that the concept had a great ethical and intellectual implication. Dr. I.B. Horner has pointed to the great conceptual change implied in it in the following words: "Hence we see that under Buddhism the great Upaniṣadic doctrine of the immanent divinity of man, expressed in the classical phrase "That art thou" (*tat tvam asi* with emphasis on *tvam*) was no longer accepted. It was replaced by a corresponding doctrine of man *becoming* Brahma-like as opposed to his *being* Brahma-like. This was the arahan theory: it claimed to see man accomplishing perfection, not simulating it."[2]

With such an ideal-accompanied by an adherence to the doctrine of *Karman* which conceives man as the inheriter of his deeds and the sole maker of his future destiny-which underlines the potential perfectibility of man and therefore the need for human exertion for its attainment, Buddhist ethics naturally does not rely on any conventional authority. It refuses to deal with any traditional morality; on the other hand, it is a universal morality free of all religious dogmas, class distinction or convictions. In the 18th-19th century Europe, too, many attempts were made to dissociate morality from religion or conventions, but all of them came to rely upon certain

[1] I.B. Horner, *The Early Buddhist Theory of Man Perfected: A Study of the Arahan*, p. 74.

[2] ibid., p. 100.

convictions. For example, utilitarianism or the class-struggle of the Marxists may be pointed out as such convictions. Buddhist morality, on the other hand, rests on human nature. Two basic factors are involved in the making of the total framework of Buddhist morality; the first is the spiritual experience of the Buddha which can be shared by anyone who is intent upon its realisation and makes right efforts therefor; the other is the analysis of human mind. In Buddhism, an attempt is made to give a psychological basis of ethical consciousness. In fact, the problem of the attainment of higher knowledge is inevitably and directly related with the nature of consciousness. 'The training of consciousness is the indispensable antecedent condition of higher knowledge, because consciousness is the vessel upon whose capacity depends the *extent* of what is to be received. Knowledge on the other hand, is the antecedent condition required for the *selection* of the material to be received, and for the *direction* of the course to be pursued for its mastery.'[1] The rejection of any external authority further necessitated an analytical and logical approach as the only convincing criterion for the acceptance of what Buddhism sought to advocate.

Concept of Analytical and Logical Methods[2]

In the Buddhist scheme of culture animism and ritualism stand automatically rejected. The warrant of this rejection lies in its rational outlook which refuses to accept anything that is beyond experience. It is this attitude which led Buddha to categorise certain questions as unanswerable (*avyākata*). But Buddha did not limit his notion of experience only to that knowledge which is made available to one with the help of the various sense-organs in companionship with the mind. He believed in two levels of reality, the phenomenal and the absolute. Whereas phenomenal reality can be a matter of objective experience and verbal communication, absolute reality cannot be so experienced and communicated. It can only be "transcendentally" experienced and is, therefore, beyond

[1]A.B. Govinda, *The Psychological Attitude of the Early Buddhist Philosophy*, p. 43.

[2]For a detailed exposition see Appendix which was originally published in the *JRAS*, 1968, 1 & 2.

logic (*atakko*).[1] Buddhism clearly is, thus, at once positivistic and mystical in its approach.

Buddhism clearly states that certain matters are "not in the sphere of *takka*."[2] In many passages, *takkapariyāhataṁ* (overcome by reasoning) and *vīmaṁsānucaritaṁ* (addicted to investigation) are used as terms of disqualification for a religious preacher or thinker.[3] Such instances may be taken as pronouncements of censure against logical reasoning and its acceptance as a valid means of knowledge.[4] But, in fact, what is rejected here is not the validity of logical reasoning as such but a vicious and unnecessary dialectic and its extreme application to such matters which belong to the realm of transcendentality. The Suttas abound in the application of logical and intellectual method. "In the Suttas no sentence occurs oftener than 'Taṁ," kissa hetu?' 'what is the reason of that'[5] The Buddhist attitude is well exemplified in the 'Brahmajālasutta' of the *Dīgha Nikāya* where Buddha has advised monks not to get angry or pleased when others belittle or applaud the Buddha, the Dhamma, or the *Saṅgha* because then they would not be able to judge the truth in their statements. They should, on the other hand, view their statements critically and comment in this manner. "For this or that reason, this is not the fact, that is not so, such a thing does not exist among us, is not in us" or "For this or that reason this is the fact. . .", etc.[6]

The scientific and logical attitude of the early Buddhists is best illustrated in their concept of law (*dhammatā*) and the concept of cause (*hetu*). In opposition to such concepts as *sassatavāda* (eternalism) and *adhiccasamuppāda* (accidental origin of things) which were held by some contemporary thinkers to explain the nature of the phenomena, Buddha propounded the doctrine of correlated action, which goes to suggest an existence of law and order in the progress of cause and effect. In Buddhist terminology the doctrine is known as *paṭiccasamuppāda*, which is meant to illustrate the law of *idappaccayatā* or the dependent origination of things.

[1] *Mv.*, p. 11.

[2] See *DN.*, I, p. 16; also ibid., pp. 20, 22, 27.

[3] ibid., I, p. 16; *MN.*, I, p. 96; ibid., II, p. 219.

[4] See, e.g., S.C. Vidyabhusan, *History of Mediaeval School of the Indian Logic*, p. 59.

[5] *ERE*, VIII, p. 132. [6] *Dial.*, I, p. 3.

The method of reasoning used in the Buddhist texts is obviously analytical. Buddha himself claimed to be an 'analyst' and not a dogmatist who gives categorical statements. Two passages from the *Vinaya*, which are quoted below, would well illustrate the analytical method employed in the early Buddhist texts, which very often takes the form of a catechism; Buddha is said to have argued like this to show *anattā* in all the five *khandhas*:

"Body, monks is not self. Now were this body self, monks, this body would not tend to sickness and one might get chance of saying in regard to body, 'Let body become thus for me, let body not become thus for me.' But, inasmuch, monks, as body is not self, therefore, body tends to sickness, and one does not get the chance of saying in regard to body, 'Let body become thus for me, let body not become thus for me," and so with the other *khandhas*.[1]

In the same context, the argument has been carried further :

"What do you think about this, monks ? Is body permanent or impermanent ?"

"Impermanent, Lord."

"But is that which is impermanent, painful or pleasurable?"

"Painful, Lord."

"But, is it fit to consider that which is impermanent, painful, of a nature to change as 'This is mine, this am I, this is my self ?"

"It is not, Lord"[2]

The analytical method of reasoning can be also seen in the *Milindapañho* or the *Questions of King Milinda* which is an early non-canonical text. It makes an attempt to answer a number of dilemmas observable in the Buddhist scheme of culture (and seeing dilemmas in the scripture itself attests a remarkable logical and scientific attitude). Even if the explanations offered might not stand up to a scientific and logical test, nevertheless they point to a questioning and reasoning mind that took trouble to seek explanations of two statements, attributed to the Master, which appeared contradictory.

In logical formulation and discussion it is essential that exact meaning of each and every word used is precisely laid down. For the first time in the history of Indian thought, the Boddhist texts manifest an explicit awareness of the concept of definition (*lakṣaṇa*). They further show the tendency to classify the objects and the topics under

[1]*The Book of the Discipline*, IV, p. 20. [2]ibid.

discussion, a tendency which is very prominently seen in the texts belonging to the *Abhidhamma Pitaka*. For an assessment of the definitions occurring in such *Abhidhamma* books as the *Dhammasañgañi, Vibhañga* and *Puggala-paññatti* we cannot do better than quote Mrs. Rhys Davids :

"Abhidhamma definitions, while they are certainly a notable psychological advance over anything achieved in earlier or contemporary Indian literature, may not be satisfying to our own logical tradition. They consist very largely of enumerating synonyms, or partly synonymous, terms, such as we might call overlapping circles. But, they reveal to us much useful information concerning the term described, the terms describing the term, and the terms which we may have expected to find, but find not. And they show the Socratic earnestness with which these early Schoolmen strove to clarify their concepts, so as to guard their doctrines from the heretical innovations, to which ambiguity in terms would yield cheap foothold."[1]

Among all the books of the *Abhidhamma*, the *Kathāvatthu* is intended to fulfil the important task of applying logical reasoning and logic to reduce all possible heterodox positions to an absurd footing. This book deals with about 200 questions on diverse issues including cosmology, psychology and ethics, etc. It is an attempt into the exercise of showing the dialectical advantage of the Theravādins over other sects of the *sāsana* of the Buddha. In every thesis put forward by his opponent, the Theravādin would point out the implications involved therein which would not be acceptable to the opposite party. Putting his opponent in a position of dilemma, the Theravādin would then refute the original thesis.[2]

Analysis of Human Personality : *Nature of Conscious Existence*

Man in Buddhism is conceived as a psycho-physical organism, as a combination of certain psychological and physical qualities, *nāma* and *rūpa*. A further analysis of *nāma* leads to its sub-division into *vedanā* (sensation), *saññā* (reaction of the mind to the sense stimuli), *saṅkhāra* (mental process) and *viññāṇa* (consciousness) which, along with *rūpā*, constitute the five stems (*khandhas-skandhas*) of the human personality. This combination of *nāma* and *rūpa*, or the five *skandhas*

[1]Mrs. Rhys Davids, *The Birth of Indian Psychology and its Development in Buddhism*, p. 369.

[2]See Appendix.

makes a person appear as an independent unit of existence, an 'individual' and is given a name. It is this which, under the influence of *avijjā*—the particular form of which is known as *sakkāyadiṭṭhi*-' leads to the notton of 'I' as a permanent substance, distinguishing and separating one from others.

But, when one proceeds to scrutinize these constituent units of human personality, one is struck by their fluxional nature. Each one of these is found to be impermanent (*anicca*) and, thus, devoid of any independent nature of its own. That physical form, or body, is impermanent and subject to change, is a matter of common experience. Mind, however, is much less lasting. Impermanence here is much more marked, as it is never the same for any two consecutive instants of time.[1] Like an ape in the forest, which leaves one branch only to catch the other,[2] mind always runs from one object to the other and is in a state of ceaseless flux. Conscious existence, thus, as the Buddhist simile goes, is 'like the current of a river' (*nadi soto viyā*), ever changing, though maintaining 'a seeming identity'.[3]

In Buddhism, *vijñāna*, *citta* and *manas* are used in the same sense, in the sense of mind and mental procession.[4] Mind may be called the foremost among the conditioned *dharmas*[5] as it is the refuge of all human activity. *Karma*, which is the *raison d'etre* of phenomenal existence, has its roots in it. Each of the five senses—seeing, hearing, smelling, tasting and touching—has its own field of functioning and corresponding objects (the visible, the audible, the olfactory, the gestatory of the tactile) and none of these enjoys the field and the object of others. The five senses take their refuge in the *manas* and it is the *manas* which enjoys their field and the objects.[6] But, as Buddhism considers all entitles to be of fluxional nature, *manas* too is not taken as

[1]*Kindred Sayings*, II, pp. 65-66.

[2]ibid.; *Viśuddhimāga* ed. Dharmarakshita, II, p. 102.

[3]Shwe Zan Aung, *Compendium of Philosophy*, Introduction, pp. 8-9; see also A.B. Govinda, *The Psychological Attitude of the Early Buddhist Philosophy*, pp. 175-76.

[4]*Viśudhimārga*, ed. Dharmarakshita, II, p. 69.

[5]In the *Abhidhammatthasaṅgaha*, Aniruddha mentions consciousness (*citta*), mental properties (*cetasika*), material and bodily qualities (*rūpa*) and *Nibbāna* as things which exist in their ultimate sense. See *Abhidhammatthasaṅgaho*, p. 1; *Compendium of Philosophy*, p. 81.

[5]*Middle Length Sayings*, I, p. 355.

a permanent entity but as something continuously changing. "This means that the fluxional character of the *manas* is nothing distinct from the *manas* itself and therefore cannot be regarded as an antecedent or subsequent event with respect to its own nature, though it may be conceived as either an antecedent or a subsequent event with respect to the immediately following or immediately preceding phase of the psychic process."[1]

Mind and the Objects : Functioning of the Mind

Conception of material phenomena and mind as a fluxional entity, however, raises a problem. If the objects, which are cognized, and mind, which cognizes, both are of fleeting character, how can there be perception ? The difficulty is resolved by introducing two different sets of duration—moments to mind and phenomena. It is conceived that every thought-moment-which may be understood as a single unit of mental activity-consists of three phases, nascent, static, arrested, and seventeen such thought-moments (*citta-kṣana*) constitute the duration of material phenomena (*rūpa-kṣana*).[2]

Individual existence, understood in Buddhism as a continuum or a process, is explained with the help of *paṭisandhi* (skt. *pratisandhi*), *bhavaṅga* (skt. *bhavāṅga*) and *cuti* (skt. *cyuti*). *Paṭisandhi* is the first thought at the time of birth which connects the stream of consciousness of the past existence with the stream of consciousness of the present consciousness. It reunites the two existences and is so called *patisandhiviññāṇa* (unifying consciousness).[3] *Bhavaṅga* denotes mind in its semi-conscious or subconscious state,[4] for example, as in a deep sleep. In *Abhtdhammattha Vibhāvanī*, a mediaeval Ceylonese commentary, it is explained as 'cause, reason, indispensable condition of our being regarded subjectively as continuous: the *sine qua non* of our existence. That without which one cannot subsist or exist.'[5] This state of mind, called *bhavaṅga-citta*, also called *vīthimutta*, is contra-

[1]Herbert V. Guenther, *Philosophy and Psychology in the Abhidharma*, p. 17.

[2]See *Abhidhammatthasaṅgaho* (*PTS* trans.), p. 125.

[3]ibid., p. 150, *Viśuddhimārga*, I, p. 54, 177, 208-209.

[4]Herbert V. Guenther, *Philosophy and Psychology in the Abhidharma*, p. 26, translates it as 'unconscious continuum'.

[5]Shwe Zan Aung, *Compendium of Philosophy*, Appendix, pp. 265-66; A.B. Govinda, *Psychological Attitude of the Early Buddhist Philosophy*, p. 180.

sted with *vīthicitta* when the objects have set vibration in the stream of being (*bhavaṅga-sota*). As has been pointed out, *bhavaṅga citta* is the self-resting, dormantm strea of consciousness whereas *vīthi-citta* is the manifest consciousness of various spiritual and external objects.[1]

Vīthi is, thus, the process of cognition. It starts when the objects (*rūpas*) come in contact with *citta* through the doors of the senses (*indriya-dvāra*) or the door of mind (*mano-dvāra*). Through these doors, the object enters the stream of being (*bhavaṅga-sota*) and sets it into vibration (*bhavaṅga-calana*). The stream is interrupted (*bhavaṅguppaccheda*) and now it 'rises above its former limitations, changing from a potential state into a state of activity'. Thereafter mind becomes aware of the object (*āvajjana*) and the aspect of consciousness which results from the stimulation of sense-organs—such as seeing, hearing etc.,–arises. Then arise one after the other receiving (*sampaṭicchanna*), investigating (*santīraṇa*) determining (*voṭṭhappana*), full cognition (*javana*) and retention (*tadārammaṇa*). After the termination of *vīthi* (*cuti*) the stream of being (*bhavaṅga*) resumes its original form. As said above, the duration of the whole process of cognition is seventeen thought-instants. The complete process takes place only when the intensity of the same object is 'very great', (*atimahanta*); if it is only great (*mahanta*), the function of registration (*tadārammaṇa*) does not take place; and if the intensity is small (*paritta*) the function of mind ceases before *javana*, i.e. full cognition does not take place at all.[2] This operation keeps on going till the last moment of ones existence.

Ethical Classifications of Psychological States

From the above it is clear that the Buddhist point of view considers psychic operation the outcome of inter-relatedness between *citta* and phenomena. Each psychic operation points to a complex situation in which too many factors are involved, these being inter-related and inter-dependent. These factors are technically called *dhammas* (*dhamma;* skt. *dharma*) and the theory evolved around it has been from the beginning one of the most important in Buddh-

[1]See Govind Chandra Pande, *BDVI*, p. 258.

[2]See *Abhidhammatthasaṅgaho* (*PTS* trans.), pp. 125 ff; *Viśuddhimārga*, ed. Dharmarakshita, II, pp. 74 ff. For an elaborate discussion see Govind Chandra Pande, *BDVI*, pp, 257-59; A.B. Govinda, op. cit., pp. 184-87; also Herbert V. Guenther op. cit., pp. 15 ff.

ism.[1] In an old passage of the Pāli *Tripiṭaka* the essence of the teachings of Buddha is said to be the discovery of *dhammas*, the fact of their casual connectedness, and instruction into the way which leads to their final termination.[2]

In Buddhism, the term 'dharma' is used in many senses.[3] In the present context, however, it means the 'elements of existence' or the 'states of mental and material existence'. The *Aṭṭhasālini* defines *dharma* in the following way: *attano pana sabhāvaṁ dhārenti ti dhammā. Dhāriyanti vā paccayehi, dhārāyanti va yathāsabhāvato ti dhammā*, i.e. 'the *dhammas* are those states which bear their intrinsic natures or which are borne by causes-in-relation or which are borne according to their own characteristics'.[4] *Dharma* is, thus, that which bears its intrinsic nature, and it is in accordanee with this notion that *Nirvāṇa* too is called *dhamma* with the qualification that its nature is transcendental and so beyond logical comprehension: it is not conditioned (*asaṁskṛtā*) and so is opposed to the worldly phenomena (*saṁsāra*) which are conditioned (*saṁskrta*). The other *dharmas* are conditioned (*pratītyasamutpanna*) and are therefore devoid of any individuality of their own (*nissatta nijjīva*).

The *Dhammasaṅgaṇi* of the *Abhidhamma piṭaka* undertakes the task of classification of these innumerable *dharmas* according to different principles. According to Buddhism, in every situation of psychic operation and comprehension of an object is involved a certain 'conscious attitude which determines the very nature of this comprehension. Apperception, in fact, is impossible without an attitude. However, it must be remembered that an attitude is not something which exists by itself; it is closely connected with the various psychic factors, but precedes them and accompanies them. Explaining it the *Aṭṭhasālinī* says that when it is announced that 'the king has arrived', it is implied that he has not come alone, without his attendants, but has come along with his retinue, so also it should be understood that an attitude has arisen in accompaniment with all the factors; it has only

[1]See Th. Stcherbatsky, *The Central Conception of Buddhism and the Meaning of the Word 'Dharma'*, pp. 2-3.

[2]*MV.*, p. 39: *Ye dhammā hetuppabhavā tesaṁ hetuṁ tathāgaṭo āha, Tesaṁ ca yo nirodho evaṁ vādī mahāsamaṇo*. p. 1.

[3]See E. Conze, *Buddhist Thought in India*, part I, ch. 7.

[4]*Aṭṭhasālinī*, II, 10: *The Expositor*, I, p. 50; see also *Abhidharmakośa*, translated by Acharya Narendradeva, I, p. 6.

come as a forerunner.[1] Admitting this overriding importance of the psychological state in relation to the objects of the sensuous world, the *Dhammasaṇgani* attempts to classify it ethically in the very first chapter.[2]

There are four planes of existence, viz., the 'realm of sensuous desire' (*kāma-loka*), 'the realm of pure Forms' (*rūpa-loka*), 'the realm of Non-Form' (*arūpa-loka*) and the 'realm of transcendence' (*lokuttara*). Accordingly, there are four planes of consciousness (*kāma-citta, rūpa-citta, arūpa-citta* and *lokuttara-citta.*[3] *Kāma-loka* does not pertain only to the human world. It consists of six planes which may be broadly classified into sub-human, human and superhuman. The sub-human has four categories, viz., the plane of utmost suffering (*niraya*), the plane of animal world (*tiracchāna-yoni*), the plane in which desire outweighs the possibility of its satisfaction (*petti-visaya*), the plane of demons who symbolise the forces of darkness (*asurā-kāya*). That of human beings (*manussā*) is the fifth plane over which is the plane of higher beings (*devaloka*). The first four are called "the abodes of misery" (*apāyabhūmi*) and the two higher ones are called "the abode of fortunate sense-experience" (*kāma-sugati-bhūmi*)[4] *Kāma-loka*, thus, stands for all the possibilities and directions along which sensuous consciousness might proceed.

Ethically, consciousness can be divided into wholesome (*kusala*), unwholesome (*akusala*) and neutral (*avyākata*) depending, with the first two, on the type of motive or root-cause (*hetu*) attached with it; the last, *avyākata dhamma*, is neutral as it has no ethical implications and this category includes within its list all the states of matter and also *Nibbāna* which is unconditioned (*asaṇkhata*). The nature of ethical consciousness is judged from the point of view whether it shows marching ahead towards the goal or a departure from it. Cra-

[1] *Aṭṭhasālinī*, III. 43.

Yathā rājā āgato ti vutte na parisaṁ pahāya ekako va āgato, rājaparisāya pana saddhim yeva āgato ti paññāyati, evamidaṁ cittaṁ pi paropaṇṇasa—kusaladhammehi saddhim yeva uppannam ti veditabbam....The Expositor, I, p. 90.

[2] *Dhammasaṅgaṇi*, 'cittuppāda-kaṇḍa'.

[3] *Abhidhammatthasaṅgaho* (*Comp. of Philosophy*), pp. 81-82.

[4] See A.L. Govinda, op. cit., pp. 246-49.

ving (*lobha*), hatred (*dosa*; skt. *dveṣa*) and delusion (*moha*) are the three unwholesome root-causes (*akusala-mūla*) which are born of ignorance (*avijjā*) and go to tarnish consciousness completely. Consciousness, under their influence, is bound to give rise to painful conditions. On the other hand, freedom from craving (*alobha*), from hatred (*adosa*) and from delusion (*amoha*) constitute wholesome root-causes (*kusala-mūla*).[1] They are born of wisdom and condition consciousness in a desirable manner facilitating the seeker's onward march toward the goal. The entire feeling and experience under wholesome consciousness is totally different from the feeling and experience under unwholesome consciousness.

Stress on the necessity of healthy attitude for the realisation of goal led the Buddhists to probe thoroughly into the framework of unhealthy attitude. The components of the framework were singled out with a view to providing a guideline to the seeker. These are called fetters (*saṁyojanāni*) for they bind man to the stream of life and death (*saṁsāra*), preventing him from realising the Truth. In the *Dhammasangaṇi* we find the conception of two sets of fetters, one as three-fold and the other as ten-fold. In the former are enumerated the belief in a permanent personality (*sakkāyaditthi*), scepticism (*vicikicchā*), and clinging to external rules and rituals (*sīlabbataparāmāsa*).[2] *Sakkāyadiṭṭhi* arises as a result of failure to see the impermanent nature (*aniccatā*) of the five stems (*skandhas*) which constitute the human personality. This failure leads one to have a false notion of 'self', the notion of 'I', which becomes a factor separating him from others. It is quite easy to see how this feeling of separateness gives all conflicts in life and operates as the support of all cravings. Scepticism prevents mind from staying with any one object and understanding its true nature; as mind keeps on doubting and so shifting from one object to other, there is a complete lack of concentration. Enumeration of clinging to external rules and rituals as a fetter[3] conforms to the intuitionist attitude of Buddhism regard-

[1]*Dhammasangani*, p. 229.

[2]*Dhammasaṅgaṇi* (Nal. ed), pp. 232-33, 276-77—*Katame dhammā dassanena pahātabbā? Tīṇi samyojanānisakkāyadiṭṭhi, vicikicchā, sīlabbataparāmāso*...

[3]In the *Aṭṭhasālinī*, III. 552 *parāmāsa* is explained as that which sets aside (*atikkamati*) the true nature of things (*dhammasabhāva*) and considers them perversely (*parato āmasati*), i.e. conceives them as eternal. *The Expositor*, II, p. 337.

ing the nature of action. Purity is not obtainable from a mere formal observance of rules and rituals. The nature of action is determined by motive and so it is the purity of motive which matters above everything. One should not attribute the fundamental and eternal importance to rituals. The external rules have a purpose to serve, no doubt, but it should also be clearly borne in mind that they themselves should not come to assume the ultimate importance. It is in this sense that in the early Buddhist texts Buddha is said to have explained the term 'Venayika' as applicable to him.[1] The other, large list, speaks of the following ten fetters (*saṁyojanāni*):[2]

1. *Kamarāga*=sensual desire.
2. *Paṭigha*=aversion.[3]
3. *Māna*=conceit.[4]
4. *Diṭṭhi* (skt. *dṛṣṭi*)=opinionatedness.[5]
5. *Vicikicchā* (skt. *Vicikitsā*)=doubt.

[1]See *Pār.*, p. 5-"*Atthi khvesa, brāhmaṇa, pariyāyo yena maṁ pariyāyena sammā vadamāno vadeyya-'Venayiko samaṇo Gotamo' ti, Ahaṁ hi, brāhmaṇa, vinayāya dhammaṁ desemi rāgassa dosassa mohassa. Aneka vihitānaṁ pāpakānaṁ akusalānaṁ dhammānaṁ vinayāya dhammaṁ desemi. Ayaṁ kho, brāhmaṇa, pariyāyo yena maṁ pariyāyena sammā vadamāno vadeyya—'venayiko samaṇo Gotamo' ti, no ca kho yaṁ tvaṁ sandhāya vedesi.*

[2]*MV.*, p. 249.

[3]It is rooted in *dosa* and is accompanied by sullenness (*domanassa*), *Dhammasaṅgaṇi*, p. 310. See also *Aṭṭhasālinī*, III, pp. 562, 564: *The Expositor*, II, pp. 341, 343. Such an attitude only rouses enmity as it finds everything offensive to his own ideas and principles and makes a person lacking in contentedness.

[4]One is drunk with his own importance and is led to showing off (*ketukāmyatā cittassa*); the state is that of desire for self-advertisement. *Dhammasaṅgaṇi*, p. 250; The *Aṭṭhasālini* V, p. 65; *The Expositor*, II, p. 479. The letter derives the word from the root 'mad', 'to get intoxicated', and gives 'arrogance' (*unnati*) as its characteristic. The *Abhidharmakośa* (tr. Narendradeva, p. 138), on the other hand, makes a distinction between '*māna*' and '*mada*' and explains it as one's feeling of superiority (*cetasa unnatiḥ*) in relation to others by actual or imaginery qualities.

[5]Holding of various opinions and theories pertaining to problems such as whether the world is eternal or non-eternal, finite or infinite, soul is the same as body or different from it, and so on. From the Buddhist viewpoint the pursuit is bound to end in frustration and is also not conducive to enlightenment. It only leads one away from the real problem and, therefore, comes in the category of unhealthy attitude.

6. *Sīlabbataparāmāsa* (skt. *Sīla-vrata-parāmarśa*)=clinging to rules and rituals.
7. *Bhavarāga*=craving for existence.
8. *Issā* (skt. *Irśyā*)=jealousy.[1]
9. *Macchariya* (skt. *Mātsarya*)=niggardliness.[2]
10. *Avijjā* (skt. *Avidyā*)=Ignorance.

The 'ten fetters' are also listed as *Kāmarāga*, *paṭigha*, *rūparāga* (craving for existence in the world of pure Form), *arūparāga* (craving for existence in the world of Non-Form), *māna*, *uddhacca* (restlessness) and *avijjā* along with *sakkāyadiṭṭhi*, *vicikicchā* and *sīlabbataparāmāsa*.[3]

The *Abhidhammatthasaṅgaha* gives a comprehensive list of immoral and moral mental properties (*cetasika*).[4] According to it, the fourteen immoral mental properties are: (1) dullness (*moha*). (2) impudence (*ahirika*), (3) recklessness of consequences (*anottappa*), (4) distraction (*uddhacca*), (5) greed (*lobha*), (6) error (*diṭṭhi*), (7) conceit (*māna*), (8) hate (*dosa*), (9) envy (*issā*), (10) selfishness (*macchariya*), (11) worry (*kukuccā*), (12) sloth (*thina*), (13) torpor (*middha*), and (14) perplexity (*vicikicchā*). The nineteen moral mental properties are: (1) faith (*saddhā*), (2) mindfulness (*sati*), (3) prudence (*hiri*), (4) discretion (*ottappa*), (5) disinterestedness (*alobha*), (6) amity (*adosa*), (7) balance of mind (*tatramajjhatatā*), (8) composure of mental properties (*kāyapasaddhi*), (9) composure of mind (*cittapasaddhi*), (10) buoyancy of mental properties (*lahutā*), (11) buoyancy of mind, (12) pliancy of mental properties (*mudutā*), (13) pliancy of mind, (14) fitness of work of mental properties (*kammaññatā*), (15) fitness of work of mind, (16) proficiency of mental properties (*paguññatā*),

[1]It arises out of covetousness for things which others possess and we want to possess ourselves. Under its influence, the *Aṭṭhasālinī* explains, a man is bound to deprive others from it (*vimukhabhāva*).

See *Aṭṭhasālini*, III, p. 563; '*Tesu issatī ti* '*issā*'. *Sā parasampattīnaṁ usūyanalakkhaṇā, tattheva anabhiratirasā, tato vimukhabhāvapaccupaṭṭhānā, parasampattipadaṭṭhānā. Samyojanāni ti daṭṭhabbā*. *The Expositor*, II, pp. 342-43.

[2]It prevents a man from sharing with others and produces a tendency in which he is unable to give to anyone what is in his possession. It goes to distort the whole mental make-up of a person, *Aṭṭhasālinī*, III, p. 563: *The Expositor*, II, p. 343.

[3]See *Viśuddhimārga*, 2, p. 270. A.B. Govinda, op.cit., pp. 146-47.

[4]*Abhidhammatthasaṅgaho* (*Comp. of Philosophy*); pp. 95-96.

(17) proficiency of mind, (18) rectitude of mental properties (*ujukutā*) and (19) rectitude of mind.

Ethical Classifications of the Path and Men

What Buddha taught was a way, *magga* (skt. *mārga*). *Mārga* or Way is a figure of speech implies going from one place to the other. It starts from *Saṁsāra*, the realm of suffering, and terminates in *Nirvāṇa*, eradication of suffering, (*Dukkha*) and attainment of perfect peace and bliss. This goal is attainable through gradual progress along the path prescribed by Buddha, in due courses. There is no long leap in spiritual journey and one has to perfect himself and undergo many stages of ethico-spiritual advancement which culminates in the attainment of the state of Enlightenment. It is with this view that the path which is one is graded as four, viz., *sotāpatti*, *sakadāgāmi*, *anāgāmi* and *Arhant*.[1] Men stationed in these respective stages represent varying degrees of ethical and spiritual perfection. As Humphreys has remarked, these stages represent 'a successive expansion of consciousness.'[2]

Buddhism believes in the equality of men as men and blasts all claims of superiority by any section on the basis of mere birth or social status. But it does make distinctions among men in respect of their ethico-spiritual potentialities and conforming distance from or nearness to the goal. In this respect not all are equal: some have not even started walking on the Way, some have covered certain part of the journey while some others might be quite in vicinity of the destination.

With variations in their attitudes and possession of different moral and immoral mental properties, men can be classified into many types. One book of the *Abhidhamma*, namely, *Puggalapaññatti*, deals with the task of the classification of human types in which ethical consideration, among others, is the most dominent principle. In the context of our discussion of the Buddhist *annattā* theory, we have seen earlier that an 'individual' in Bhuddhism cannot be conceived as something ultimately real (*paramatthasacca*), but so long as the *khandhas* are there we can talk of 'a being' in the same way

[1]See *Visuddhimagga*, ch. XXII.

[2]Christmas Humphreys, *Buddhism*, p. 119.

as the term 'chariot' is used by the co-existence of its various parts in interdependent relationship.[1]

The most common division of men that Buddhism makes is that between the *Puthujjana* (skt. *Pṛthagjana*) and the *Ariyajana*. The former designates the average and undertrained men of the world who live entrapped in the snares of sensual desire and have not yet been touched by the spark of the Truth. They remain bound to the world of suffering by the various fetters. The *Puggalapaññatti* has thus made the distinction between an average person and a person belonging to the Ārya family. "The person whose three fetters[2] have not been put away and who is not proceeding to put these away–such a person is said to be an average person." Contrary to such a person, "the person who is endowed with those conditions immediately after which there is the advent of the Ariyan (noble or elect) nature is said to be one become of the Ariya family."[3]

By entering into the 'stream' that finally leads a man from *Saṁsāra* to *Nirvāṇa* thus, one becomes the member of the Ariya family and is designated as 'one who has entered the stream' (*sotāpanna; śrotāpanna*). The stage is characterised by the destruction of the first three fetters. The journey to *Nirvāṇa* has been started. It is connected with the 'seeing' (*darśana* of *Nirvāṇa-Nirvāṇa* is now 'seen' for the first time.[4] The second stage, that of the 'once-returner' (*sakadāgāmi; sakṛdāgāmin*), is marked by the destruction of the first three fetters, passions, hatred and delusion and that

[1]*The Questions of King Milinda*, I, *SBE*, XXXV, p. 45. For the Puggalavādin's view of 'puggala' ('being') in the *Kathavatthu*, see Bimala Charan Law, *Designation* or *Human Types* (translation of *Puggala-paññatti*), Introduction, pp. vii-viii.

[2]Viz., *sakkāyadiṭṭhi*, *vicikicchā* and *sīlabbataparāmāsa*.

[3]*Puggala-paññatti* (*PTS*, trans.), p. 19.

[4]'Seeing' is, however, not the experiencing of *Nirvāṇa*. The *Aṭṭhasālinī* has explained the whole thing with the help of an analogy. As a person comes to see the king on a certain errand and has seen the king from a distance riding on the back of an elephant on a certain road, when asked if he has seen the king, would reply that he has not seen the king as his errand was not accomplished, in the same way the cognitive moment (*gotrabhū*) has just got a glimpse of *Nirvāṇa* for the first time; the task has not been achieved yet. So, it is not seeing in the true sense. This cognition only adverts one in the Path. *Aṭṭhasālinī*, II. p. 24: *The Expositor*, I, p. 56,

of the fourth and fifth fetters partly. Such a person comes back once only to this world.[1] The stage of the 'non-returner' *anāgāmi* (*anāgāmin*) has been thus described: Here a person, having completely destroyed the five fetters, causing rebirth in the lower worlds, becomes a 'being of apparitional rebirth' (i.e. a deva, without parents); attaining the final release in the self-same state, he is not liable to return from that region."[2] When all the 'ten fetters' are done away with; one becomes 'arahā (*arhat*). "The person whose attachment to form and the formless, to pride, haughtiness and ignorance has been entirely put away is said to be an Arahant."[3] With the realisation of this stage, the goal of spiritual journey is accomplished. One of the *Arahant*-formulas[4] thus describes the accomplishment:

Khiṇāsavo vusitavā katakaraṇīyo ohitabhāro anuppattasaddattho parikkhīṇibhavasaṁyojano sammadaññā vimutto-'Canker-waned, who has lived the life done what was to be done, laid down the burden, attained his own goal, whose fetters of becoming are utterly worn away, who is freed by perfect profound knowledge.

The above discussion makes evident the close relationship between psychology and ethics as it was conceived in Buddhism. The cosmological attitude of the Buddhists led them to find in psychology a sound and objective support for their ethical framework. The analytical and logical methodology, inherent in Buddhism from the very beginning, enabled them to make remarkable advancements in their pursuit of psychological analysis which one finds culminating in the books of the *Abhidhamma*. The *Abhidhamma* is an outcome of great insight into psychic operations, a patient observation of mind and its properties and also a keen desire of classifying them into logical categories. The Buddhist psychological analysis, however, is inseparably linked up with the spiritual experience of its teacher and aspires to go beyond the realm of modern psychological analysis into the realm of transcendental reality which is characterised by complete restfulness of mind and thought. Its goal is to make possible to the spiritual seeker the depth-experience of *Nirvāṇa*.

[1] *Puggala-paññatti* (*PTS* trans.), p. 24, 26.
[2] ibid.
[3] ibid., p. 27.
[4] For four notable formulas about *arahant* see Jan T. Ergardt, *Faith and Knowledge in Early Buddhism*, Introduction, pp. 3-4.

CHAPTER 4

Ethical Ideals

The Buddhist texts introduce a dramatic element in the career of Buddha as a founder of religion and a teacher. It is said that in the beginning he was reluctant to teach, fearing that the subtle *Dhamma* he had realized would not be comprehensible to the worldly people who were entrapped in the snares of desires and attachment. He was however, persuaded by the entreaties of Brahmā and, driven by compassion (*Kāruññataṁ*); when he glanced his Buddha-eyes (*Buddha-cakkhūni*) down on earth, he noticed that there were men of different spiritual calibres—some with thick layer of blemishes and not afraid of evil or the life here after but some others with little blemishes, fearful of evil and full of concern with the life hereafter.[1] Finally, he decided that it was worth-while to teach, and he began his teaching activity by delivering his first sermon at Ṛṣipattana (modern Sārnāth) to the band of five monks, who had attended on him during the period of his severe penance prior to Enlightenment but had later left him when he came to consider this course futile and abandoned it. Soon a large band of spiritual seekers gathered around him and, as was the custom of the age, this led to the foundation of a new religious order, the *Buddha-sāsana* or the *Saṅgha* of Buddha. The vision of Buddha became the goal of attainment for these seekers and, as a teacher, Buddha instructed them into the way through which it could be attained. An individual event of realization of a spiritual vision, thus, got transformed into an institutionalized religion. So far as Buddha was concerned, he had seen the Truth face to face and, like one who had reached the other shore of the river, needed no more the 'raft of the law.' He was now, in a sense, personally, above morality, beyond the duality of good and evil. But, the others, who had yet to reach the desti-

[1] *MV.*, p. 9.

nation needed it greatly as a necessary means to reach them there. The process is the same with regard to all the religions of the world. A religious teacher, having attained the goal and decided to preach, seeks to instruct his followers into some methodology, assuring them that its observance would lead them to the realization of that Truth which he himself had realized. As the disciples do not obviously have the same wisdom and capacity as the teacher has, they require guidance in the form of moral and spiritual prescriptions which would, on the one hand, check them from going astray and, on the other, hasten their progress toward the goal. In other words, every religion involves an ethical code of conduct; it is difficult to conceive of a religion which does not refer to some system of ethics. To quote Professor Lewis, "Although ethical truths require no direct support from religion, except in so far as we have some specifically religious duties like acts of worship in mind, there can be no adequate presentation of religious principles that does not make a very fundamental use of ethical objectivity."[1] Buddism takes Gnosis to be the culmination of morality; an immoral person can never dream of attaining to it.

Ascetic Tenor

Earlier, we have discussed the generic connection of Buddhism with the Śramaṇic ideology. Though Buddhism is not anti-social or a-social in its attitude—as we shall see a little later in this chapter—in a sense, asceticism stands for withdrawal from the world and the worldly objects which produce sense-pleasures, enchaining man by arousing in him an insatiable thirst and craving for them. According to the ascetic contention, happiness cannot be obtained through the fulfilment of desires for the worldly objects but only though the purification of mind resulting from cessation of desires. Asceticism may be said to stand on two legs: a firm faith in the undesirabilty of material life, and an equally firm faith in spiritual happiness which points to a state of transcendence. Mental quietude born in a stage of desirelessness, thus, becomes the supreme virtue. In the *Saṁyutta Nikāya*, this idea has been illustrated with the help of an analogy: A jackal wanted to eat a tortoise; seeing the jackal coming to him, the tortoise drew its neck and four limbs into its

[1]H. D. Lewis, *Morals and the New Theology*, p. 26.

shell, and the jackal had to go away disgusted. In the same way, it is stated, Māra (Evil personified) cannot overcome a man who has withdrawn his senses from worldly objects.[1] Buddha admonished people to abandon the habit of keeping worldly treasures for themselves in a deep cellar but to acquire merits which would guarantee happiness 'on the other side'.[2] The *Khuddaka-pāṭha* elaborates: 'A man buries a treasure in a deep pit which, lying day after day concealed therein, profits him nothing. But there is a treasure that man or woman may possess, a treasure laid up in the heart, a treasure of charity, piety, temperance, soberness. A treasure secure, impregnable, that cannot pass away. When a man leaves the fleeting riches of the world, this he takes with him after death. A treasure unshared with others, a treasure that no thief can steal'.[3]

Foundational Norms and General Orientation

In its overall manifestation Buddhism appears as a form of rationalism. To quote from one of my earlier writings: 'By rejecting animism and ritualism and emphasizing a rational outlook which treats reality as a causally and functionally determined system of plural synergies (*saṁskāras*), the emergence of Buddhism marks an important event in the history of Indian thought. The most distinctive feature of Buddhist ethics is its freedom from theism, which leaves room for rationalism and rules out submission to some super-

[1]*Kindred Saying*, IV, pp. 12-13. Compare the *Gītā* II. 58: *Yadā Saṁharate cāyaṁ kūrmoṅgānīva sarvaśaḥ, indriyānīdriyārthebhyaśca tasya prajñā pratiṣṭhitā*.

[2]*Kindred Sayings*, I, p. 83; *Psalms of the Sisters*, 283, p. 127: The recluses are said to be dear to Buddha because 'they lay not up a treasure for the flesh...'

[3]*Khuddaka-pāṭha*, VIII, translation by R. C. Childers. One may compare here *Matthew*, 6, 19-20 where Jesus has spoken of the need 'to lay up for yourselves treasures in heaven, where neither moth nor rust consumes and where thieves do not break in and steal,' see Hajime Nakamura, *Buddhism in comparative Light*, p. 75. It may, however, be noted that asceticism is not as essential and dominant characteristic of the teachings of Jesus as it is of the teachings of Buddha. It has been observed about the ethics of Jesus that it is, 'heroic' and not 'ascetic'; that 'Jesus does not preach asceticism; in this teaching there is no trace of contempt for the life of the senses or for pleasure as such, nor does He glorify poverty for its own sake'. Ernst Troeltsch, *The Social Teaching of the Christian Churches*, p. 59.

human power controlling the world-process'.[1] Buddha condemned personality-cult[2] and emphasized self-experience.[3] On the one hand, he disallowed the notion of any power or entity apart from man controlling his destiny and, on the other hand, preached *Karmavāda* which made man his own master. Thus, in place of a theological basis, Buddhist morality rests on a rational basis. Buddha pointed to the analytical character of his approach and the rejection of any form of dogmatism therein.[4] Addressing the *Kālamas*, a republican clan of his time, Buddha is reported to have said, 'You should be carried away in favour of a doctrine, O Kālāmas, neither by hearsay, nor by tradition, nor by scriptual authority, nor by mere logic or argumentation, nor even by the teacher's personal charm, and such other things. You should accept a doctrine only after employing your own reason and discretion, after having known it to your utter satisfaction and conviction'.[5] The religion of Buddha was a 'come and see religion' (*ehipassika dhamma*)[6] which repudiated all external authorities as a means for the attainment of the *summum bonum* and recommended the use of one's own reason and personal exertion.

Often the passage, cited above, relating to Buddha's address to the Kālāmas is quoted to point out the rational element in Buddhism. It, however, deserves a more careful attention and sensitive treatment that is usually given to it. From what Buddha said to the Kālāmas, however, it is clear that according to him rationalism is not mere logic or power of argumentation. A distinction is to be made between reasoning and bad reasoning, the latter being of no profit to the spiritual seeker. His rationalism is also not agnostic rationalism but the one which believes in a transcendental reality as an object of

[1]G.S.P. Misra, 'Logical and Scientific Method in Early Buddhist Texts', *JRAS*, 1967-68, p. 54. See also Trevor Ling, op. cit., pp. 140-41, who quotes this passage and elaborates the point.

[2]See *Kindred Sayings*, III, p. 103: When a disciple, Vakkali, lamented over not having been able to see the Master for long, Buddha is reported to have retorted, 'Hush, Vakkali! What is there in seeing this vile body of mine? He who seeth the Norm, Vakkali, he seeth me...'

[3]*Kindred Sayings*, I, p. 147.

[4]*MN*, II, p. 469: '*Vibhajjavādo... ahaṁ...nāhaṁ ekaṁsavādo*,.

[5]'Kālāma Sutta' in the *Aṅguttara Nikāya*.

[6]*Middle Length Sayings*, 'Vatthūpamasutta', I, p. 47.

seeking and also contains within it a profound sense of human freedom.

In a recent article aimed at a critical examination and comparison of the views on the Buddhist *Nibbāna* put forth by two modern Sinhalese scholars, viz., K.N. Jayatilleke and David J. Kalupahana, A.D.P. Kalansuriya makes an interesting point about the nature of Buddhist ethics. He writes: "...Methodically, the Buddha moves from facts to ethics... The Buddha starts with an empirical fact or a psychological fact and then goes on to work out its implication. Then a moral procedure is designed to eliminate the empirical or psychological fact in question." There is suffering is a statement of fact; it constitutes the starting point of Buddhism. Suffering may be in the form of physical pain or an empirically observable phenomenon; it may be in the form of anguish or a feeling of sorrowfulness —a psychological fact. From the recognition of suffering—as an empirical or a psychological fact—Buddha proceeds to prescribe the way through the observance of which it could be removed; it is necessarily an ethical procedure. That the methodology of Buddha synthesizes two logically different contexts viz., facts and ethics, and thus amounts to a philosophical error (See Wittegenstein, *Philosophical Investigations*) does not have any relevance for, 'these highly developed conceptual distinctions were primarily non-existent in the Buddha's time, especially in the context of the ancient Indian Buddhist Dhamma... There was at that time no meta-ethics, the study of the statements about the good and the right, but only ethics, which is concerned with the study of the good and the right...'[1] It may, however, be remarked that this Humian sundering of fact and value need not be acceptable as a universal postulate of philosophy.[2] The basis of Buddhist ethics is not the empirical perception of *duḥkha-saṁvedana* but the spiritual intuition of *duḥkha-satya*. The former is accessible to any *pṛthagjana*, the latter only to an Ārya.

Buddha believed that virtue lies in the avoidance of extremes.[3] If in the realm of metaphysics he sought to reject the extreme notions

[1]A.D.P. Kalansuriya, 'Two Modern Sinhalese Views of Nibbana', *Religion*, 9, Spring 1979, pp. 5-6.

[2]Cf. Govinda Chandra Pande, *Mūlya-Mīmāṁsa*, p. 282; Muirhead in *Mahatma Gandhi*, ed. Radhakrishnan, p. 382.

[3]The view has striking similarity with the Aristotelian view. According to Aristotle also, the right action is the middle course, the *via media;* 'virtue is

of 'eternalism' (*sassatavāda*), and 'annihilationism' (*ucchedavāda*) and advocated in their place the notion of 'becoming' (*pratītyasamutpāda,*) in the realm of ethico-spiritual practice, he denounced, on the one hand, extreme sense-indulgence and, on the other, practice of severe self-mortification. He rejected the gross materialism preached by Ajita Kesakambalin and also decried the Jaina belief in self-mortification as a means to liberation. He discovered that both these ways are futile for spiritual life and, therefore, preached the Middle-Way.[1] According to him, extreme ascetic practices, involving a lot of physical discomfort and self-torture, could not be taken as a measuring-yard of Samaṇaship or Brāhmaṇaship.[2] When Kassapa, the naked ascetic, put to Buddha 'How hard then, Gotama, must Samaṇaship be to gain, how hard must Brāhmaṇaship be', Buddha is said to have replied thus :

"That, Kassapa, is a common saying in the world that the life of a Samaṇa and of a Brāhmaṇa is hard to lead. But if the hardness, the very great hardness of that life depended merely on this asceticism, on the carrying out of any or all of these practices you have detailed, then it would not be fitting to say that the life of the Samaṇa, of the Brāhmaṇa, was hard to lead. It would be quite possible. . .for anyone. . .to say: 'Let me now go naked, let me become of low habits' and so on through all the items of those three lists of yours. . .

"O Kassapa, a Bhikkhu has cultivated the heart of love that knows no anger, that knows no ill-will—from the time when, by the destruction of the deadly intoxications. . .he dwells in that emancipation of heart, in that emancipation of mind, and that he, while yet in this visible world, has come to realize and know—from that time, O Kassapa, is it that the bhikkhu is called Samaṇa, is called a Brāhmaṇa!"

This long passage was quoted here only to show that, according to Buddha, the essense of spiritual exertion did not lie in mere formal observance of hard ascetic penances but in the training of mind.

In his quest for the Truth, Buddha had himself practised severe

located as a mean between two-extremes: the vice of deficiency found on the one side, and the vice of excess on the other; but in between *est modus in rebus*'. William S. Sahakian, *Systems of Ethics and Value Theory*, p. 10.

[1]*Kindred Sayings*, II, p. 52.

[2]*Dial.*, 'Kassapa-Sīhanāda-Sutta', I, pp. 223-40.

penances amounting to near death, and, thus, the realization of the futility of the course was a result of his personal experience. Buddha was a rational thinker and had a good understanding of human nature as well. He knew it too well that moral practice is not mathematics and that regulation of life by absolutely unbending rules would only result into childishness of character and conduct. He also felt that regulation of life by much to stringent rules might cause aversion to them. His attitude is reflected in his formulation of the monastic rules purported to guide the life of the monks and the nuns in the Saṅgha. Whereas the Jaina standard of monastic behaviour was really strict in which self-mortification was considered a moral virtue and the practice of *ahiṁsā* and the vow of non-possession were taken to the farthest limit possible,[1] the Buddhist rules were much more favourable and much less stringent.[2]

In the ethical framework of Buddhism, the problem starts with Ignorance owing to which man fails to see the real nature of his own self and the world around him. As a result, one feels attached to them, expressing this attachment in the diverse forms of desires which are never finally satiated; one desire, even when satisfied, gets replaced by another desire and the process goes on subjecting man to suffering and pain. This is the evil inherent in human existence as such. It is to be squarely faced and its nature needs to be understood. The moral procedure starts with this basic understanding and would acquire perfection through the harnessing of action on the right way and exercising control on the dallying nature of mind. Suffering is an existential reality but it is not recognized by Buddha as the final reality for man. The recognition of the fact of suffering in human existence on the part of Buddha should not be understood as an advocacy of pessimism. It is wrong to characterize Buddhism—as S.k. Mitra does—as an ontological passimism;[3] Suffering or *Dukkha* is, rather, explained by Buddha in terms of psychological and physical experience. To overlook or ignore a fact does not amount to optimism but only to escapism which, however, cannot do away with it. Buddha was a realist, as he asserts: 'There are religious teachers who, living in the state of bewilderment, do not recognise

[1]S.B. Deo, *History and Doctrine of Jaina Monachism*, p. 11.
[2]G.S.P. Misra, *The Age of Vinaya*, ch. IV.
[3]S.K. Maitra, *The Ethics of Hindus*, p. 276.

the difference between night and day, but I would treat night as night and day as day'.[1] On the emperical and relative level Buddha did not reject the existence of pleasure and satisfaction; if the worldly existence contained pain, it also contained satisfaction. "Now, herein, monks, if there were not satisfaction to be found in the world. beings would not be attached to the world. If there were not misery in the world, beings would not be repelled by the world. . . If there were no escape from the world, beings could not escape therefrom. . ."[2] It was only in the ultimate analysis that even that which apparently looked satisfaction came to be nothing but suffering. He recognized the fact of suffering, but he, however, did not end there. Like a good physician,[3] he saw the disease, diagnosed it and proceeded to cure it by prescribing a Way. There was no need of any ethical procedure if there had not been the possibility of its eradication.

Prescription of a way by Buddha implies his belief in the possibility of improvement in human character.[4] The potentiality of improvement is there if only one is awakened from one's slumber and exercises one's will. There is, however, no big-leap through which one can reach the goal. As Buddha says, a wise way-farer 'trains himself in the training',[5] implying thereby that training is not a hasty affair but a matter of constant effort through which a gradual moral and spiritual uplift is attained. It is significant that the Eightfold Path (*aṭṭhaṅgika-magga*) is also called by Buddha *paṭipadā*

[1]*MN*, 'Bhayabherava-sutta', I, p. 29: *Middle Length Sayings*, I, p. 27.

[2]*Gradual Sayings*, I, p. 238.

[3]To Buddha has been attributed the epithet '*Vaidyarāja*, 'a great physician', *Lalita-vistara*, pp. 3, 263, 307 etc. Significantly, in a Sūtra called *Vyādhisūtra*, the Four Truths have been compared with the medical counterparts of it, viz., disease, diagnosis, cure and medicine. See Poussin, *JRAS*, 1903, pp. 570-80. Scholars have pointed to a connection between the Buddhist formula and the current medical science, Kern, *Manual of Indian Buddhism*, pp. 46-47; Poussin, *JRAS*, 1903, pp. 570-80; See also Stcherbatsky, *The Central Conception of Buddhism*, p. 8, fn. 22.

[4]For a discussion on the possibility of change in human nature by Harold Kelman, Frederick, A. Wiss, Paul Tillich and Karen Horney see "Human Nature Can Change: A Symposium", *American Journal of Psychoanalysis*, 12, 1952, pp. 62-68—incorporated in Harold H. Titus/Morris T. Keetan, *The Range of Ethics*, ch. 3.

[5]*Middle Length Sayings*, 'Sekhasutta', II, p. 20.

suggesting that the path leading to the eradication of suffering (*dukkhanirodhagāminī*) has to be walked on step by step and not in reckless jumps. It is illustrated in the practice of the *Brahmavihāras* and also in the schematization of the Eightfold path.[1]

It has been noted with dissatisfaction by Copleston that in Buddhist ethics negative elements are more predominant than the positive elements.[2] Let us examine this point. It need not be emphasized that the very conception of ethics is rooted in a desire of removing certain undesirable things which are supposed to hinder the progress of an individual or a society and mar its peace and harmony. Westermarck brings the point home when he says, "Nobody would ever have dreamt of laying down a moral rule if the ideas of its transgression had not presented itself to the mind."[3] A teacher needs both affirmation and negation and he is the best judge to see which of the two would be more effective in bringing his audience on the right track. Also, as has been pointed out by Nakamura, the famous Japanese scholar, the Indians are fond of using the negative in their language and to them the negative form of expression has more positive and powerful meaning; to the Indian mind expressions like 'non-idleness' (*apramāda*), 'non-grudge' (*avera*), 'non-violence' (*ahiṁsā*) etc., "appeal as more positive virtues than 'exertion', 'tolerance', 'peace' etc."[4] Moreover, nobody can miss the significance of such virtues as *mettā, karuṇā* and *dāna* which are clearly positive in character as well as in their phraseology. Buddhist *sīla* or morality consists both of negative virtues (*vāritta sīla*) and positive virtues (*cāritta sīla*).

To some scholars, Buddhism appears as preaching egoism, a religion which emphasizes knowledge to the exclusion of love. Paul Dahlke, for example, comments: 'Buddhism, although the most sympathetic of all religions, is not the religion of love, but of knowledge'.[5] The Buddhist belief in the doctrine of *Karman* and its rejection of a creator God, according to him, account for the above.

[1]See *The Age of Vinaya*, pp. 97-98.

[2]Copleston, *Buddhism*, p. 100.

[3]Westermarck, op. cit., p. 135.

[4]H. Nakamura, *Ways of Thinking of Eastern Peoples, India, China, Tibet, Japan*, pp. 52-53.

[5]Paul Dahlke, *Buddhist Essays*, p. 130.

He writes: "That cordiality which forgets itself for others, that affection which breeds tenderness and emotion, is entirely wanting here. The whole moral scheme in Buddhism is nothing but a sum in arithmetic, set down by a clear, cold egoism;. . .Kamma is the most exact arithmetician in the world. . . Here is wanting that great centre of love, that father-god, with whom, in loving, I become one; that father-god who loves me and whom I love in return; whose children all men are, and who thus through his all fatherhood changes the whole world into one vast family of brothers and sisters, whose natural duty it is to love one another. In Buddhism only Kamma reigns."[1]

Sometimes Buddhism is interpreted as individualism purporting to emphasize an unconcern for social and political affairs.[2] Elsewhere I have tried to discuss and answer this charge at some length.[3] Here, I would only like to point out that Buddhism is no doubt individualism in so far as it lays stress on self-experience for the attainment of the *summum bonum*, which is individual happiness, and *Karman* as the divider of individuals, but it would be utterly wrong to conclude thereby that it breeds egoism or lacks concern for others. This wrong notion about buddhism derives from a failure to comprehend the doctrine of *Karman* and understand the notion of the individual in the general context of Indian thought. Nakamura, after making a detailed comparison between eastern and western ways of thinking, points out that in Indian thought the individual is not different from the universal. "According to the way of thinking of most Indians, therefore, the essence of the individual or the particular is no more than the universal by virtue of which the individual or the particular is grounded and realized."[4] Buddhism does not teach confinement to I-ness or cessation of active love, it teaches just the opposite. In Buddhism, however, the feeling of

[1] *Buddhist Essays*, p. 132.

[2] Max Weber, *The Religions of India : The Sociology of Hinduism and Buddhism*, pp. 204 ff. Weber emphasizes the individualistic character of Buddhism and calls it "a specifically unpolitical and antipolitical status religion" in which the "specific social character of all genuine mysticism is ... carried to its maximum".

[3] G.S.P. Misra, 'The Buddhist Conception of Social Change and the Buddhist Social Ethics', *Indica*, 5, no. 2, pp. 69-71.

[4] H. Nakamura, *Ways of Thinking of Eastern Peoples*, p. 47.

love derives not from a belief in a Father-God but from right view (*samyak dṛṣṭi*) about the 'self and the world'. As regards the place of love in Buddhism, let us quote a passage from the *Dīgha Nikāya* which should settle the issue : "All the means that can be used as bases for right action are not worth the sixteenth part of the emancipation of the heart through love. This takes all others into itself, outshining them in glory. Just as whatsoever stars there be, their radiance avails not the sixteenth part of the radiance of the moon, just as the sun, mounting up into a clear and cloudless sky, overwhelms all darkness in the realms of space. . .so all means toward right action avail not the sixteenth part of the emancipation of the heart through love."[1] *Mettā* (amity), *Karuṇā* (compassion) and *Dāna* (charity) are exalted virtues in Buddhist ethics. Buddha himself is said to have decided to preach to the worldly people out of compassion for them. In this connection, Buddha's words to his first band of disciples, ready to move out for the propagation of his teachings, are noteworthy: 'Walk, monks, on tour for the blessing of the manyfolk, for the happiness of the many-folk, out of compassion for the world, for the welfare, the blessing, the happiness of devas and men."[2] (*bahujanathitāya bahujanasukhāya lokānukampāya. . .*)

Śramaṇic ideology is the core of Buddhism and, hence, it is quite natural that it attaches great value to the homeless life of the anchorite. As compared to the worldly life of the householders, it provides much greater opportunities for moral and spiritual perfection. Free from all social and economic relations, the adopters of this life voluntarily imposed on themselves the vows of non-possession and poverty; through constant vigilance and practice, they could devote all their energies on overcoming their boldily appetites and egoity for the realization of the truth. Buddhism recognizes the inherent difference between living the life of a householder which is 'an oppression, a dust-hole sort of life' and the wanderer's life which is 'a life in the open air'.[3] Compared to ascetic life, householder's life—which by its very nature involves all sorts of social and economic tensions and occasions for the origination of blemishes like anger,

[1]*Dial.*, III, p. 185.
[2]*The Book of the Discipline*, IV, p. 28.
[3]*Kindred Sayings*, V, p. 306.

aversion attachment, etc.—is called 'lower life'.[1] Those who had chosen the life of a recluse and accepted the spiritual leadership of Buddha, became members of the *Buddhasāsana* or the Buddhist Saṅgha. The denial of the material world had led them to the membership of a spiritual community, living in which they could expect to hasten the process of Truth-realization under the guidance of someone who had himself realized it.

However, the householders, who were not yet moved to renounce the worldly life and embrace the life of homelessness, were not a doomed people. They too had the potential of *Bodhi* which they would realize sometime in future. Some had left the material world as a matter of spiritual contingency but they could not afford to be indifferent or antipathetic to those who were still there. Not only that the various necessary items of physical living became available to the recluses from such people, even their own effort at the actualization of the spiritual goal required a congenial atmosphere. The seeking for perfection is to take place within the scope of day-to-day existence and points to the necessity of providing moral guidance to the worldly people. It was the responsibility of the enlightened men to shape the society along right lines by trying to make its members moral. As I have observed elsewhere, 'The Buddhist definition of a saint does not necessarily require the person to be completely cut off from the world and worldly affairs; the only necessary attribute of a saint is his non-egotistical nature and the feeling of universal love that is born thereof'.[2] Buddha himself had mediated in the conflict that arose between the Śākyas and the Koliyas on the issue of the storing of water and had made efforts to check Viḍūḍabha, the ruler of Kośala, from launching an attack on the Śākyas.

The Buddhist ethical ideals may, thus, be broadly classified under two categories: those laid down for the monks and nuns, and those which were to guide the worldly people. The former were naturally of a more advanced nature and as such the observances involved in them were more stringent. In the context of the worldly life, Buddhism recognizes the unique status of state in society

[1] *Gradual Sayings*, III, p. 3; *Kindred Sayings*, I, p. 105; see also, ibid., V, p. 306; *Dial*, pp. 282-83.

[2] G.S.P. Misra, 'The Buddhist Conception of Social Change and the Buddhist Social Ethics', *Indica*, 15, no. 2, p. 72.

and hence the special responsibility of the one who happens to be at the helm of it. Buddhism lays down some guiding principles in this regard which came to be concretized in the personality of the great Buddhist king Aśoka. It has been rightly pointed out by scholars that the Buddhist social ethics revolves round three focal points, viz., the *Sañgha*, the worldly society of the common people, and the state, and the status and welfare of the three are correlated and interdependent.[1] We propose to study the Buddhist ethical ideals as divided in and applicable to these distinct groups: monastic, laic and political.

Saṅgha as the Basis of an Ideal Social Order

Underlining the significance of a monastic establishment on the part of Buddha Sir Charles Eliot has observed: "The great practical achievements of the Buddha was to found a religious order which has lasted to the present day. It is chiefly to this institution that the permanence of his religion is due".[2]

Buddhism makes a distinction among men in accordance with their moral and spiritual stature. Broadly speaking, there are the *Ārya-janas* (literally 'noble men') or the men of right vision and the *Pṛthag-janas* (*Pāli Puthujjana*) or the 'common folk' who are under the sway of the process of *Avidyā* (Ignorance) and have false vision about the nature of things and also about themselves. The early Buddhist texts leave no doubt about their denigrating and condemnatory attitude towards the latter; they are, generally, slaves to sense-pleasure, greedy, lacking in wisdom, and, therefore, bound to suffer. However, that is not their fate for eternity. Instructed by those who know the truth they too will obtain deliverance at some stage.

In contrast to this society of the uneducated common folk, there stands the *Saṅgha*, the Order founded by the Buddha. It is also a society of men, but of a different nature. It is a spiritual society wherein men have come together, after leaving the world of material pleasures and selfish desires, to seek the highest goal of life, and are bound to one another through a common spiritual purpose. As such there are no conflicts and clashes of interests, no bickerings, no

[1]A. Gard, *Buddhism*, p. 193; Ling, op. cit. p. 179.

[2]*Hinduism and Buddhism*, I, p. 239. Gokul Das De, *Democracy in Early Buddhist Saṅgha*, preface p. xi says that the very nature of his *dhamma* required for its successful propagation the help of a well-trained *Saṅgha*.

occasion for grief or frustration resulting from unfulfilment of worldly desires. Its members practise renunciation of sensual pleasures, make efforts to transcend the sense of 'egoity' and cultivate love for all sentient beings through the universalization of their own self. The *Saṅgha* is thus an ideal society, a model to be emulated by the worldly people. It is obvious that by entrusting the *saṅgha* with this role, Buddha laid great responsibility on its members. They are to maintain very high standards of conduct and give expression in all their activities to the essence of *Dhamma* taught by Buddha. It is for this purpose that a code of conduct (*Vinaya*) was laid down for them which the monks and nuns were to observe rigorously.[1] They have to train themselves in goodness, be always watchful in respect of their physical, vocal and mental action, and cultivate virtues of universal friendship (*maitrī*) and compassion (*karuṇā*). It is not that the *Saṅgha* always maintains this pristine and ideal character, but it is at least expected of it: otherwise it is bound to decline.[2]

As noted above, the 'uneducated many-folk' too have a future, provided they opt for it and are prepared to be guided by *Dharma* taught to them by the wise ones. In the Buddhist structure of social ethics, the laity and the *Saṅgha* are conceived as complementaries to each other and Buddha always thought in terms of a healthy relationship between the two.[3] The members of the *Saṅgha*, for their sustenance, depend on the former. But they could not be considered parasites as the society is compensated in other ways for what it gives to them. In return for the alms the monks instructed them in moral and religious teachings. Speaking of the six ways in which the recluses and the Brāhmins show their love for the laity, a passage of the famous 'Sigālovāda-Sutta' says: "they restrain him from evil, they exhort him to be good, they love him with kindly thought; they teach him what he had not heard, they correct and purify what he has heard, they reveal to him the way of heaven."[4] The ascetic life practised by the members of the *Saṅgha* had an indirect impact on the men of the worldly society. Regarding the impact of ascetic

[1] '*Patimokka-saṁvara-saṁvuto*' 'controlled by the control of the obligations' is the definition of a good monk. On *Pātimokkha* see below.

[2] *Gradual Sayings*, IV, p. 13.

[3] G.S.P. Misra, *The Age of Vinaya*, p. 129.

[4] *Dial.*, III, p. 123.

life on people in general, let us consider the following passage: "... it is...a good thing that the ascetic ideal be incarnated eminently in certain persons, whose speciality, so to speak, it is to represent, almost with excess, this aspect of the ritual life, for they are like so many models inciting to effort Such is the historic role of the great ascetics. When their deeds and acts are analyzed in great detail, one asks himself what useful end they can have. He is struck by the fact that there is something excessive in the disdain they profess for all that ordinarily impassioned man. But these exaggerations are necessary to sustain among the believers a sufficient disgust for an easy life and common pleasures. It is necessary that an elite put the end too high, if the crowd is not to put it too low. It is necessary that some exaggerate, if the average is to remain at a fitting level." This is a passage from Durkheim which Ling has quoted and he remarks on it: "Whether these words of Durkheim are true for any other system or not, they are certainly true of early Buddhism."[1]

'Pātimokkha-Saṁvara—Saṁvuto'—'Controlled by the Control of Obligations'

Buddha conceived discipline as a gradual process, leading to perfection through unfailing vigilance and constant effort on the part of the seeker. Those who had opted for the ascetic life greatly needed a set of rules to guide them in respect of their general conduct. *Pātimokkha* (skt. *Prātimokṣa*) was the name for such a set of rules which Buddhism provides for its elite adherents, i.e., monks and nuns. The *Dīgha Nikāya* thus describes a person who abandons the worldly life and embraces the homeless life of a recluse symbolized by cutting off of his hair and beard and wearing of orange-coloured robes: "When he has thus become a recluse he lives self-restrained by that restraint that should be binding on a recluse (*Pātimokkha-saṁvara—saṁvuto*). Uprightness is his delight, and he sees danger in the least of those things he should avoid. He adopts, and trains himself in the precepts. He encompasses himself with good deeds in act and word. Pure are his means of livelihood, good in his conduct, guarded the door of his senses, Mindful and self-possessed he is altogether happy."[2] The *Pātimokkha* rules were thus

[1]Trevor Ling, op. cit., p. 170.
[2]*Dial.*, I, p. 79.

intended to transform the whole personality of the seeker in the monastery with a view to enabling him to realize the goal for which he had forsaken his earlier life and become a recluse. The very fact that the *Vinayas* of all the Buddhist schools bear reference to some of the *Prātimokṣa* rules, though varying in details,[1] points to the important position assigned to it in the Buddhist monastic framework. There is no doubt that it belongs to the oldest stratum in the corpus of the *Vinaya* literature.[2]

In its extant form, the *Prātimokṣa* in the Pāli *Vinaya* consists of 227 rules covering the entire range of a monk's life—clothes, food living-place, medicine, relationships with others, etc. This set of rules was recited by the monks twice a month on the occasion of the *Uposatha* ceremony and a monk was expected to admit before the assembly if any violation had been committed on his part. Except in the case of the four gravest offences (*Pārājikas*), which amounted to expulsion from the Order, a monk guilty of any violation had to undergo some punishment, which amounted to a loss of certain privileges, and were supposed to serve as a corrective measure against its repetition. The rules are framed in conformity with the Buddhist psychological and moral beliefs with a view to providing a real spiritual training to the disciples. As these rules pertained exclusively to the monastic dwellers, its recital in the presence of the householders was disallowed.[3]

Avoidance of sense-objects

Desire or craving is the cause of suffering and the aim of a spiritual seeker is to overcome it. When does craving arise? It arises when sense-organs come in contact with sense-objects. The first requisite, therefore, is not to contemplate on them as it supplies fuel to the lamp;[4] 'sense should be covered up and the impressions should be shut out,' as Copleston remarks.[5] Sense-objects, involving

[1]See G.S.P. Misra, *The Age of Vinaya*, pp. 12ff.

[2]For the divergent views of T.W. Rhys Davids, Oldenberg, Frauwallner, N. Dutt and I.B. Horner see ibid., pp. 29-30.

[3]*MV.*, p. 177.

[4]*Dial.*, 'Mahāparinibbāna-sutta', II, p. 154. See *Aṭṭhasālinī*, *PTS* trans, pp. 142-43 for an explanation of why contact comes first.

[5]Copleston, op. cit., pp. 138-39.

any possibility of leading one off the track, should be avoided as much as possible. When Ananda asked Buddha how a monk should behave towards women, the latter said that, in the first instance, he should try not to look at them or speak to them:

'Kathaṁ mayaṁ, bhante, mātugāme paṭipajjāma'? ti
'Adanassaṁ Ānanda' ti'
'Dassane, bhagavā, sati kathaṁ paṭipajjatabbanti?'
'Anālāpo Ānanda' ti'[1]

Like a tortoise, says the *Saṁyutta Nikāya,* who drew its neck and four limbs into its shell in order to protect itself from the jackal who wanted to eat it, one should withdraw his senses from the worldly objects; such a man cannot be overtaken by evil.[2]

But living in the world, as it is, it is not always possible to be completely away from the undesirable sense-objects. It is not always in the hands of man to let not the sense-objects come near him. Does training consist only in the crippling of our senses? Could one get rid of the undesirable urges of the sensory organs by somehow managing to put them to constant disuse? Buddha's answer is in the negative. The above advice is regarded only as a preliminary stage in training.

Exercise of Control over Mind

Man lives in the midst of innumerable sense-objects, complete avoidance of which is an impossibility. Besides, man is not a tamed animal of the circus or a dog of a household. Animal training admits of no exception and is just behavioural, absolutely conditioned by an outside agency. Man, on the other hand, has to train himself and learns it by the application of his watchfulness. As far as possible, the way-farer should try to avoid the sense-objects, but if they come to confront him he should possess restraint enough to stand against their temptations. Mind, dallying by nature as it is, is the main source of trouble and, in the ultimate analysis it is mindfulness that Ānanda is advised to cultivate and exercise with regard to his behaviour towards women—*sati, Ānanda, upaṭṭhapeta-*

[1] 'Mahāparinibbāna-sutta,' *Dīgha Nikāya.*
[2] *SN,* pp. 12-13. Compare *Gīta,* II, 98.

bbati.[1] Buddha's stand is clear from an account in the *Majjhima* which contains his criticism of the teaching of a Brahmin teacher, Pārāsariya, who taught perfection in man's conduct regarding senses (*indriya bhāvanā*) through such external means. When Buddha was told by Uttara, the informant youth, that the training consisted in not seeing material shapes and not hearing sounds, he denounced the teaching:

"This being so Uttara, then according to what Pārāsariya, the Brahmin teacher, says a blind man must have his sense-organs developed, a deaf man must have his sense-organs developed. . ."[2]

The *Cullavagga* relates the story of a monk who, in order to be free from sex-instinct, amputated his sex-organ; Buddha condemned his conduct and observed—*aññamhi so, bhikkhave, moghapuriso chhetabbamhi, aññaṁ chhindi*, i.e. the foolish man did not severe what he actually ought to have severed.[3] Buddha, thus, taught that the evil impulses should be mastered and controlled by a firm determination and not by severence or disuse of the senses. The whole purpose of the training is defeated if the mind is not under control and still clings to worldly objects. As to how Buddha desired the application of this theory in the practical monastic code of his Order is evident from an incident related in the 'Pavāraṇākkhandhaka' of the *Mahāvagga*:[4] Once a group of monks of Śrāvasti, with a view to avoiding disputes, decided to observe the rain-retreat period (*Vaṣrāvāsa*) without speaking a word. When Buddha came to know about it, he condemned the practice commenting that observance of dumbness like the sheep was not conducive to any gain: he declared that the *Varṣāvāsa* had not been spent in an appropriate manner.

Thus, Buddha aims at mastery over the restless mind. It is a constant training of mind wherein one tries to cultivate an attitude of indifference toward worldly objects—it is in one word 'a sane distate'.[5] Morality is a matter of how one looks at things and not a matter of what things one looks at.

[1]See above, 'Mahāparinibbāna-sutta'.

[2]*Middle Length Sayings*, III, p. 347.

[3]*CV.*, p. 199. [4]*MV.*, p. 167.

[5]*Psalms of the Brethren*, p. 401.

Ethical Aspect of the Middle Path

The Middle Path doctrine of Buddha has both philosophical as well as ethical aspect. Philosophically, it meant avoidance of certain extreme assertions which were in vogue in Buddha's time, such as 'the world is eternal' (*sassato loko*), 'the world is not eternal' (*asassato loko*); 'the world is finite' (*antavā loko*), 'the world is not finite' (*anantavā loko*); 'the soul is identical with the body' (*taṁ jīvaṁ taṁ sarīraṁ*), 'the soul is different from the body' (*aññaṁ jīvaṁ aññaṁ sarīraṁ*), etc. Ethically, it stood for the avoidance of the extremity of self-indulgence (*kāmasukha*), on the one hand, and the extreme of self-mortification (*atta-kilamatha*) on the other. The householders, who led the common life of worldly indulgence, were generally too much involved with sensual pleasures. As against it, there were recluses who, in a very strong reaction to such a life. believed in taking up the course of severe penance amounting to torture to the body. The inherent logic in such a thinking was that since body, as the receptacle of various sensual pleasures, was the source of suffering, the extreme opposite of sensual pleasures, i.e. inflicting pain to the body, would lead to cessation of all suffering. In Buddha's time, severe penance was generally considered the source of emancipation among the ascetics. It is clear from the remark of the 'Pañcavaggiya monks'[1] when Buddha, after his Enlightenment, came to them to Isipatana and declared that he had realized the Truth: '*Tāya pi kho tvaṁ, āvuso Gotama, tāya paṭipadāya, tāya dukkarakārikāya nevajjhagā uttarimanussadhammaṁ alamariyañāṇadassanavisesaṁ kiṁ pana tvaṁ etarahi bāhullaka padhānavibbhanto āvatto bāhullāya, adhigamissasi uttarimanussadhammaṁ alamariyañāṇadassanavisesaṁ' ti?*[2] Buddha, however, preached that if pursuit of sense-pleasures as practised by the worldly people was condemnable, inflicting pain to the body by the way of austere penance too was devoid of any gain. Buddha explained the Middle Way to Soṇa, who in his overenthusiasm sought to overexert, with the help of the simile of lute: Just as sweet notes can be obtained only when it is tuned neither too high nor too low, in the same way goal is realized only

[1]The 'Five Monks' who had attended on Buddha when the latter, prior to his Enlightenment, had taken up to austere penance but had abandoned his company when he decided to leave this way.

[2]*MV.*, p. 12.

when the two extremes are avoided. He pointed to him the evils involved in the extreme of over-exertion and that of non-exertion and advised to follow the mean.[1]

The Middle Way is the Eightfold path (*aṭṭhaṅgika magga*) which includes all the aspects of the seeker's training, physical, mental and intellectual (*sīla, samādhi* and *paññā*).[2] Herein, *sammā vāca, sammā kammanta and sammā ājīva,* 'practically include the whole code of moral laws'.[3] Others pertain to purification of mind and intellect.

Basic Moral Obligations: The Ten Sikkhāpadas

An unordained novice in the Order was called *Sāmaṇera*. Such a new entrant was yet to be trained in the subtleties of the doctrine; it could not be expected of him to conform to those heights of ethical and spiritual standards which the monastic dwellers of experience had obtained. He was first to be trained in the basics of moral precepts which a seeker needed to observe for his very entitlement of being a recluse and as a guarantee of his onward progress. *Sāmaṇera* is required to assiduously follow ten basic moral precepts.[4]

These are couched in negative phraseology but are positive in fruition. The first five are equally applicable in the case of a householder; a more faithful layman or laywoman may observe the first eight on the *Uposatha* days. Buddhaghosa has therefore called them *gahaṭṭha sīlas,* i.e., the precepts for the householder.[5] The application of the last five in the case of the recluses involves a distinction between the ascetic life and the worldly life of the householders, In the former, anything adding fuel to sensuality is to be overcome.

1. *Pāṇātipātā veramaṇī*—'I refrain from injury to living things'. It refers to the Buddhist doctrine of *Ahiṁsā* which has far-reaching implications. As an extension, it includes within it such virtues as amity (*mettā*) and compassion (*karuṇā* or *anukampā*). It emanates from the belief in the oneness of all forms of life and refers not only

[1]ibid., p. 202: '*evameva kho, Soṇa, accāraddhaviriyaṁ udhaccāya saṁvattati, atilīnaviriyaṁ kosajjāya saṁvattati. Tasmātih tvaṁ, Soṇa, viriyasamataṁ adhiṭṭhaha, indriyaraṁ ca samataṁ paṭivijjha, tattha ca nimittaṁ gaṇhāhi.*

[2]N. Dutt, *Early Monastic Buddhism*, I, p. 199ff. For a detailed enumeration of the 'Eight Steps' see Christmas Humphreys, *Buddhism*, pp. 108ff.

[3]N. Dutt, *Early Monastic Buddhism*, I, p. 200.

[4]See *MV.*, p. 87.

[5]*Viśuddhimarga* (ed. Bhiksu Dharmarakshita), pp. 17-18.

to non-killing but to all forms of cruely, harm and oppression. Buddha was opposed to such Brahmanical sacrifices which entailed killing of and cruelty to animals.[1] A *Jātaka* story puts forth that one single act of *hiṁsā* bears its result in hundreds of births.[2] The Buddhist viewpoint is expressed in these words: 'As I am, so are these. As these are, so am I. Thus identifying himself with others the wise man neither kills nor causes to be killed.'[3]

2. *Adinnadānā veramaṇī*—'I refrain from taking that which is not given'.

This refrain refers to all forms of theft and is linked up with the first one in the sense that taking a thing from someone without his consent or by cheating him would cause injury to him. Moreover, the physical act of stealing springs forth from mental covetousness which is a blemish by itself.

3. *Abrahmacariyā veramaṇī*—'I refrain from sexual misconduct'.

Buddha recognized that 'of all the lusts and desires, there is none so powerful as sexual inclination'.[4] In the appetite for flesh, according to Buddhism, was embodied the high watermark of man's attachment with the world and sensual desires, and also his incapacity to see the transitory nature of bodily existence in which lies the essence of Ignorance. Buddhist texts speak of body as a 'citadel of bones' (*aṭṭhīnaṁ nagaraṁ*), 'plastered over with flesh and blood' (*maṁsalohitalepanaṁ*) in which dwell old age and death, pride and deceit.[5] The *Visuddhimagga* has illustrated the analogy by a story: once the hermit Mahā-Tissa was walking near Anuradhpura meditating on the transiency of life. A woman who had quarrelled with her

[1]See 'Kūṭadanta-sutta' in the *Dīgha Nikaya*; *Gradual Sayings*, II, pp. 42-43; ibid., IV, pp. 42-45,

[2]'Matakabhatta Jātaka', *Jātaka*, 1, p. 53.

[3]See *Dhammapada*, 'Daṇḍavagga'. From the Buddhist viewpoint the act of 'killing' is done when the following five conditions are present: (i) the fact and presence of a living being, (ii) the knowledge that the being is a living being, (iii) the intent or resolution to kill, (iv) the act of killing by appropriate means, (v) the resulting death. 'In the absence of any one of these conditions, the act would not constitute 'killing' even though death should follow; the event would be considered an accident, and would not entail any evil effect for the performer of the act.' See H. Saddhatissa, *Buddhist Ethics*, p. 89.

[4]Beal, *A Catena of Buddhist Scriptures*, p. 198 quoted in Christmas Humphreys, *Buddhism*, p. 112.

[5]*Dhammapada*, 150.

husband, passed by him. She was gaily dressed and smiled at him. When the husband, who was pursuing her, asked the Thera whether he saw a woman, the Thera replied, 'I saw only a skeleton, whether it was man or woman I know not'.[1] A recluse who had left world in the high pursuit of self-relisation and was to overcome all passions must try hard to have control over this carnal desire. The *Dhammapada* declares: 'As long indeed as the desire, however small, of man for woman is not destroyed, so long is his mind attached (to existence) as a sucking calf is to its mother.'[2]

We have quoted earlier Ānanda's query to Buddha as to what should be a monk's attitude toward women and the latter's guideline in this regard. The final remedy lies in control of mind—in control of mind, not in its suppression.

4. *Musāvādā veramaṇī*—'I refrain from falsehood'.

It refers to adherence to truth in speech. Lying implies a deliberate motive of distorting the truth. False-speaking and slandering should be strenuously avoided.

5. *Surāmerayamajjapamādaṭṭhānā veramaṇī*—'I refrain from liquors which engender slothfulness.'

The goal which the recluse has set for himself requires unfailing watchfulness and mental fitness. Slothfulness is a great hindrance in his pursuit. Intoxicant drugs and drinks affect the taker adversely and, therefore, should not be taken.

6. *Vikālabhojanā veramaṇī*—'I refrain from untimely food'.

The means of sustenance for the recluse was by begging alms from the householders. In comparison to Jaina and Brāhmaṇical rules, the Buddhist rules regarding food-taking are quite liberal and, generally, a monk could accept anything in alms. Over-eating, however, was to be avoided and he could eat only once a day before mid-day.[3] Alms-begging time was to be adjusted accordingly which was also intended to take care of the convenience of the householders.[4]

[1]Quoted by Radhakrishnan in his translation of the *Dhammapada*, p. 109.

[2]*Dhammapada*, tr. Radhakrishnan, p. 284.

[3]The *Pac.*, p. 121 defines *vikāla* as '*majjhantike vitivatte yāva araṇuggamanā*'.

[4]Compare *Manu Smṛti*, VI, 56. Manu lays down that an ascetic should go to beg when no smoke ascends from the kitchen, when the pestle lies motionless, when the people have finished their meal and the remnants of dishes have been removed.

7. *Naccagītavāditavisūkadassanā veramaṇī*—'I refrain from seeing the performance of dancers, musicians and jesters'.

8. *Mālāgandhavilepana-dhāraṇa-maṇḍana-vibhūsaṇaṭṭhānā veramaṇī*—'I refrain from adoring my body in various ways'.

The above two relate to sensual pursuits and are evidently unprofitable to a recluse.

9. *Uccāsayanamahāsayanā-veramaṇī*—'I refrain from the use of high and comfortable bed'.

10. *Jātarūparajatapaṭiggahaṇā veramaṇī*—'I refrain from taking gold and silver'.

It is obvious that the purpose of these precepts is to tune the entrant into the order to the new life he has voluntarily accepted for himself—a life which is harder, requiring great physical and mental discipline on his part. It is to be noted, however, that all these precepts are not of the same gravity and few of them got changed and modified in due course when Buddhism developed in terms of time and space. As early as the time of the second Buddhist Council nos. 5, 6 and 10 had been modified by the Vesālian monks. In Tantric Buddhism, taking of liquor received sanction and the Japanese priests even today take liquor and call it 'Wisdom Water'.[1]

Practices as Aids to Moral and Spiritual Progress of the Seeker

In Buddhism, morality and spirituality are intermixed with each other. Again, true morality is not confined to the external acts of the doer but, rather, relates to his mental purity. He has not only to put a curb on ethically wrong actions but also, through conscious efforts, to constantly train his mind to deter from harbouring ethically wrong notions and desires. There should be perfect harmony between his actions and thoughts, ethically pure actions springing forth from an ethically pure mind. To ensure this, a recluse is advised to undertake a number of practices supposed to help him in such an enterprise.

Buddha laid great stress on solitude. He himself retired in solitude from time to time.[2] The *Sutta-Nipāta* observes that companion-

[1]See Nakamura, *Buddhism In Comparative Light*, p. 91.

[2]*Kindred Sayings*, V, p. 11: "Monks, I desire to dwell in solitude for half a month. I am not be visited by anyone save by him alone who brings my food." ibid., p. 283.

ships breed fondness which, as its consequence, leads to suffering; hence, a recluse must live alone.[1] Buddha recommends it even to the householders.[2] Solitude provides an opportunity for self-introspection, a faculty which has to be exercised constantly in order that one may assess his progress from time to time. In solitude the recluse, through meditation, may try to reach the depths of his mind and attain mental quietude,[3] Meditation holds the most important place in the Buddhist spiritual practice : Buddha himself had obtained the Truth through it. The *Milindapañho* speaks of meditation as the chicf of all good qualities—"As all the rafters of the roof of a house. . . go up to the apex, slope towards it, are joined on together at it, and the apex is acknowledged to be the top of all; so is thc habit of meditation in its relation to all other qualities."[4] The texts frequently refer to *Jhāna* or meditation into the form of a fourfold formula practised in succession.[5] The description leaves no doubt about their ethical purposefulness. Making an observation on the meditational process Mrs. Rhys Davids says ". . .the four stages describe the man as eliminating successively the intellectual activity present in the first, when he may be said to win the second, and the hedonic factors of consciousness when he may be said to win the third. The fourth is the winning of perfect sati (lucid, alert mentality) and of indifference (upekkha) or poise."[6] mental health is

[1]*Sutta-Nipata*, 36.

[2]*Gradual Sayings*, III, p. 152: Buddha says to Anāthpiṇḍaka, 'Come now, let us, from time to time, enter and abide in the zest that comes of seclusion. Verily, train yourself thus, householder'.

[3]Conze notes four disabilities from which the practice of Buddhist meditation in the modern times suffers, one of which is excess of noise. He quotes an old saying which says, "Noise is a thorn in the side of dhyana". See Edward Conze, *Buddhist Meditation*, pp. 38-41.

[4]*The Questions of King Milinda*, I, *SBE*, XXXV, p. 60.

[5]For example, see *Middle Length Sayings*, III, pp. 63-64: "... And what kind of meditation ... does the Lord praise? As to this, ... a monk, aloof from the pleasure of senses, aloof from unskilled states of mind, enters and abides in the first meditation which is accompanied by initial thought and discursive thought, is born of aloofness, and is rapturous and joyful, By allaying initial and discursive thought with the mind subjectively tranquilled and fixed on one point, he enters and abides in the second meditation which is devoid of initial and discursive thought, is born of concentration, and is rapturous and joyful ... he enters and abides in the third meditation and the fourth meditation ..."

[6]Mrs. C.A.F. Rhys Davids, *The Birth of Indian Psychology*, p. 332.

the goal of meditation but, as Conze has pointed out, it is not the same as modern psycho-therapy as 'they differ profoundly in their definitions of mental health, in their theoretical assumptions about the structure of the mind and the purpose of human existence, and in the methods which they prescribe for the attainment of mental health.'[1]

Closely connected with meditation is the virtue of mindfulness. The great value that is attached with it in Buddhism becomes evident by the fact that Buddha has called the fourfold setti ng of Mindfulness (*Sati*), "the one and only path. . .leading to the purification of beings, to passing far beyond grief and lamentation, to the dying out of ill and misery, to the attainment of right method, to the realisation of Nirvāṇa."[2] The four stations of mindfulness are thus described: "Herein a monk dwells, as regards body, contemplating body (as transient), by having restrained the dejection in the world arising from coveting. He dwells as regards feeling.. . .He dwells as regards mind, contemplating mind (as transient) ardent, composed and mindful. . .He dwells as regards mind—states, contemplating mind-states (as transient), ardent, composed and mindful, by having restrained the dejection in the world arising from coveting."[3] It is obvious that mindfulness in Buddhism is not an effort to grasp something abstract: it refers to fact and consists in a conscious mental application. It is probably for the first time in the teaching of Buddha that mindfulness comes to have an ethical implication. The idea is that the mind should not lose poise and balance and remain constantly alert. Commenting on the virtue of mindfulness E. Conze remarks, "Whereas faith and vigour, when driven to excess, must be restrained by their counterparts i.e. wisdom and tranquil concentration, the virtue of mindfulness does not share this disability. Mindfullness should be strong everywhere. For it protects the mind from excitedness, into which it might fall since faith, vigour and wisdom may excite us; and from indolence into which it might fall since concentration favours indolence."[4]

The Buddhist texts speak of many forms of meditation. Of these,

[1]Edward Conze, *Buddhist Meditation*, p. 38.
[2]*Dial.* II, 'Mahāsatipaṭṭhānasutta' pp. 326; *Kindred Sayings*, V, pp. 119-20.
[3]*Kindred Sayings*, V, pp. 119-20; ibid., p. 150, 160.
[4]Edward Conze, *Buddhist Thought in India*, p. 51.

the one which has an obvious ethical character relates to the set of four moods (or attitudes) called *Brahmavihāras*. They are: *Mettā* (Amity or Friendliness), *Karuṇā* (Compassion), *Muditā* (Sympathy i.e. feeling of happiness in the happinass of others), and *Upekkhā* (Impartiality or Indifference), The *Vihāras* are mentioned in the early Pāli texts, in varying contexts.[1] An elaborate treatment however, is given to them in a chapter of the *Visuddhimagga* devoted exclusively to this topic.[2] Though the exact origins of the *Brahmavihāras* is not very clear,[3] it appears, as G.C. Pande says, 'to have been a feature of original Buddhism, if not an original feature of Buddhism.'[4] In the practice of the *Brahmavihāras*, one begins with the cultivation of the feeling of friendliness (*Mettā*) which is made to keep on enlarging its area in the successive states of meditation to the point of encompassing all the creatures within it; in order that the course becomes easy and the person is not caught by repulsion in the very beginning, it is suggested that one makes the start by first meditating on his own good, then makes his preceptor the object of his meditation and include his enemies only in the final stages. In the ultimate stage, however, there should not remain any distinction between himself and any other person, and complete identity with all should be established. After *Mettā*—feeling is perfected, one takes up *Karuṇā*-feeling and tries to perfect it in the same way. In the third (*Muditā*) the seeker practises feeling of joy at the happiness of others. Then is developed the feeling of complete indifference

[1]See 'Makhadevasutta' of the *MN* where Makhadeva, the king of Mithilā is made to practise it; The 'Mahāgovinda-sutta' of the *DN* mentions a Brahmin minister of bygone days, Mahāgovinda, who, through the practice of one of these *Viharas*, is supposed to have reached the Brahman-world. The 'Tevijja-sutta' of the *DN* however contains the best *Nikāyan* account of the use of the *Brahmavihāras* as a form of meditation.

[2]'Brahmavihāra-niddesa' in the *Visuddimagga*.

[3]According to Mrs. Rhys Davids, *JRAS*, 1928, pp. 271ff, it did not derive originally from Buddha but was founded by an ex-Brāhmaṇa Parivrājaka. E. Conze, *Buddhist Thought in India*, p. 80, thinks that it may have been borrowed from other Indian religious systems. G.C. Pande, *Studies*, p. 529, gives his opinion on this issue in the following words: "All this, however, only suggests that the doctrine of the Four Vihāras originated in an atmosphere full of Brahmanic ideas, and that at one period of its history it became a common possession of many different sects".

[4]G.C. Pande, *Studies*, p. 529.

(*Upekkhā*) toward all things. No one can miss the ethical character of the first three practices which also represent a subtle process through which the individual ego would get so universalized as to lose it menacing habit of creating distinctions and, consequent upon it, occasions for rifts and clashes. After such a state of mind has been achieved, one must practise meditation on the fourth which amounts to an intellectual indifference towards all phenomena.

It was a popular belief in Buddha's time that the practice of various religious austerities such as mindfulness, meditation and the like brought various super-human powers (*iddhis*) to him with the use of which he could perform any marvel of wonder.[1] The *Nikāyan* passages describe these powers as follows: "From being one he becomes many, from being many he becomes one; manifest or invisible he goes unhindered through a wall, through a rampart, through a mountain, as if it were through air. He plunges into the earth and shoots up again as if in water. He walks upon the water without parting it, as if on solid ground. He travels sitting cross-legged through the air, like a bird upon the wing. Even this moon and sun, though they be of such mighty power and majesty, he handles and strokes them with his hand. Even as far as the Brahma World he has power with his body".[2] Buddha was regarded by his contemporaries as one who possessed great psychic powers.[3] In fact, anyone who had made considerable advancement on the spiritual path was considered possessing such super-human powers, as is evidenced in the case of some of his prominent disciples.[4] Buddha does appear

[1] *CV.*, pp. 199-200. All the prominent religious teachers of the age, viz., Pūraṇa Kassapa, Makkhali Gosāla, Ajita Kesakambala, Pakudha Kaccāyana, sañjāya, Belaṭṭhaputta, and Nigaṇṭhanātaputta are mentioned as claiming such powers.

[2] *Kindred Sayings*, V, p. 236; *Dial.*, I, pp. 88-89; Gradual *Sayings*, III, p. 203.

[3] *Middle Length Sayings*, II, p. 331; ibid., p. 285. This belief about Buddha was held even by the ascetics belonging to other sects. See *Middle Length Sayings*, 'Upālisutta', II, p. 40, and ibid., 'Abhayarājakumārsutta', p. 60.

[4] See, for example, *CV.*, pp. 199-200 where Mahāmoggalāna and Piṇḍola-Bhāradvāja have been called *iddhimā* (possessors of *iddhis*) and the latter performs a supernormal feat. The *Theragāthā* gives the following story: in the middle of the night the stream rose in flood causing great panic among the younger brethren. The Exalted One sent venerable Gavaṁpati to arrest the rising stream, who 'by his mystic power did so, and stopped the stream afar so that it stood up like a mountain-peak'. *Psalms of the Brethren*, p. 43.

to believe in the *iddhis* as an ingredient of advanced spiritual life.[1] but he discouraged its display to the householders,[2] and did not like his disciples to indulge in them.[3] "An ordained disciple must not boast of any superhuman perfection. The disciple who boasts of a superhuman perfection, be it celestial visions or miracles, is no longer a disciple of the Sakyamuni."[4]

General Code of Conduct as Member of an Āvāsa

Both men and women, who took up to ascetic life under Buddha's guidance, constituted the Church, or *Saṅgha* as it has been called in the texts. Besides his own, many other sects were operating at this time, for the most part, within the same geographical area of the Kosala and Magadha dominions. Among the others, the one founded by Mahāvīra is the most important in comparison with which the Buddhist *Saṅgha* shows some interesting distinctive and novel features.[5]

Theoretically, the Buddhist *Saṅgha* appears to have been divided into (1) *Sammukhībhūta Saṅgha* i.e. the local *Saṅgha* and (2) *Āgatānāgatassa Cātuddisa Saṅgha* i.e. the *Saṅgha* belonging to all the ages and places. The latter stands for the *Saṅgha* in its idealized form including even those who would embrace the Order of Buddha in future. With the spread of Buddhism to distant places, the former came to be divided into a number of units. Ideally speaking, each of these '*Sammukha Saṅghas*' was considered a part of the *Cātuddisa Saṅgha*. Generally, the boundaries of an *Āvāsa* were fixed and the monks and nuns residing within the area formed a distinct and separate body, enjoying a common community life and observing the various ascetic ceremonies like *Upostha* and *Pavāraṇā* together. Though during his own life-time Buddha's own position in his *Saṅgha* was not different from other *Saṅgha*-heads, contrary to the

[1]See *SN.*, IV, pp. 217-18, 247-48—*Iddhipādas* as leading to *Nibbara*; ibid., p. 248—*Iddhipādas* as essential to *Vimutti:* see also *DN.*, III, pp. 87-88 where a distinction between 'Ariya' and 'No-Ariya' *iddhis* has been made.

[2]*CV.*, pp. 200-201.

[3]See *DN.*, 'Sāmaññaphala Sutta' and 'Patika Sutta'.

[4]Paul Carus, *The Gospel of Buddha*, p. 98.

[5]For a detailed discussion, see G.S.P. Misra, 'Some Reflections on Early Jaina and Buddhist Monachism,' *Jijñāsā*, 1, nos. 3-4, July-October 1974, pp. 4-15.

prevalent custom in the contemporary ascetic sects, Buddha preferred for his *Saṅgha* the abstract guidance of *Dharma* to the tangible control of a leader and deviated from the time-honoured practice of choosing a successor to guide it after his death; his *Saṅgha* came to be based on the ideas of a corporate life organized on the model of a republican state in which members decided their affairs on the basis of common participation and deliberation. The *Vinaya* lays down elaborate rules relating to the functioning of the Order in all its dimensions.[1]

The monks and nuns formed a spiritual society united together by adherence to a common faith and a common monastic code. They were like members of family in which harmony and mutual help was to mark the total way of life. Concluding the 'Tittira Jātaka' in the *Vinaya*, Buddha says that they were expected to respect and help each other and lead a co-operative life.[2] For the maintenance of proper discipline, seniority was given due consideration and the seniors enjoyed preference over the juniors in respect of seat, water or food.[3] In other matters, however, the juniors had equal rights and in illness could expect all care and service from the senior monks. If, a monk happened to be *upādhyāya* or *ācārya*, he was to be attended upon by the novice associated with him; if a junior monk fell ill, it was the duty of the *upādhyāya* or *ācārya* to attend upon him; or else, the duty fell on a resident monk. At one place Buddha admonishes his disciples that as in the *āvāsa* there was no father or mother to take care of them, they have to look after each other, and that one who wants to attend upon him should attend upon an ill monk—*natthi vo, bhikkhave, mātā natthi pitā ye vo upaṭṭhaheyyuṁ. Tumhe ca, bhikkhave, aññamaññaṁ na upaṭṭhahissatha, atha ko carahi upaṭṭhahissati? Yo, bhikkhave, maṁ upaṭṭhaheyya so gilānaṁ upaṭṭhaheyya.*[4]

A newly ordained monk, to be properly trained in the new ethical and spiritual life, was provided with an *upādhyāya* or *ācārya*. Every junior monk was to select an *upādhyāya* and an *ācārya* who would guide him in all matters. The *ācārya* officiated for the *upā-*

[1]See G.S.P. Misra, *The Age of Vinaya*, ch. IV.
[2]See *CN.*, p. 214.
[3]ibid., p. 257.
[4]*MV.*, p. 317.

dhyāya in his absence and thus a novice was never left without guidance. The novice, called *saddhivihārika* or *antevāsika*, was expected to be in his behaviour respectful and serviceable to his preceptors,[1] and, in turn, it was the duty of the latter to see that he was in possession of all required articles and also to attend on him in his illness. The ideal of relationship between the two was to be that of father and son, the same as one finds conceived in the Brahmanical system between a *guru* and a *śiṣya*.[2]

A monk was generally required to avoid unnecessary mixing with the lay people. By mixing too much with the worldly people, Buddha maintained, he would form ties which is to be avoided by one who had opted for ascetic life. Generally, he would come in their contact on his alms-begging tour or when he goes to them to teach the Norm. Buddha wanted a very healthy relationship between the *Saṅgha* and the society and many of the monastic rules were formulated by him on such considerations. The *Sekhiyas* include many rules which express Buddha's keen desire to make the monks decent in their behaviour with regard to the people. If a monk insulted a faithful householder he became liable to '*Paṭisāraṇīya*' punishment and, accordingly, was required to seek his pardon.[3] In certain circumstances, the monks were even allowed temporary relationship with their former families—a monk, for example, could break his *varṣāvāsa* if there was a call from his sick father or sick mother;[4] he could give surplus clothes to them if they were in need.[5]

The life and conduct of the nuns was not much different from that of the monks. They had their own *Prātimokṣa* rules to guide them. They were, however, subjected to eight strict rules (*garudh-*

[1] *MV.*, pp. 46-47; Compare *Pāraskara Gṛhyasūtra*, p. 310; *Āpastamba Gṛhyasūtra*, p. 7, pp. 22-25.

[2] *MV.*, p. 43; Compare, *Sāṅkhayana Gṛhyasūtra*, p. 65, *Āśvalāyana Gṛhyasūtra*, p. 190, *Gṛhyasūtra of Hiraṇyakeśin*, p. 152.

[3] *CV.*, pp. 32-40.

[4] *MV.*, p. 154.

[5] ibid., p. 313. See the *Sāma Jātaka*, *Jātaka*, VI, no. 540—A monk, after twelve years of renunciation, came to know that his parents were in miserable condition. Then he thought that the Master had said, 'A son, who has become an ascetic, could he helpful to his parents in misery and need.' He started supporting them by what he received in alms, and his conduct was later on praised by Buddha.

ammā),[1] a condition on which Buddha had allowed women entrance in the Order. In all matters they were under the guidance and supervision of the *Bhikkhu-Saṅgha*. The *Vinaya* contains elaborate rules with a view to establishing pure and healthy relationship between the monks and nuns.[2] Forest-dwelling was not permitted to nuns nor were they allowed to go alone to a village or tour lonely at night.[3]

× × ×

Conception of Society and Social Change

In order to understand properly the type of social structure that Buddhism recommends, it is necessary to comprehend and appreciate the Buddhist notion of the origin of the world and human society. This would lead one beyond perceived phenomena into the realm of cosmology from which could be derived the cosmic and metaphysical background of social change as conceived in Buddhism. At the outset it should be noted that Buddhism believes in many world-systems or planes of existence (*cakkavālas*) apart from that of our own, each of unthinkable duration. The 'Patika Sutta' and the 'Aggañña Sutta' of the Pāli *Dīgha Nikāya*—especially the latter-provide the earliest Buddhist description of changes in the cosmic order, a restatement of which is also found in Buddhaghosa's *Visuddhimagga* and the *Mahāvastu* of the *Mahāsāṅghika* school. According to this account, the world-process or *saṁsāra* is constituted over long ages (*kappas*), of involution (*samvaṭṭa*) and evolution (*vivaṭṭa*). Each *kappa* or world-age has four aeons in it, viz., aeon of involution (*samvaṭṭa-kappa*), continuance of involution (*samvaṭṭaṭṭhāyi*), aeon of evolution (*vivaṭṭa-kappa*) and the continuance of evolution (*vivaṭṭaṭṭhāyi*). These four are called *asaṁkheya-kappas* signifying that these are vast periods of time which can be grasped only intuitively and not by any arithmetical computation. When asked about the measurement of an aeon, the Buddha is reported to have replied : "Long, brother, is an aeon. It is not easy to reckon how long by saying so many years, so many centuries, so many thousand centuries". When asked if any illustration could be

[1]*The Age of Vinaya*, p. 130.
[2]*CV.*, pp. 382-93.
[3]ibid., p. 399. In case of the Jaina nuns, see S.B. Deo, *History of Jaina Monachism*, p. 504.

given in this regard, the Buddha continued : "Suppose, brother, there were a great crag, a hill, one yojna wide, one yojana across, one yojana high without chasms and clefts, a solid mass. And a man at the end of every hundred years were to stroke it once each time with a Kasi cloth. Well, that mountain in this way would be sooner done away with and ended than would an aeon. So long, brother, is an aeon. And of aeons long more than one has passed, more than a hundred have passed, more than a hundred thousand."[1]

Apart from this objective world, Buddhist cosmology significantly posits a subjective world, viz., *Brahmaloka*. It is here that beings, inhabiting various planes of existence, are reborn during the time of involution. With the advent of the aeon of evolution the world-system re-evolves and the beings of *Brahmaloka* are reborn on earth, following for a long time, however, the same mode of life as they had been enjoying in *Brahmaloka*. They are radiant beings, made of mind, feeding on rapture, and sexually undifferentiated. Gradually, earth comes into existence, then in due course plants and cereals for which the beings develop taste and sport feeding on them, which causes them to lose their radiance and ethereal bodies and they become more and more gross and solid. Bisexuality, which was thus far absent among them, comes into existence and the sex-awareness, as an inevitable outcome, brings with it lustful feelings, attachment, hatred, enmities, etc. Social and political institutions are formed, sense of property is created, notions about crime and law are born and formulated. In short, we now have the world of our experience, a realm of lust and passions, hatred and selfish attachments, conflicts and wars, all making life full of frustration and suffering. Man becomes full of differences and so does the society formed by him.

From the above two points are derived : (1) that the world or society is not static but changing, and (2) that this evolution in the objective world is twofold : it not only signifies material progress but also a spiritual and moral degeneration. Under the force of *Avidyā* (Ignorance), by which the beings of this world are influenced and guided, the world continues to be a miserable thing.

Thus far the situation appears quite hopeless and one only wonders if there can be any escape from it. But, apart from the one

[1]*Kindred Sayings*, II, pp. 121-22.

mentioned above, there runs also another line of descent in which are born the *Buddhas* and *Bodhisattvas*, the beings who make a rediscovery of the eternal truth for the ignorant, lead them on to the right path and serve humanity in every possible way. There are men of false vision (whom Buddha calls *Pṛthagjana*), but there are also men of right vision (who are called *Ārya-jana*). Buddhism considers man the converging point of the force of *Avidyā* (ignorance) as well as the force of *Prajñā* (wisdom); man is the psychological unit from which the human journey can start in either direction, in the direction of deliverance or in the direction of bondage. *Bodhi* or *Prajñā* (wisdom) is not something alien to man but inherent in him and he has only to put it in operation. Such an operation, the spiritual quest and seeking, turns the same individual into an all-enlightened person. Such a person teaches the truth to others also. The 'Buddha' as is well known, is a generic term, Gautama the Śākya being only one of the many Buddhas and considered the founder of Buddhism only because he belongs to our aeon and is nearer to us than the other Buddhas. All the traditions of Buddhism believe in the existence of many Buddhas, the Buddhas of the past, of the present and of the future. However, seeing the immenseness of the world-systems and considering the fact that some aeons are devoid of a Buddha (*suñña-kappa*), the coming of a Buddha is a rare and an important phenomenon. In the early Sthaviravādin tradition, there occurs refecence only to seven Buddhas, from Vipassī to Gotama, but in the later Sthaviravādin tradition twenty-one more Buddhas are added to the list. The Mahāyāna Buddhism considers their number incalculable. In the Sthaviravādin tradition Bodhisattvahood stood for the previous lives of Gautama the Buddha, whereas in Mahāyāna a Bodhisattva is one who is eligible for Buddhahood but, out of compassion for others, postpones its attainment till others are liberated. He cherishes the ambition of universal emancipation and helps people in this direction. In the later tradition, thus, the Bodhisattva and the Buddha are closely and causally connected with each other, though from the human point of view there is no qualitative difference between the two as both tend to serve the same purpose. The Buddhas and the Bodhisattvas, i.e. the enlightened and saintly beings, too are an integral part of the phenomenal existence and, from time to time, the social good and well-being of humanity is assured through them.

Social change implies change in the form of social structure, change in various institutions which are designed to serve the various needs of its members, change in their material needs, their approach and attitudes. However, despite all these changes, the basic malady remains the same and so does the goal, i.e. deliverance from the miseries of the world. From the Buddhistic point of view, in a similar manner, *Dharma* too has a twofold character. It is eternal (*sanātana*); the Buddha said, his teachnig is not new but 'an ancient law' (*porāṇa dhamma*) taught by other Buddhas of the past.[1] But the content of *Dharma* does not remain the same in all ages and is transformed according to changed historical situations. It is in this sense that we come across prophecies in the Buddhist texts about the disappearance of *saddharma*.[2] Skilfulness in means (*upāya-kauśalya*) is an important characteristic of an enlightened being who is always aware of his audience and situation. It is in consonance with this notion of *sādhana-bheda* (difference in means) that the later Buddhist tradition came to believe not in one *Dharma-cakra-pravartana* (i.e. the beginning of the teaching mission of Buddha) but three *Dharma-cakra-pravartanas*: the one preserved in the Hīnayāna tradition, the second in the Mahāyāna tradition, and the third in the Vajrayāna or Tantrayāna tradition. Though historically belonging to later dates, the Mahāyānists and the Vajrayānists both claim their teaching to have originated from Buddha himself. Implicit here is the notion that the same teachings of the Master have assumed different forms according to historical needs. The basic purpose of the teaching is, however, the same, viz., making people good, and then happy. A Bodhisattva, who has made it the aim of his life to help all other beings and give them whatever they might need, supplies them with different kinds of things starting from material things to the teaching on *Dharma*. However, the former is considered the lowest in the hierarchy of things to be given. A *sūtra* preserved in Chinese translation reads:

"What is bad means (*anupāya*)? When, by the practice of the perfections the Bodhisattvas help others, but are content to supply

[1]*Kindred Sayings*, II, p. 74.

[2]See, for example, *Gradual Sayings*, IV, pp. 184-85; on the gradual decline of the Buddha *sāsana* see *Anāgatavaṁsa* trans. I. B. Horner, in Edward Conze, *Buddhist Texts Through the Ages*, pp. 47-50.

them with merely material aid, without raising them from their misery or introducing them into beatitude, then they are using a bad means.

Why? Because material aid is not sufficient. Whether a dunghill be large or small, it cannot possibly be made to smell sweet by any means whatsoever. In the same way, living beings are unhappy because of their acts, because of their nature; it is impossible to make them happy by supplying them with merely material aids. The best way of helping them is to establish them in goodness."[1]

The Five Sīlas

In the first section of this chapter we have enumerated the ten negatively phrased rules of conduct which every monk was to take on himself as a voluntary vow. The first five of these are applicable in the case of a householder also. These five precepts, as Edmond Holmes says, 'indicate five arterial directions in which the Buddhist self-control is to be exercised. Thus, the first rule calls upon him to control the passion or anger, the second, the desire for material possessions, the third, the lusts of the flesh, the fourth, cowardice and malevolence (the chief causes of untruthfulness), the fifth, the craving for unwholesome excitement.'[2]

The Ideals Governing Social Relationships

The Buddha looked at the life of a householder as the complexity of different types of social relationship and conceived the happiness of a houseman as depending on the proper performance of his duties in the context of each one of them. It is in these, he explained to Uggatasarīra, a Brāhmaṇa, that the fire of a householder (*gahapataggi*) was contained. "Consider, brāhman, the man who honoureth his son, womenfolk, slaves, messengers, workmen—this is called the fire of the householder. Therefore, brāhman, this fire of the householder, when esteemed. . .must bring best happiness."[3]

There are many passages in the early Buddhist Canon which record the discourses of the Master relating to the moral code of conduct which the laymen are exhorted to observe. However, three

[1]Quoted by Henri de Lubac, *Aspects of Buddhism*, p. 24.
[2]Edmond Holmes, *The Creed of Buddha*, p. 73.
[3]*Gradual Sayings*, IV, p. 26.

Suttas, viz., the 'Sigālovāda-Sutta' of the *Dīgha Nikāya*, the 'Uggahasutta' of the *Aṅguttara Nikāya*, and the 'Mahāmaṅgala-sutta' in the *Sutta-Nipata* of the *Khuddaka Nikāya* deserve special mention as they preserve the essence of the Buddhist ethical code for the laity.

The 'Sigālovāda-sutta' is called the 'Vinaya of the Houseman', as it contains a comprehensive account of the social and domestic duties which can be posited with regard to the life of a householder. It speaks of six sets of moral duties which a householder has to perform. A householder has to worship six quarters: parents as the east, teachers as the south, wife and children as the west, friends as the north, servants and other employees as the nadir, the recluses (the Sramaṇas) and the Brāhmaṇas as the zenith. These, in fact, are the different types of inter-relationships which exist in a society. The duties are conceived in reciprocal terms. Every person should suppose and look after parents in old age and make himself worthy of his heritage; the parents too have some duties towards the son: they should love him, restrain him from vice and inspire him to be virtuous, train him to a profession, arrange a suitable marriage for him and hand over the inheritance to him at the proper time. The pupils should show respect to the teachers by rising from their seat in salutation, by waiting upon them, by showing a desire to learn, by doing personal service and by being attentive to the lessons; the teachers in their turn should love their pupils, train them in morality, inspire them to learn and protect them from any danger. A husband should treat his wife with respect, courtesy and faithfulness should give to her the due rights and provide her with ornaments; similarly, a wife should attend on her husband well, perform her duties well, show hospitality to her husband's relatives and friends, be faithful and diligent. One should be generous, courteous and benevolent towards friends and be good to them; the friends and companions should also show their love to him, protect him and his property when they are unguarded, be a refuge in the times of danger and be sympathetic to his family. A master should treat his servants and employees properly by assigning them work according to their ability, by providing them food and wages, by attending on them when they are sick, by sharing with them unusual delicacies and by granting them leave in time; the servants and employees should show their gratitude to their master by rising at his approach, by being out of bed before him and going to bed after him, by doing the assigned work well and by spreading his fame. Lastly, a householder should treat the recluses and the Brāhmaṇas as the zenith by showing affection for them in action, speech and thoughts, by giving them warm welcome and providing them with their needs; the recluses and the Brāhmaṇas in return should have feelings of sympathy for the householder, should restrain him from vice and exhort him to virtue, teach him what he has not heard and correct him in what he has heard.[1]

The above is thus an exhaustive analysis of social relationships. It also includes the recluses as an integral part of the social structure and affirms even the rights and privileges of servants and employees.

In the 'Uggaha-Sutta', the Buddha exhorts the girls of the householder Uggaha as to their duties after marriage. The five qualities desirable in married girls are noted as following: they should rise early and be the last to retire, should be willing workers, order things sweetly and be gentle-voiced; they should be respectful to all whom the husband holds in esteem; they should be deft and nimble at the husband's homecrafts; they should know all about the husband's household, about the slaves, messengers and workmen, should know the work of each of them and give them food, etc.; they should keep safe watch and ward over the money, corn, silver or gold which the husband brings home.[2]

We may also consider here the Buddha's discourse to the daughter-in-law of Anāthapiṇḍika, Sujātā, wherein he speaks of seven types of wives. These, as he designates them, are: the wife who is like a slayer, like a robber, like a mistress, like a mother, like a sister, like a companion, or like a headmaid. The one who is pitiless, of corrupt thinking, unamiable, aroused by others, unfaithful, of murderous inclination and neglectful is a slayer-wife. The one who robs her husband of his wealth is a robber wife; the one who is sluggish and lazy doing nothing herself but full of praise for her husband's zeal and industriousness is a mistress-wife; the one who takes care of her husband as a mother does toward his only son is a mother-wife, the one who regards her husband as her elder sister is a sister-wife; the one who behaves like a friend and helpmate is a companion wife;

[1]*Dial.*, III, pp. 180-83.
[2]*Gradual Sayings*, III, pp. 29-30.

and the one who is not afraid of lash or stick, is of calm disposition, is pure in heart and obedient to her husband is a headmaid wife. The Buddha concludes that the first three types are immoral and lacking in the desirable qualities and subject to great miseries in hell after death; the last four types have their place in heaven after death.[1]

In the 'Mahāmaṅgala-sutta' the Buddha is requested to preach about the highest blessing (*mahāmaṅgala*) which may be devised for happiness. He enumerates: "Not cultivating (the society of) fools, but cultivating (the society of) wise men, worshipping those that are to be worshipped, this is the highest blessing; to live in a suitable country, to have done good deeds in a (former) existence, and a thorough study of one's self, this is ..; great learning and skill, well-learnt discipline, and well spoken words, this is...: waiting on mother and father, protecting child and wife, and a quiet calling, this is ..; giving alms, living religiously, protecting relatives, blameless deeds, this is ..; ceasing and abstaining from sin, refraining from intoxicating drink, perservance in the *Dhamma*, this is...; reverence and humility, contentment and gratitute, the hearing of *Dhamma* at due seasons, this is...; penance and chastity, discernment of the noble truth, and the realisation of *Nibbāna*, this is...; he whose mind is not shaken (when he is) touched by the things of the world (*lokadhamma*) (but remains) free from sorrow, from defilement, and secure, this is...; those who, having done such (things), are undefeated in every respect, work in safety everywhere, this is the highest blessing."[2]

The Buddhists Conception of an Integrated Social Order

In their bid to understand the social significance of the teachings of Buddha, the scholars find themselves generally taking either the view that Buddha was only a spiritual teacher with emancipation from spiritual suffering as his sole aim, or that he was a social reformer and a conscious crusader against the inequities of the Brāhmaṇical caste-system. V.P. Verma, who has attempted to study the origins of Buddhism with a sociological orientation,[3] rightly

[1] *Gradual Sayings*, IV, pp. 56-58.

[2] *Sutta-Nipāta*, trans. Fausboll, pp. 43-44.

[3] Vishwanath Prasad Varma, *Early Buddhism and its Origins*, pp. 366ff.

says that Buddha was a spiritual and religious teacher but that 'social, economic and political consequences do follow from his teachings, sometimes directly and sometimes indirectly.[1] However, pointing to intensifying caste-consolidation as a great factor which Buddha had to face, he makes the following curious observation : '. . . He (i.e Buddha) cannot be regarded as the defiant and declared spokesman of the Kṣatriyas but it is clear from the Buddhist dialogues of the Tripiṭakas that he had anti-Brahmanical prejudices and was interested in addressing his sermons to Kṣhatriya youths of good family status (*Kulaputra*)...But both Buddha and Māhavira belonged to the Kshatriya clans of eastern India. Hence they could not act as the conscious exponents of the interests of the proletariat and the agricultural labourers who formed the numerous assemblage of the Shudras.'[2]

We have argued earlier that the Śramaṇa movement was a classless and casteless movement, and the teachers of the sixth century B.C. were definitely not preyed by the modern notion of class-conflict of the exploiters and the exploited. The teachings of Buddha, however, had serious social implications. His teaching of the doctrine of *Karman* as a cosmic principle and the sole arbiter of human destiny was logically bound to take away all weightage from birth and lay emphasis on right conduct. Accordingly, he declared that what really mattered was not one's birth in a particular *gotra* or family but one's moral accomplishment.[3] He repudiated the Brāhmaṇa and Kaṣtriya claims of superiority due to their lineage[4] and advocated

[1]V. P. Varma, op. cit., p. 367.

[2]ibid., pp. 372-73.

[3]See 'Sundarika Bhāradvāja-sutta' of the *SN*; also 'Vasala Sutta' in the *Sutta-Nipata*: 'Not by birth does one become a Brahmin; by deeds one becomes an outcaste; by deeds one becomes a Brahmin.' Also the verses of 'Brāhmaṇavagga' in the *Dhammapada* wherein a Brahmin is defined on the basis of the possession of various moral attributes.

Regarding the use of the term '*brahmana*' in the *Nikayas*, H. Saddhatissa *Buddhist Ethics*, p. 118, has made this observation: "Of the numerous *vaggas* in the *Nikāyas* bearing the titles *Brāhmaṇavagga* and *Gahapativagga*, the term 'brāhmaṇa' does not generally refer to members of the Brahman caste; 'Brahmam' is taken in the titles, to signify the ideal type". See also A.K. Coomaraswamy and I.B. Horner, *La Pansee de Gotama le Bouddha*, p. 48.

[4]'Ambaṭṭha Sutta' of the *DN*.

absolute equality of all the four classes of the society;[1] both in this world and the world hereafter the evil deeds are to be punished and the virtuous deeds are to be rewarded.

In conformity with the above notion he conceived the general framework of his spiritual order, namely, *Saṅgha*. Admission to it was open to men of all sections of the society. As after merging into the Great Ocean all rivers lose their former identity, so the monks lose all their former distinctions after joining the *Saṅghā*, Buddha said.[2] His Order, accordingly, included the Brahmin Kassapa, the Kṣatriya Ānanda, the barber Upāli, the fisherman Svāti, the low-caste Sunīta, and many others from different strata of society. The underlying social implication is 'not to give any place to caste in associations, groups and organizations.'[3]

× × ×

Political Ethics and the Ideal of State

The state is the third point of the Buddhist social structure. From the general Buddhists viewpoint, it can be a state of any form or complexion,[4] monarchical, democratic, socialistic, or communistic,though, placed in a particular historical situation, it has considered the problem in terms of a monarchical state. Buddhism believes in a social-contract theory of the origin of state and kingship.[5] The prevailing disorder in the society led people to ask the most worthy among them to serve as the king who would have to perform certain obligations to

[1]'Madhuriya Sutta' of the *MN*.

[2]*CV.*, p. 356.

[3]V.P. Varma, op. cit., p. 377.

[4]Though it is generally believed by scholars that the Buddha had sympathy for republican form of state. The fact that he himself hailed from a republic and that he employed the same style of functioning in his Order which prevailed in the contemporary republican states are considered sufficient evidence to support this contention. His discourse to the Vajjians on the various conditions of welfare ('Mahāparinibbāna-sutta', *Dial.*, II, p. 73) and his remark 'so long as the Vajjians will be well instructed in those conditions, so long may one expect them not to decline, but to prosper' are also taken as supporting points for this contention. It may, however, be noted that the Buddha's age was marked by ascendence of the monarchies. His various statements relating to state and state-activities have a monarchical form of government in view, though the theoretical position about the origin of kingship is that of an elected representative of the people (*Mahājana-sammata*).

[5]See the 'Aggañña-sutta' and the 'Cakkavatti-Sīhanāda-sutta' of the *DN*.

the people in return of which he was entitled to a proportion of the agricultural produce (rice). '*Mahāsammata*', meaning 'chosen by the people', was the first standard appellation of a king. This ideal gets soon replaced by the ideal of 'cakravartin' or a universal monarch which becomes very strong and popularly accepted one. Buddhaghosa, a later day Buddhist, says that this king 'Mahāsammata' is no one else but the Bodhisattva himself.[1] The king is in fact conceived as the temporal counterpart of a Buddha, and it is not without significance that in an early passage of the Pāli Canon a parallelism has been drawn between a Buddha and a *Cakravartin* king, both of whom, according to the passage, hold the same esteemed place in the eyes of the people and, after their demise, deserve erection of relics (*stūpas*) on their bodies.[2] It appears that from the Buddhist point of view the king is not only the leader of the society but also a patron of the *Saṅgha*; he should always rule under the guidance of *Dharma*, which is eternal and universal. A *bhiksu* once asked the Buddha, "But, who, Lord, is the king of the king ?" Buddha is reported to have replied, "It is Dhamma, O Bikkhu."[3] Through the personal moral conduct of the king expressed in political affairs, 'universal righteousness' would come to prevail on earth and deliverance would become an easy thing for all.

There are many Suttas in the *Dīgha Nikāya*, *Saṁyutta Nikāya* and the *Aṅguttara Nikāya* and a number of Jātaka stories which contain discussions on kingly conduct. Among the *Nikāyan* passages the 'Mahāsudassana-sutta' holds the most important place. In all of them, the personal righteous character of the ruler is especially emphasized, which not only inspires righteousness in all his officials and subjects, but even moves the gods and natural forces to favour his domain. Significantly, a Buddhist definition of king, in the

[1] Bhikshu Dharmarakshita, trans. *Viśuddimarga*, II, p. 41: Nanamoli trans. *The Path of Purification*, p. 460.

[2] 'Mahaparinibbāna-sutta' of the *DN*.

[3] *Gradual Sayings*, III, pp. 144ff.

The Buddhist ideas on kingship are closely related with the concept of *dhamma*. In the Buddhist conception of state, the state is not only a punitive instrument but is also responsible for the moral upliftment of its members. All state enterprises should be inspired by moral earnestness. The moral training of king was therefore necessary. See Balkrishna G. Gokhale, 'Early Buddhist Kingship', *The Journal of Asian Studies*, XXVI, no. 1, November 1966, pp. 20-21.

Vinaya, includes, along with the ruler, his officials also.[1] A passage of the *Aṅguttara-Nikāya* reads:

"When kings are righteous, the ministers of kings are righteous. When ministers are righteous, brahmanas and householders are also righteous. Then townsfolk and villagers are righteous. This being so, moon and sun go right in their course. This being so, constellations and stars do likewise: days and nights, months and fortnights, seasons and years go on their courses regularly; winds blow regularly in due season. Thus the *devas* are not annoyed and the *sky-deva* bestows sufficient rain. Rain falling seasonably, the crops ripen in due season, men who live on those crops are long lived, well-favoured, strong and free from sickness."[2]

This notion that the general righteousness of the people depends on the king's personal righteousness lays a moral pressure on the ruling agent to be good and righteous; it imposes all responsibility of any untoward happening in the country on him.

Economic Welfare of the People as a Safeguard against Crimes

The 'Kūṭadanta-sutta' of the *Dīgha Nikāya* suggests that the economic prosperity of the people should be a special concern of the state and the king. A certain king, desirous to offer a sacrifice for the good fortune he had enjoyed thus far and for further continuance of prosperity in his domain, is advised by his counseller that instead of such a sacrifice it would be more advisable for him to take preventive measures to check the occurrence of crime. He says that it could be achieved by the removal of the causes of economic discontent among the people, for which he lays down some positive guidelines: he (the king=the state) should give to farmers subsidy of food and seed; sources of capital for investment should be made available to merchants and traders; those in government jobs should get proper wages and food. If this is done there would be no danger for the state; on the contrary, "the king's revenue will go up; the country will be quiet and at peace, and the populace, pleased one with another and happy, dandling their children in their arms, will dwell with open doors". The account says that the king, convinced about the soundness of this advice, acted accordingly and things took place

[1] *Pār.*, p. 57.
[2] *Gradual Sayings*, II, p. 85.

as the councillor had predicted.[1] On the other hand, 'Cakkavatti-Sīhanāda-Sutta' tells how a king caused chaos and confusion and various other evils in his kingdom by not giving due attention to the economic well-being of the poor.[2]

Aśokan Ideal

According to the Buddhist conception, the *Saṅgha*, the worldly society, and the state are inter-dependent and the condition of each affects the condition of the other two. Aśoka, the ideal Buddhist ruler, aspired to found such a society in which all these three units enjoyed sound condition. B.G. Gokhale has rightly pointed to the difference between the Kauṭilyan conception of state and the Buddha's conception of state; between the two Aśoka professed the latter wherein the state was conceived not as an end in itself but as a means to attain the higher ideal of *Dhamma*. "For Ashoka the state was not an end in itself but rather a means to an end higher than the state itself, namely, *dharma*, or morality. . . If for Kautilya the state was a punitive instrument, for Ashoka it was an educative institution. For the dichotomy between force and morality, between Kautilya and Buddha, had existed for a long time. Ashoka felt that his most glorious mission was to resolve this dichotomy and endow the mechanism of the Kautilyan state with a moral soul".[3] This *Dhamma* of Aśoka,which he so fondly mentions in his edicts and desires his subjects to follow, has been an enigma to scholars.[4] The

[1] *Dial*, I, p. 175f.

[2] ibid., III, p. 59ff.

[3] B.G. Gokhale, *Ashoka Maurya*, p. 107.

[4] This enigma is exemplified by the following views expressed by competent scholars from time to time: According to Fleet (*JRAS*, 1908), the *Dhamma* of Aśoka was *rāja-dharma* 'ordinary dharma of kings which is laid down in the *Mānava-dharmaśāstra* I, 114, as one of the topics of that work'; R.K. Mookerji (*Aśoka*, pp. 67-68) has sought to make a distinction between his personal religion and the religion he wished to preach to his people—'It was certainly not Buddhism ... The Dharma of the edicts is not any particular Dharma or religious system but the moral law independent of any caste or creed, the sara or essence of all religions'.; J.M. Macphail (*Aśoka*, pp. 56-57) too believes that 'Dhamma does not stand for Buddhism, but for the simple piety which Aśoka wished all his subjects of whatever faith to practise'. Smith (*Aśoka*, pp. 36-37) writes: ... No foundation either of theology or of metaphysics is laid, and the ethical precepts inculcated are set forth for purely practical purposes as being self-evidently true'. *cont.*

scholars have generally failed to reconcile the non-sectarian character of Aśoka's *Dhamma* as he enumerates it in his edicts with the fact that his personal faith was Buddhism. The modern notion of secularism, which fails to appreciate the generally prevalent feeling of mutual tolerance and understanding among the followers of various religious sects in ancient India, appears to lay down a trap in which these scholars have fallen. We are inclined to agree with Trevor Ling when he says: "The word *Dhamma* was used widely, not only by Buddhists, and could bear a quite general meaning, such as 'piety'. But when the whole range of Ashokan inscriptions is taken into account, there seems little room left for doubt that when Ashoka used the word he meant Buddha-Dhamma".[1] The First Minor Rock Edict, which Ling too quotes in support of his view, should settle the issue. In it, after greeting the *Saṅgha* and expressing his respect in the Buddha, the *Dhamma* and the *Saṅgha*, Aśoka lists some Buddhist texts and concludes, " . . . these sermons on the *Dhamma*, Sirs, I desire that many *bhikkhus* and *bhikkhunis* should hear frequently and meditate upon, and likewise laymen and laywomen. I am having this engraved, Sirs, so that you may know what I desire."[3] The social ethics which Aśoka propagates through his proclamations has been aptly put in this way: 'Buddhist Ethical Values+The wheel of Social Action=Asokan Action.'[3]

F.W. Thomas (*Cambridge History of India*, I, pp. 454-55) says that 'The degree of Asoka's appreciation of Buddhism is not very easily definable; ...' He points to the absence of mention of Four Great Truths, the Eightfold Path, the Chain of Causation, Nirvāṇa etc., in his edicts and concludes: 'Aśoka, therefore. is no theologian or philosopher'.

Romila Thapar (*Aśoka and the Decline of the Mauryas*, p. 149) has this to say—'*Dhamma* was Aśoka's own invention. It may have borrowed from Buddhist and Hindu thought, but it was in essence an attempt on the part of the king to suggest a way of life which was both practical and convenient, as well as being highly moral . . . If his policy of *Dhamma* had been merely a recording of Buddhist principles, Aśoka would have stated so quite openly, since he never sought to hide his support for Buddhism'. Senart (*Les Inscriptions de Piyadasi*, p. 322), Mrs. Rhys Davids (*Buddhism*, pp. 226ff) and D.R. Bhandarkar (*Aśoka*, pp. 72ff) are of opinion that the *Dhamma* of Aśoka was original Buddhism as preached by the Buddha.

[1]Trevor Ling, op. cit., p. 194.

[2]Rendering by Romila Thapar, *Aśoka and the Decline of the Mauryas*, p. 261.

[3]Michael Irwin Roehm, 'The Wheel of Asokan Action', *The Mahabodhi*, Vaishakha Number, 1967, p. 190.

A perusal of Aśokan inscriptions clearly points to their emphasis on the purity of public life and harmony in domestic affair by laying down guidelines in respect of diverse social relationships. The 11th Major Rock Edict, which extols *Dhamma*, enumerates in no ambiguous words the social ethics which Aśoka had in mind. Let it be quoted in full:

"Thus speaks the Beloved of the Gods, the king Piyadasi: There is no gift comparable to the gift of *Dhamma*, the praise of *Dhamma*, the sharing of *Dhamma*, fellowship in *Dhamma*. And this is—good behaviour towards slaves and servants, obedience to mother and father, generosity towards friends, acquaintances, and relatives and towards *sramanas* and brahmanas, and abstention from killing living beings. Father, son, brother, master, friend, acquaintance, relative and neighbour should say, 'this is good', 'this we should do'. By doing so, there is gain in this world, and in the next there is infinite merit, through the gift of *Dhamma*."[1]

At many places in his edicts, Aśoka lays emphasis on service and respect to father and mother,[2] elders[3] and teachers,[4] proper treatment towards Brāhmaṇas and Śramaṇas,[5] relatives,[6] friends, companions, acquaintances, Śervants and slaves,[7] and liberality to Brāhmaṇas and Śramaṇas, friends, companions, relatives and the aged.[8] He underlines the importance of the habit of spending little (*apavyayatā*) and accumulating little (*apabhāṇḍatā*).[9] As a convinced Buddhist, he preaches abstention from slaughter of living beings and non-violence towards life.[10]

As head of the state, Aśoka knew that for the accomplishment of his goal to bring about purity in public life and introduce moral and healthy social habits among the people the state has to introduce certain legislations to that effect but he was equally convinced that

[1]See Thapar, *Aśoka and the Decline of the Mauryas*, pp. 254-55.
[2]Rock Edict 3, 4, 11, 12, Pillar Edict 8.
[3]Rock Edict 4, Pillar Edict 7.
[4]Rock Edict 9, 13, Pillar Edict 7; Minor Rock Edict 2, Brahmagiri version.
[5]Rock Edict 4, Pillar Edict 7.
[6]Rock Edict 4, 12, Minor Rock Edict 2.
[7]Rock Edict 13, Pillar Edict 7.
[8]Rock Edict 3, 8, 9, 11.
[9]Rock Edict 3.
[10]Rock Edict 3, 4, Pillar Edict 7.

persuasion would be a more effective measure. So he states in the 7th Pillar Edict: 'The advancement of *Dhamma* amongst men has been achieved through two means, legislation and persuasion. But of these two, legislation has been less effective and persuasion more so. I have proclaimed through legislation for instance that certain species of animals are not to be killed, and other such ideas. But men have increased their adherence to *Dhamma* by being persuaded not to injure living beings and not to take life."[1]

He did not believe in mere sermonizing. He was aware that the people look to the person on top and emulate his character in conduct as a standard.[2] He took on himself those ethical obligations which he preached to his subjects. He restricted to only three the number of animals killed for the royal kitchen whereas hundreds and thousands were killed earlier and was determined to stop even that much of killing in future. He renounced the pleasure-tours customary for the kings of earlier times and took upon himself the task of educating his people through what he calls *Dhamma*-tours during which "meetings are held with ascetics and Brahmanas, gifts are bestowed, meetings are arranged with aged folk, gold is distributed, meetings with the people of the countryside are held, instruction in *Dhamma* is given, and questions on *Dhamma* are answered."[3]

He felt concerned about the welfare of his subjects, not only here in this life but also in the other world, as a father does with regard to his children—'all men are my children', he proclaimed.[4] As measures of public welfare, he had banyan trees planted on the roads to provide shade to beasts and men, got wells dug and rest homes built at every eight *kos*, had many watering places made for the use of beasts and men.[5] He realised that the head of the state cannot afford to be lazy and should be in constant touch with public business; he has no time of his own; as such, he ordered that his informants should always keep him in touch with public business whether he is eating or is in the women's apartments, in his inner apartment, at

[1]Thapar, *Aśoka and the Decline of the Mauryas*, p. 266.

[2]Cf. *Gītā*, III. 21: *Yadyadācarati śreṣṭhaḥ tattadevetaro janaḥ/Sa yatpramāṇaṁ kurute lokastadanuvartate.*

[3]Rock Edict 8: Thapar, op. cit., p. 253.

[4]Second separate Edict: Thapar, p. 258.

[5]Pillar Edict 4.

the cattle-shed, in his carriage or in his gardens.[1]

Aśoka appears to have been inspired by the Buddhist ideal of *cakravartin*. The 'Ambaṭṭhasutta' of the *Dīgha-Nikāya* describes the attributes of a *cakravartin*. A *cakravartin* represents the same universal principle on the secular plane as a Buddha does on the spiritual plane; both are endowed with 'mahāpuruṣalakṣanas' or the various characteristic signs of a great man. Early Pāli canon contains references to legendary *cakravartins* of the past. One such king, Sudassana, is frequently referred to in the 'Mahāsudassana-sutta';[2] Daḷhanemi (Skt. Dṛḍhanemi, 'he the felly of whose wheel is firm') is another who is mentioned in the 'Cakkavattisīhanāda-sutta'.[3] Reason justice, compassion and understanding are the great virtues which adorn the personality of a *cakravartin*. "The early Buddhist attitude to warfare, agriculture and meat-eating was more mixed than was its attitude towards blood sacrifices. It made no whole-hearted condemnation of these three practices although they all entail the taking of life. But it did what it could do to lessen their incidence and popularity".[4] A *cakravartin* conquered his enemies not through force and war but through *Dhamma*, his moral perfection and moral glory. After his acceptance of the Buddha's creed, moved immensely by the killing and suffering of the people in the Kalinga war, Aśoka turned to conquest by *Dhamma* which he calls the 'true conquest'. Pertaining to various contemporary political powers and people Aśoka makes the following claim:

'The Beloved of the Gods considers victory by *Dhamma* to be the foremost victory. And moreover the Beloved of the Gods has gained this victory on all his frontiers to a distance of six hundred *Yojanas* (i e. about 1500 miles), where reigns the Greek king named Antiochus, and beyond the realm of that Antiochus in the lands of the four kings named Ptolemy, Antigonus, Magas, and Alexander; and in the south over the Colas and Pandyas as far as Ceylon. Likewise here in the imperial territories among the Greeks and the Kambojas, Nābhakas and Nābhapanktis, Bhojas and Pitinikas, Āndhras and Parindas,

[1] Rock Edict 6.

[2] Sutta no. 17 of the *DN*.

[3] Sutta no. 26 of the *DN*.

[4] I.B. Horner, 'Early Buddhism and Taking of Life' in *B.C. Law Volume*, I, p. 443.

everywhere the people follow the Beloved of the God's instructions in *Dhamma*. . .

What is obtained by this is victory everywhere, and everywhere victory is pleasant. The pleasure has been obtained through victory by *Dhamma*. . .[1]

Aśoka clearly aspires here to concretize in him the Buddhist ideal of a *cakravartin* who does not evoke in the neighbouring kingdoms a feeling of awe and fear but that of understanding. Aśoka had a sound and moral international vision which the modern world today aspires to achieve.

[1]Rock Edict no. 13: Thapar, *Aśoka and the Decline of the Mauryas*, p. 256.

CHAPTER 5

Compassion and Perfection

A New Spiritual Insight: Emergence of Mahāyāna

It may be generally said that the form of Buddhism which prevailed till the time of Aśoka is manifested in the Pāli *Tipiṭaka* along with the Pāli *Aṭṭhakathās* and some other related texts. However, it is manifest that differing trends existed with regard to interpretation and understanding of the Master's teachings from the very beginning. The incidence of Purāṇa, recorded in the *Cullavagga* of the Pāli canon, clearly shows that the verdict of the monks constituting the First council was not acceptable as totally representing the *Buddha-vacana* to all the immediate disciples of the Master.[1] This differing trend appeared in quite marked form a century later when 'ten points' regarding monastic conduct preached by the Vesālian monks and 'five points' of doctrinal import preached by Mahādeva, the head-monk of the Kukkuṭārāma *vihāra* of Pāṭaḷiputra according to the *Abhidharma-Mahāvibhāṣāśāstra*,[2] combined to divide the order in two schools, viz., the Sthaviravāda and the Mahāsāṅghika. The process of division of the Order did not stop here and the *Dīpavaṁsa* records that between the Second Council and the Third Council as many as eighteen sects of Buddhism had emerged from these two parent schools. The Third Council, convened in the time of Aśoka, did make an effort to provide a monolithic shape to the Order by specifying '*vibhajjavāda*' to be the true doctrine of the Master as represented by the Sthaviravāda school,

[1]At the time of the Council, Purāṇa, along with five hundred other monks, was away in Dakkhiṇāgiri. When he came back after the conclusion of the Council and was told that the *Dhamma* and the *Vinaya* had been recited by the monks in the Council, he remarked that he would prefer to understand the same as he had himself heard from the Master: "*Susaṅgītāvuso, therehi bhikkhūhi dhammo ca vinayo ca. Api ca yatheva mayā bhagavato sammukhā sutaṁ, sammukhā paṭigahītaṁ, tathevāhaṁ dhāressāmī*" *ti*.

[2]Watters, *On Yuan Chwang's Travels in India*, I, pp. 267-68.

but the developmental process of Buddhism could not be checked and it continued imbibing new ideas and rendering new interpretations or laying new emphasis on certain points.

The Mahāsāṅghika school represented the liberal trend in Buddhism. Manifesting a democratic spirit, it also undermined the hierarchical superiority of the '*Arhats*' which was claimed for them in the orthodox Sthaviravāda school. Further, it believed in the transcendental character of Buddha's personality—a notion which was imbued with significant doctrinal and ethical repercussions. In course of time many other schools emerged out of the Mahāsāṅghika, each of them revolving around certain points which bear Mahāyānic tenor in an embryonic form. In the various traditions on the origins of sects[1] it is said that Lokottaravāda, Ekavyāvahārika, Kaukkuṭika or Gokulika, Bahuśrutīya, Caityaka, Āndhraka, Pūrva-Śaila, Apara-Śaila, Prajñaptivāda, Rājagirika and Vaitulyaka schools arose from the Mahāsāṅghika. According to A. Bareau, the Lokottaravādins were not different from the Ekavyāvahārikas[2] while N. Dutt takes the Lokottaravādins to be identical with the Caityakas.[3] It is the Mahāsāṅghika, along with its offshoot-schools, which paved the way for the emergence of the later day full-fledged Mahāyāna.

At the time of the second Buddhist Council, the Mahāsāṅghika school had its stronghold in Vaiśāḷī and Pāṭaliputra. From here it journeyed to the Āndhrapatha region where its existence, in its various sub-schools, is attested in various inscriptions discovered from Amarāvatī and Nāgārjunīkoṇḍa.[4] After a thorough and critical scrutiny of the different sources and traditions, Professor Pande concludes that it was in the Pūrvaśaila and Vaitulyaka sects of the Mahāsāṅghika that Mahāyāna took its birth in the first century BC.[5] From Āndhrapatha it reached Magadha and, then, following the familiar trade-route which connected the Uttarāpatha region with Magadha, to north. Kuṣāṇa

[1]For a critical account of these traditions, see A. Bareau, *Les Sectes Bouddhiques du Petit Véhicule;* N. Dutt, *EMB.*, G.C. Pande, *BDVI.*, J. Masuda, *Origin and Doctrines of Early Indian Buddhist Schools of Vasumitra's Treatise.*

[2]A. Bareau, op. cit., pp. 75-76.

[3]N. Dutt, *EMB.*, p. 51.

[4]Caitikīya, Caityaka, Caitya, Śailīya, Mahāvanśailīya, Apara-Mahāvanaśailīya, Pūrvaśaila and Aparaśaila are the names of the various sects which are mentioned in these inscriptions.

[5]*BDVI.*, pp. 320-21. *Prajñāpāramitā Sūtra* is considered the earliest of the

emperor Kaniṣka's patronage to Buddhism and the nature of Kuṣāṇa empire which, apart from the Indian regions, included Afghanistan and parts of Central Asia, were, naturally, greatly helpful in the spread of Buddhism in the trans-Indian regions of the north; by the end of the first century AD it had crossed the boundary of India and from the second century onwards it spread to Central Asia and China through the Parthian and the Khotanese monks.

It has been rightly stated by Prof. Pande that the main inspiration behind Mahāyāna was the life of the Master which provided a guideline for others to follow.[1] Though it is undeniable that the seeds of various Mahāyānic principles were present in Hīnayāna which were gradually developed through an autonomous process of further reflections on them, a number of external factors also operated in giving Mahāyāna a concrete form as a distinctive and separate movement within the framework of Buddhism. The spread of Buddhism to distant regions and the desire of the missionary monks to popularise it among alien peoples were bound to take away from Buddhism its strict and rigid ascetic tenor and provide it a more attractive form. From the second century BC starts the inflow of the successive waves of foreigners in India whose presence exercised great pressures on Indian society to change itself in many ways. It would not be unnatural to expect that Buddhism too was ready to undergo some modifications to accomodate such alien elements. The patronage that Buddhism continued receiving from the foreigners in the North-west since the time of Aśoka and particularly the attraction of Kujul Kadphises and Kaniṣka toward Buddhism may be properly understood in this light. It is also imperative to take into consideration the emergence of Bhāgavatism as a dominant movement within Brahmanical religion with its ideas of *Bhakti* and *Avatāra* (incarnation of God) which were more appealing to the psychology of the common

Mahāyāna Sūtras. The *Aṣṭasāhasrikā-Prajñāpāramitā* clearly attests the Southern origin of *Prajñāpāramitā*, a point agreed upon by its different recessions, preserved in Chinese, except one, See E. Conze, *The Prajñāpāramitā Literature*, pp. 10-11. E. Lamotte ('Sur la formation du Mahāyāna' *Asiatica*, 1954) has, however, challenged this theory and argued for North-West and the region of Khotan as the place of its birth. Conze (loc. cit., p. 12), comments: "I believe that he (i.e. Lamotte) has shown no more than the Prajñāpāramitā had a great success in the North-West at the Kushana period . . . and its Southern origin has not, I think, been definitely disproved.

[1]*BDVI.*, p. 316.

people than the notion of individual salvation through individual efforts. The new movement of the Bhāgavatas, and also that of the Śaivas, in Brahmanical religion was quite vigorous and forceful; it, in fact, posed a great challenge to Buddhism and the latter could not afford to ignore it. Har Dayal has rightly observed: "The Buddhist leaders, who inaugurated the Mahāyāna movement, saved Buddhism from shipwreck by popularising it and inventing compassionate *bodhisattvas* as Buddhist counterparts of the Hindu deities and their Incarnation."[1] There are many common verses in the *Gītā* and the *Saddharma puṇḍarīka* and one can easily see abundant traces of the influence of the former in the Mahāyānaśraddhotpāda-śāstra of Aśvaghoṣa.[2] The notion of *Bhakti*, by its inherent logic, demanded a statue of Buddha as an object of devotion and worship; as a result of it the images of Buddha came to be made which, in turn, gave birth to various rules and rituals of worship in texts and in practice. In short, it can be said that the attempt to give Buddhism a popular form suited to the intelligence of common people, which started from the time of Aśoka, ultimately culminated in the emergence of Mahāyāna Buddhism.[3]

Though, historically speaking, of later origin, the general Mahāyānic outlook can be clearly seen as having its rooting in various Nikāyan passages.[4] The seed of Mahāyāna is there. Then comes the transitional phase in which the Buddhist writers have their one foot in Hīnayānism and the other in Mahāyānism.[5] The literature called 'Mahāyāna Sūtras'[6] present the first systematic formulations of Mahā-

[1]Har Dayal, *Bodhisattva Doctrine*, p. 38.

[2]Hemchandra Raychaudhari, *Materials for the Study of the Early History of the Vaishnava Sect*, pp. 124-25.

[3]Pandey, *BDVI.*, pp. 308-9.

[4]See N. Dutt, *Mahayana Buddhism*, ch. II, pp. 71 ff.

[5]B. Puri, 'Ideology and Religion in the Kushan Epoch' in *Proceedings of the International Conference of the History, Archaeology and Culture of Central Asia in the Kushan Period*, II, p. 186.

[6]For a list of the extant and published Mahāyāna Sūtras see G.C. Pande, *BDVI*, pp. 328-29, fn. 117. The *Śikṣāsamuccaya* and the *Mahāvyutpatti* contain long lists of Mahāyāna Sūtra works. See ibid., pp. 329-32, fn. 119-20. Of these, nine, called 'Vaipulya Sūtra' are assigned special reverence. They are: *Aṣṭasāhasrikā-Prajñāpārmitā*, *Saddharma-Puṇḍarīka*, *Lalita-vistara*, *Laṅkāvatāra*, *Suvarṇa-Prabhāsa*, *Gaṇḍavyūha*, *Tathāgata-guhyaka*, *Samādhirāja* and *Daśabhumīśvara*.

yāna doctrines and also an exposition of the distinction between Hīnayāna and Mahāyāna. The *Aṣṭasāhasrikā Prajñāpāramitā* is probably the earliest work of the Mahāyāna Sūtra literature and is placed in the first century BC.[1] In due course, Mahāyāna received its classical shape in the writings of such Buddhist teachers as Nāgārjuna, Asaṅga and Vasubandhu who are generally known in association with the two most important Mahāyāna schools, viz., the Śūnyavāda and the Vijñānavāda.

Significance of Mahāyāna

Apparently, the Mahāyāna is of a late historical origin. However, it claims to be the original teaching of the Master and attempts to provide this claim an historical authenticity by ascertaining two *Dharma-cakra-pravartanas* by the Buddha, the one marked by his address to the 'Five Monks' at Ṛṣipattana (Sāranāth) in Vārāṇasī and the other by his address to the assembly of the *Bodhisattavas* on the Gṛdhrakūṭa mountain of Rājagṛha.[2] According to it, the former was the teaching of the Hīnayāna while the latter is represented by the Mahāyāna. The necessity of two different sets of teaching by the Tathāgata is accounted for by pointing to skilfulness of means (*upāya-kauśalya*) as a necessary characteristic of a good teacher which Buddha was; the Hīnayāna was preached by him for the sake of comparatively less deserving and spiritually less advanced disciples while the teaching of the Mahāyāna was his real teaching.[3] Clearly, the Mahāyāna bases itself on the notion of *sādhanabheda* (divergence in means) in spiritual matters, i.e., the spiritual teacher, while teaching, has to take into account the potentiality and receptivity of his disciples.[4] With *sādhana-bheda* (divergence in means) is associated the notion of

[1]N. Dutt, *Aspects of Mahayana Buddhism and its Relations to Hinayana*, pp. 323 ff.

[2]*Sad. Puṇḍ BST.*, 6, p. 50: *Pūrvaṁ bhagavatā Vārāṇasyāmṛṣipattane mṛgadāve dharmacakraṁ pravartitam. Idaṁ punarbhagavatā adya anuttaraṁ dvitīyaṁ dharmacakraṁ pravartitam.*

[3]ibid., pp. 53 ff.

[4]See ibid., pp. 28-29: *Ahamapi Śāriputra . . . sattvānāṁ nānādhātvāśayānamāśayaṁ viditvā dharmaṁ deśayāmi. Ahamapi Śāriputra krameva yānamārabhya sattvānāṁ dharmaṁ deśayāmi yadidaṁ buddhayānaṁ . . . apitu khalu punaḥ Śāriputraḥ yadā . . . samyaksaṁbuddhāḥ kalpakaṣāya votpadyante. Evaṁrūpeṣu kalpasamkṣobhakaṣāyeṣu bahusattveṣu lubdheṣvalpakuśalamūleṣu tadā . . . samyakasaṁbuddhā upāyakauśalyena tadaivaikam buddhayānaṁ triyānanirdeśana nirdiśanti.*

yuga-bheda, i.e., spiritual means need to undergo change in accordance with the changed times. Thus, the Mahāyāna would signify the necessity of some modifications in the understanding of the teachings of the Tathāgata. Mahāyāna does not discard Hīnayāna. It says that the Hīnayāna, also called Śrāvakayāna, too is helpful to some as it enables them to be free from egoity, attachment, malice and delusion etc., and, thereby, attain the state of Arhathood. But this venture, which is individualistic, serves only as a means to the attainment of Buddhahood, and it is because of this that the Mahāyāna texts call it Hīnayāna,[1] or 'Petty Vehicle.' Mahāyāna, or 'Great Vehicle,' on the other hand, is so called because it has scope in it for an infinite number of beings.[2] However, it is only in view of the 'upāya-kauśalya' of the Master that the 'way' (or 'vehicle=*yāna*') is known as *Śrāvaka-yāna*, *Pratyekabuddhayāna* or *Bodhisattvayāna*;[3] in essence, there is only one *yāna* and that is Buddhayāna.[4] Mahāyāna asserts that the element of Buddhahood is present in every being and it is to be perfected by everyone. One who has undertaken this spiritual task on oneself is called a *Bodhisattva*. He reaches the goal through a number of spiritual stages. But, his spiritual venture is not individualistic; rather, his concern is the attainment of Buddhahood to every being and he assiduously works for it. Mahāyāna is thus guided by the notion of *sarvamukti* or 'liberation for every being' and is basically universalistic in temperament.

Hīnayāna is chiefly characterized by an ascetic tenor. The Hīnayānic texts, primarily, contain injunctions which centre around a person who has left his home to embrace the state of homelessness. Buddha

[1] *MSL, BST.*, 13, p. 4; *Sad. Puṇḍ.* 'Adhimukti-Parivarta'.

[2] As the *Aṣṭ. Pr. BST*, 4, p. 12 says: *yathā ākaśe aprameyāṇāmasaṁkheyānāṁ sattvānāmavakāśaḥ evameva bhagavani asmin yāne aprameyāṇāmasaṁkheyānāṁ sattvānāmavakāśaḥ*. For various Mahāyānist authors claiming the relative superiority of Mahāyāna over Hīnayāna see Lalmani Joshi, *Studies in the Buddhistic Culture of India*, pp. 4-5.

[3] *Śrāvaka*, *Pratyeka-buddha* and *Bodhisattva* denote three categories of spiritual seekers: the *Śrāvakas* are those seekers who receive injunctions from Buddha and reach the state of Arhathood; The *Pratyeke-buddhas* are neither disciples nor teachers; the *Bodhisattvas* are those who attain enlightenment through their own previous virtuous actions and wisdom and are distinct from the *Śrāvakas* and *Pratyeka-buddhas*.

[4] *Sad. Puṇḍ BST.*, 6, p. 31—*Ekaṁ hi yānaṁ dvitīyaṁ na vidyate . . . ekaṁ hi kāryaṁ dvitīyaṁ na vidyate, na hīnayānena nayanti buddhāḥ*. Also ibid., p. 90.

had preached to the householders as well but this aspect of his teaching was naturally not of much concern to the ascetic compilers of the *Buddha-vacana* which we find in the Hīnayāna canon. Mahāyāna, on the other hand, shows great consideration for the householders. 'Mahāyāna Buddhism is primarily a religion for layman.'[1] This increased concern for the household life was backed up by a new philosophical and metaphysical understanding offered by Mahāyāna of the world (*saṁsāra*) in its relationship to the *summum bonum* (*Nirvāṇa*). The ideal state of *Nirvaṇa* is not to be found in any heaven apart from the human world but very much within it. As the great Mahāyāna teacher asserts, "*Saṁsāra* is in no way distinguishable from *Nirvāṇa*, *Nirvāṇa* is in no way distinguishable from *Saṁsāra*."[2] Sorrow and pain are our subjective production and, so, the realization of the Absolute can be accomplished only when our subjectivity is transcended and not by mere formal renunciation of the world. As, according to Mahāyāna, every sentient being is possessed of the seed of enlightenment (called *Bodhicitta*) 'Nirvāṇa consists not in escape from the world, but in the unlocking of the hidden nature, the development of the sleeping Buddha, the unfolding of potentialities. It is the fruition of life rather than its denial . . . .'[3] In its expanded form, with a large area and diverse communities of people within its sphere of influence, Buddhism was bound to shake off its rigorous ascetic tendency and lay down a simpler spiritual course which would be attractive to the general psychology of the common people. The ideas of *Bhakti* and grace were taken up and perfected in Mahāyāna to such an extent that, apparently, it could hardly be distinguishable from the various theistic sects of the Hindu religion. The notion of innumerable Buddhas and Bodhisattvas as 'saviours' was naturally much more appealing than the notion of a Buddha as a mere 'good friend' (*kalyāṇa-mitra*) who would only show the way. In its bid to be popular in the new areas of its influence and among different peoples, Mahāyāna showed great accomodative spirit in providing room for different shades of beliefs and practices.

[1]B.L. Suzuki, *Mahayana Buddhism*, p. 75.
[2]*Mūlamadhyamakārikāḥ*, XXV. 19;
Na saṁsārasya nirvāṇāt kiṁcid asti viśeṣaṇam,
Na nirvāṇasya saṁsārāt kiṁcid asti viśeṣaṇam.
The Laṅkāvatārasūtra (trans. Daisetz Taitara Suzuki), p. 38.
[3]W.M. McGovern, *An Introduction to Mahāyāna Buddhism*, pp. 31-32.

On the intellectual and philosophical side, Mahāyāna takes the idea of selflessness of everything (*sabbe dhammā anattā*) to its ultimate limit. The earlier Hīnayānic belief in the multiplicity of separate *dharmas* as constituting the ultimate reality and the Abhidharmic interest in the review and analysis of these *dharmas* was nullified by Mahāyāna by its denial of the multiplicity of *dharmas* (because all is one) and assertion of non-production of *dharmas*.[1] It claimed that even the ultimates of analysis do not have any real existence and are mere words. The doctrine of *Pudgalaśūnyatā* was thus replaced by that of *Dharmaśūnyatā*. Mahāyāna shows too great an interest in the Absolute and uses such words as *Tathatā* and *Śūnyatā* to connote it; it, however, clarifies that these connotations for the Absolute are used only for the sake of convenience as it transcends all speech and thought.[2] It is, thereby, led to conceive of Reality at two levels: the phenomenal or the relative level (*saṃvṛti satya*) and the absolute level (*paramārtha satya*). At the absolute level, Reality is a state of transcendence, beyond all verbal formulations.

To sum up this discussion, Mahāyāna signifies a distinctive growth of Buddhist spiritual experience. It was a growth bothways—in depth and height as well as in growing out of the monastic cell. As a concrete result of it, in place of the earlier ideal of '*Ārya*' or '*Arhat*' the ideal of '*Bodhisattva*' came to the surface.

Buddhological Developments and the Bodhisattva Ideal as the Foundational Ground of Mahāyāna Ethics

[1]Nāgārjuna XVIII. 7 says that the true nature of *dharma* is like *Nirvāṇa*:
Nivṛttam abhidhātavyaṁ nivṛttaś cittagocaraḥ.
Anutpannā niruddhā hi nirvāṇam iva dharmatā.

[2]In a *Kārikā* of Nāgārjuna the point has been brought home with the help of 'Eight Notes':
Anirodhaṁ anutpādaṁ anucchedaṁ aśāśvatam.
Anekārthaṁ anānārtham anāgamam anirgamam.
'No annihilation, no origination, no destruction, no continuity, no unity, no plurality, no coming in, no going out.'

About the nature of Tathāgata, Nāgārjuna says that it cannot be said that he is *Śūnya* or *Aśūnya*, or both or neither and that he is given a name only conventionally—
'*Śūnyam iti na vaktavyam aśūnyam iti vā bhavet.*
Ubhayaṁ nobahyaṁ ceti prajñaptyarthaṁ tu kathyate.
—Mūlamadhyamakārikāḥ, XXII. 11.

Mahāyāna is marked by great Buddhological developments. The earlier notion of the uniqueness of a Buddha[1] developed into the Mahāsāṅghika belief of the transcendental character of his existence; Mahāyāna carries the trend further so as to raise him to the status of divinity, an object of worship, to be approached for his compassion and grace. In Hīnayāna and the early Mahāyāna Sūtras there existed the conception of the 'Two Bodies' (*kāya*) of Buddha viz., the *rūpa-kāya*, later called *nirmāṇakāya* (i.e. his mortal form through which he taught to the worldly people), and the *dharmakāya* (i.e. the sum total of his teachings which was said to be his real form). Later, especially in the Vijñānavādin texts, it culminated in the conception of 'Three Bodies' (*trikāya*) of Buddha, the additional one being the *saṁbhoga-kāya* (Body of Recompense or Bliss) which stands between the *nirmāṇakāya* and the *dharmakāya* and is assumed for the sake of instructing the *Bodhisattvas* and is visible to them only.[2] While granting the supremacy of *dharma*, the Hīnāyāna accepted the historical career of Buddha as a human individual who was born in this world, had attained the highest spiritual wisdom through his efforts and had imparted this wisdom to others out of compassion. Mahāyāna, on the other hand, came to conceive Buddhahood as an eternal fact: the real Buddha is never born, he does not come from anywhere, he does not go anywhere; he is ever-existent in the form of 'suchness.' As the *Saddharma-Puṇḍarīka* states, Buddha attained Buddhahood innumerable *kalpas* ago and that his life-span is immeasurable.[3] Father of all beings of the world, he is self-born whose permanent abode is the Gṛdhrakūṭa mountain.[4] Though Hīnayāna also believed in more than one Buddha, there was now a tremendous increase in the number of Buddhas; there are more Buddhas than sands in the Gaṅgā.[5] There is

[1]This uniqueness is underlined by the distinction that is maintained between a Buddha and *Arhat*.

[2]On the doctrine of *Trikāya* and its significance see Daisetz Teitaro Suzuki, *Outlines of Mahayana Buddhism*, Ch. X; B.L. Suzuki, *Mahayana Buddhism*, pp. 38 ff; G.C. Pande, *BDVI.*, pp. 341 ff; M.C. McGovern, *An Introduction to Mahā-yāna Buddhism*, pp. 47 ff. For a sound and detailed discussion on *Trikāya* doctrine and its close relationship with the development of the Idea of *Bhakti* in Mahāyāna see Susmita Pande; 'Conceptual Background of the Development of Bhakti in Mahayana Buddhism', *Buddhist Studies*, A Yearly Research Journal of the Department of Buddhist Studies, University of Delhi, 1980.

[3]*Sad. Puṇḍ*, *SBE.*, XXI, pp. 306, 309.

[4]ibid., pp. 309-10. [5]ibid., pp. 409, 413.

hardly any difference between the Buddha of the Mahāyāna and the Kṛṣṇa of the *Gītā*. Buddha is now called the supreme God (*devātideva*) who, through his grace, is the saviour (*santāraka*) of the world.[1] In the Mahāyāna, thus, grace of the Buddha assumes much greater importance than self-exertion.

The greatest development, however, was made in the conception of *Bodhisattva* who was conceived as the aspirational ideal of the Mahāyānic ethico-spiritual seeking. In Hīnayāna, the term was used to denote the lives of Buddha prior to his Enlightenment. *Bodhisattva* is the future Buddha. Mahāyāna took up this notion to exalt it to the farthest limit so much so that there ceased to be any difference between a Buddha and a *Bodhisattva*. The Mahāsāṅghikas had already paved the way by emphasising, along with that of the Buddha, the transcendental character of the *Bodhisattva*. According to them, the *Bodhisattvas* have only 'mind-forms;' they appear as men only because of their concern for the welfare of the world. The Ekavyāvahārikas even said that they have no forms and the Vaitulyakas went to the extent of saying that there was only one incarnation of *nirmāṇakaya* from the *Tuṣita*-heaven (the abode of the *Bodhisattvas*) through the womb of Māyādevī.[2]

According to Mahāyāna, a Bodhisattva is one who has successfully practised the various perfections such as *dāna* (charity), *śīla* (morality) etc., and is thus fit to be a Buddha. He, however, refrains from entering into the state of Buddhahood and enjoying its bliss because of his compassion for others. He sees no justification for it as his fellow-beings are still subject to fear and pain.[3] All beings, according to Mahāyāna, are potential Buddhas, but all are not capable of attaining this state by themselves without taking the help of an enlightened being. The *Bodhisattvas*, innumerable, are such beings who are there to render this help. A *Bodhisattva* is so called as his 'intention is concentrated on Illumination.'[4] One who is desirous of putting an end

[1]ibid., *BST.*, 6, p. 35, pp. 100-01. See Susmita Pande, 'Conceptual Background of the Idea of Bhakti in Mahayana Buddhism', *Buddhist Studies*, 1980, p. 84.

[2]See G.C. Pande, *BDVI.*, p. 357.

[3]*Śikṣā.*, first verse:
Yadā mama pareṣāṁ ca bhayaṁ duḥkhaṁ ca na priyam,
Tadātmanaḥ ko viśeṣo yāttaṁ rakṣāmi netaram.

[4]*Bodhicaryavatāra—Pañjikā* by Prajñākaramati *BST.*, 12, p. 200: *Tatra bodhiḥ sattvam, abhiprāyosyeti bodhisattvaḥ.*

to pain and gaining bliss should strengthen one's faith and direct one's thought towards '*bodhi*' (Enlightenment), says the *Śikṣāsamuccaya*.[1] And added to this is the fact of his immeasurable compassion for all suffering beings. As D.T. Suzuki quotes Nāgārjuna's work on *Boddhicitta*, "The essential nature of all Bodhisattvas is a great loving heart (Mahākaruṇācitta), and all sentient beings constitute the object of his love."[2]

A New Ethical Dimension: Exaltation of Positive Virtues

It is clear from the above that the Mahāyāna conceives of *Prajñā* (Perfect Wisdom) and *Karuṇā* as inseparable properties constituting the personality of a Buddha and a *Bodhisattva*. Accordingly, "the Mahāyāna stands firmly on two legs, Prajñā and Karuṇā, transcendental idealism and all embracing affection for all kinds of beings, animate as well as inanimate."[3] Perfection and compassion go together; to be enlightened means to be compassionate. Such a being is the ideal person to be emulated if salvation is set as the goal. This special emphasis on compassion introduced a new orientation in the ethical framework as it demanded from the seeker not to be satisfied with his personal spiritual gain but to work actively for the welfare of others. A feeling of complete identity with others was evoked so that one's individual liberation is tendered incomplete and meaningless if all others are not liberated. It is not that the earlier Hīnayānic ideal of *Arhat* was devoid of the attribute of non-selfishness (transcendence of narrow selfishness was here also the primary characteristic) but the positive attitude of completely identifying oneself with others and, consequently, exerting vigorously for others was not so much highlighted in it as came to be the case with the Mahāyānic ideal of *Bodhisattva*. While an *Arhat* exerts for his individual liberation and is content with its achievement, a *Boddhisattva* is moved to place the liberation of others as the primary goal of his spiritual exertion in preference to which his individual liberation comes to have a secondary place. It is from this stand that the Mahāyānists viewed the Hīnayānic ideal of *Arhat* as selfish.

[1] *Śikṣā.*, p. 1.
Duḥkhāntam kartukāmena sukhāntaṁ gantumicchatā.
Śraddhāmūlaṁ dṛḍhīkṛtya bodhau kāryā matirdṛḍhā.

[2] D.T. Suzuki, *Outlines of Mahayana Buddhism*, p. 292.

[3] ibid., quot. B.L. Suzuki, *Mahayana Buddhism*, p. 1.

The Mahāyāna added a new dimension in the ethical framework of Buddhism by its exaltation of positive virtues. This new orientation derived from the change in the conception of relationship between mind and the world. Believing in a dichotomy of mind and matter, early Buddhism conceived the material world as a corrupting force which does not allow mind to be restful and in a state of equanimity. The individuating and activating mind, thus, became an object of great attention and stress came to be laid on the practice of the detachment of mind. In this process cultivation of negative virtues—not-wishing, not-acting, not-wanting—would naturally be an aid in the achievement of perfection. In the Mahāyāna, mind creates matter; world itself is a projection of mind. In such a conception of relationship between mind and the world mere negative virtues are not adequate. Evil is not removed by merely neglecting them or suppressing them. What we call evil is only a perverted form of the original nature of mind. With the introduction of the ideas of Suchness (*Tathatā*) the outlook of the Mahāyāna was greatly widened. As the *Tathāgatagarbha* was conceived as the source of both *Saṁsāra* and *Nirvāṇa*, the latter ceased to be a mere transcendental entity attainable after the stream of *Saṁsāra* has been crossed; the life of becoming that we are living (i.e. *Saṁsāra*) is itself *Nirvāṇa*. Therefore, the necessity is not to negate *Saṁsāra* and its objects but to find ourselves. What is needed is the transmutation of mind (*parāvṛtti*) which, as a result of it, discards its evil orientation and attains purification.[1] It is through the transmutation of mind that the erotic thing becomes aesthetic. As a corrolary to this viewpoint, the Mahāyāna lays down that positive virtues have to be cultivated and perfected in order to strengthen mind so that it can interfere in the world purposefully and effectively. As regards the true nature of the ethical achievement, while one version considered mental quietude the ultimate state, another version believed that everything remains as it is but understanding of it changes; there was yet another version—

[1]The idea of *parāvṛtti* is discussed in the *Mahāyāna-sūtrālaṅkāra* of Maitreya-Asaṅga. It speaks of '*parāvṛtti* of maithuna' and states that it leads to the origins of great power in '*Buddhasaukhyavihāra*' and '*dārāsaṅkleśadarśana*'. From what has been said earlier in the text (*avaśiṣṭaih ślokaiḥ manovṛttibhedena vibhutvabhedaṁ darśayati*), it is clear that the term has been used in the sense of transmutation of mind. See *MSL*. ed. S. Lévi, p. 41. For a detailed philosophical treatment, see G.C. Pande, *BDVI*., pp. 464-65. Pande connects the idea of *parāvrtti*, especially that of *parāvrtti* of *maithuna*, with tantricism. ibid.

the popular one—which claimed creation of a blissful world to be the real purpose.

Metaphysical Base of Ethics: Prajñāpāramitā

Bodhisattvahood stands for complete self-effacement. It is co-terminous with what is called 'Immaculate Wisdom' (*Prajñāpāramitā*), the climax of spiritual attainment according to Mahāyāna. Attainment of this wisdom is the necessary pre-condition for the eradication of suffering.[1] 'Immaculate wisdom,' said to be the very same as *Tathāgata*, is non-dualistic[2] knowledge which leaves no room for any distinction and, consequently, for any conflict or hostility between oneself and others; it, thus, emphasises unity of all life. This wisdom is the same which amounts to seeing things as they are (*Tathatā*), that is realizing the fact that things of the world have no nature of their own (*niḥsvabhāva*) and they exist in 'Emptiness' (*śūnyatā*). What follows from it is summed up by L.M. Joshi thus: "Thus the logic of the doctrine of Prajñāpāramitā indubitably leads to universal love and sympathy; when all beings are devoid of ego; when all beings have the seed of Buddhahood; and when all beings hate pain and fear, and need perfect freedom and peace, all beings are, and must constitute the object of a Bodhisattva's love. There can be no moral or logical justification for an egoistical effort; the ego does not exist. Moral and spiritual perfection is possible only on this profound principle of Prajñāpāramitā."[3]

Cultivation of Bodhicitta—Its Ethical Content and Significance.

Bodhi or *Sambodhi*[4] ('Wisdom'; derived from the root *budh*) is the supreme object of a *Bodhisattva's* aspiration, the ultimate goal of his spiritual seeking. In the Mahāyāna texts, it is usually qualified by *anuttara* (pre-eminent, unsurpassed) and *samyak* (perfect), the complete phrase being *anuttarā samyak sambodhi*, 'the unsurpassable, perfect wisdom.'[5] As has been observed by Har Dayal, in the Buddhist Sanskrit texts the attainment of this wisdom is considered to be of a

[1] *Bodhic*. IX. 1.

[2] *Prajñāpārmitā jñānam advayam sā Tathāgataḥ*, *Prajñāpāramitā-Piṇḍārtha* (ed. in *BST*., 4, p. 263) quoted in L.M. Joshi, op, cit., p. 149 fn. 70.

[3] L.M. Joshi, op. cit., p. 121.

[4] The prefix *sam* before the word *bodhi* denotes its excellence and completeness.

[5] For example, *Sad. Puṇḍ*. ed. Vaidya, pp. 13, 27, 28, 106; *Śikṣā*., pp. 9, 101-02, 167; *Sukhāvativyūha* in *Mahāyānasūtrasaṁgrahaḥ*, pt. I, pp. 225 ff; *MSL*., ed. Bagchi, p. 4; *Śat. Pr*., p. 91.

greater importance by a *Bodhisattva* than even the attainment of *Nirvāṇa*.[1] Will to attain this Wisdom (*bodhicitta*) is of the greatest importance. The Mahāyāna texts acknowledge its glory in too many words. It produces immeasurable virtue (*puṇya*)[2] and is the cause of both *abhyudaya* and *niḥśreyasa*.[3] It nullifies even the operation of the law of *karman*, cancelling out completely all the sins and transgressions of past lives.[4] *Bodhicitta* is said to be the store-house of innumerable qualities[5] and is likened to a tree (*bodhcittavṛkṣah*) which is ever fruit-giving and never comes to a state of non-production.[6] A passage in the *Mahāvastu* says that it is easy to count the stars in the sky but it is impossible to estimate the virtues and merits associated with the *Bodhicitta*.[7]

Cultivation of *bodhicitta* is, thus, considered highly precious in the spiritual seeking as prescribed by the Mahāyāna. It is noteworthy that though the cultivation of *bodhicitta* would naturally result in a *Bodhisattva's* individual perfection, the feeling of altruistic love (*karuṇā*) is clearly said to be the guiding force of this undertaking. The essence of the matter, as the *Bodhisattvabhūmi* clearly specifies, is that the Thought has two objects (*ālambanas*)—the object of *bodhi* and the object of the welfare of all living beings.[8] It is, in fact, this moving concern for others, the motive to help and save all other creatures, which has led one to resolve to become a *Bodhisattva*. In the *Bodhicaryāvatāra*, the following statement is put in the mouth of a *Bodhisattva*: "As the Buddhas of yore embraced *bodhicitta* and observed the discipline of the *Bodhisattvas*, so do I, too, cultivate *bodhicitta* for the welfare of the world (*jagaddhite*), and I will observe this discipline in the appropriate manner."[9] He values it for he thinks that

[1]Har Dayal, op. cit., pp. 11-13.

[2]*Bodhic*., I. 26 . . . *Cittaratnasya yatpuṇyam tatkathaṁ hi pramīyatam*. In his *Pañjikā* Prajñākaramati elaborates: *Cittaratnasya badhicittasya yatpuṇyam tat katham hi pramīyatam . . . Ativipulatayā pramātumaśakyatvāt*. ibid., p. 15.

[3]*Bodhicaryavatāra-Pañjikā*, ibid., p. 15.

[4]*Bodhic*., I. 13; I. 35.

[5]*Śikṣā*., pp. 6-7.

[6]*Bodhic*., I. 12.

[7]*Mahāvastu*, trans. J.J. Jones, II; p. 334, also *Bodhic*., p. 9.

[8]*Tasmātsa cittotpādo bodhyālambanaḥ sattvārthālambanaśca*, *Bbhū*. Book I. ch. II '*Cittotpādapaṭalaṁ*', p. 8.

[9]*Bodhic*., III, 22-23: *Yathā gṛhītaṁ sugatairbodhicittaṁ purātanaiḥ. Te bodhisattvaṣikṣāyāmanupūrvyā yathā sthitāḥ. Tadvadutpādayāmeṣa bodhicittaṁ jagaddhite, Tadvadeva ca tāḥ śikṣāḥ śikṣiṣyāmi yathākramam*. In the *Aṣṭasāhasrikā*-

in it he has found a means to remove all the poorness of the world (*jagaddāridryaśamanam*),[1] a cure to all the ills of the world (*jagadvyādhipraśamam bhaiṣajyam*),[2] a tree to provide rest to all the beings of the world who are tried of the tortuous journey of *saṁsāra* (*bhavādhvabhramaṇaśrāntajagadviśrāmapādapaḥ*),[3] a bridge to take all the seekers to the other side (*setuḥ sāmānyaḥ sarvayāyinām*).[4] The *Śikṣāsamucaya* quotes Buddha in the *Āryasiṁhapaṛiprcchāsūtra* as saying that the 'Thought of *bodhi*' is to be cultivated for the liberation of all beings (*sarvasattva-pramokṣāya*).[5] The same concern for all other beings in the world is further expressed in the resolve (*praṇidhāna*) that a *Bodhisattva* makes after having cultivated the *bodhicitta*. The formula of *praṇidhāna* as given in the *Aṣṭa-sāhasrikā-prajñāpāramitā* reads as following: "We have crossed over, we shall help beings to cross over. Freed we shall free them! Recovered we shall help them to recover! Gone to Nirvana we shall lead them to Nirvaṇa![6] In the *Lalita-vistara*, Siddhārtha, who is at the moment a *Bodhisattva*, is reminded of the resolve that he had made in his previous birth: "I will attain the immortal, undecaying and pain-free *bodhi*, and free the world from all pain."[7] A much more elaborate form of *praṇidhāna* can be seen in the *Sukhāvatīvyūha-sūtra*[8] wherein a *Boddhisattva* named *Dharmākara* aspires to free all the creatures from the fear of being born in a miserable state such as animals, *pretas*, *asuras*, etc., and to gain for them all good things and, finally, their final liberation before he himself is liberated.

Obviously, in the conceptions of *bodhicitta* and *praṇidhāna* the two ideals of individual perfection and all-pervasive compassion (*karuṇā*) are welded together into one. Perfection and compassion, according to Mahāyāna, cannot be separated, both being innate characteristics of the one who is released and liberated. Both perfection and com-

Prajñāpāramitā, the Lord says to Subhūti that the *Bodhisattvas* are favoured by the Tathāgata 'because these bodhisattvas have practised for the wealth and happiness of many, out of pity for the world. Out of pity for Gods and men, for the benefit, the weal and the happiness of a great man of people do they want to win the supreme enlightenment, and thereafter to demonstrate the supreme dharma'. *Aṣṭa. Pr.*, trans. Conze, p. 77.

[1]ibid., III, 28. [2]ibid., III, 29. [3]ibid.

[4]ibid., III. 30. [5]*Śikṣā.*, p. 6.

[6]*Aṣṭa. Pr.*, p. 108, 177.

[7]*Lalita-Vistara, BST* 1, pp. 112-14, 117.

[8]*Mahāyānasūtrasaṁgrahaḥ*, part I, pp. 225 ff.

passion, inseparably, constitute the object of aspiration of the one who wants to attain the state of final emancipation. It may be said that according to Mahāyāna individual liberation is no liberation at all. Though in the course of training there may be some *Bodhisattvas* who exert for their individual happiness and spiritual gains, but it is not a desirable thing; a *Bodhisattva* should primarily exert for the good of others (*parārtha*).[1]

Practical Ethics of Mahāyāna: The Pāramitās[2]

The *Pāramitās* contain the essence of practical ethics that the Mahāyāna prescribes for a *Bodhisattva* who is on the spiritual journey to freedom.[3] They represent the highest virtues without practising which it is impossible to attain the goal. The *Laṅkāvatāra* says that Buddhahood is realised by fulfilling the six *Pāramitās*.[4] According to the *Aṣṭasāhasrikā-prajñāpāramitā*, "All the six perfections, in fact, are the good friends of a *Bodhisattva*. They are his Teacher, his path, his light, his torch, his illumination, his shelter, his refuge, his place of rest, his final relief, his island, his mother, his father."[5] The *Mahāyāna-sūtrālaṅkāra* defines the six *Pāramitās* as fulfilling certain specific spiritual and moral virtues[6] and says that they bring welfare, happy rebirths and lead to serenity, great spiritual attainment, good concentration and supreme knowledge.[7] In a number of Mahāyāna Sanskrit

[1]See *Bbhū.*, book I, ch. III, *Svaparārthapaṭala*'.

[2]On the etymology of the word 'Pāramitā' see Har Dayal, op. cit., pp. 165-66. T.W. Rhys Davids and W. Stede, in their *Pali Dictionary*, have translated it as 'completeness, perfection, highest state'. The explanation of the word, by Bohtlingk and Roth, Monier Williams, E. Burnouf, B. Hodgson and M. Vassilief, as consisting of two words, *param* (the opposite bank) and *ita* (gone, from the root *i* to go) does not find favour with Har Dayal who prefers to derive it from *parama* (supreme or the highest). According to the explanations given in the *Bodhisattva-Bhūmi*, *Pāramitās* are so called because they are acquired during a long period of time (*paramena kālena samudagatāḥ*), are absolutely supremely pure in their nature (*paramāya svabhāvaviśuddhyā viśuddhāḥ*) and lead to the attainment of the highest result (*paramaṁ ca phalam anuprayacchanti*). As such, Har Dayal opines: "It simply means, "highest condition, highest point, best state, perfection."

[3]*Ye sada pāramitāsu carantī te pratipanna iho mahāyāne*. *Ratnolkādharaṇī* quoted in *Śikṣā.*, p. 6.

[4]*Laṅkāvatāra Sūtra*, trans. Suzuki, p. 204.

[5]*Aṣṭ. Pr.*, p. 158.

[6]*MSL.*, *BST.*, 13, p. 99.

[7]ibid., pp. 97-98.

texts, wherein these virtues are discussed and elaborated,[1] their number is given as six and they are named: *Dāna*, *Śīla*, *Kṣānti*, *Vīrya*, *Dhyāna* and *Prajñā*. Later, four more—*Upāya-Kauśalya*, *Praṇidhāna*, *Bala* and *Jñāna*—were added to the list[2] thus making them ten in number. In his *Madhyamakāvatāra*, Candrakīrti connects the ten *Pāramitās* with ten *bhūmis* (stages of spiritual growth) in the same order.[3]

It has been stated in the *Mahāyāna-Sūtrālaṅkāra* that the practice of each *Pāramitā* necessitates the cultivation of the preceding one.[4] It is evident that 'they imply one another and form a progressive scheme of action.'[5] Each *Pāramitā* is divisible in three categories: (1) the worldly one which the ordinary people of the world practise in order to attain happiness in this life and the life hereafter, (2) the super-worldly one—a category superior to the former one—which the Hīnayānists practise with the aim of attaining personal *Nirvāṇa*, and (3) the highest super-worldly category which the *Bodhisattvas* practise with the aim of liberating all beings.[6] The degree of excellence in them is clearly based on the aim keeping which in view it is practised and since liberation of all (*sarva-mukti*) is the noblest aim conceived in Mahāyāna, the last one naturally finds the place of highest importance. The six *Pāramitās* are:

1. *Dāna*. The list of perfections starts with *Dāna*, the act of giving. It is clearly grounded in such virtues as universal friendliness (*maitrī*) and compassion (*karuṇā*) which, from the beginning, had been so much emphasised in the teachings of Buddha. I have discussed elsewhere that by the time of the advent of Buddha a number of factors had operated in preparing the ground for the emergence of philanthropic idea in assertive form with a special stress on its realiza-

[1]For example, *Lalita-Vistara*, *BST.*, 1, p. 25; *Mahāvastu*, trans. J.J. Jones, III, p. 221; *Avadāna-śataka*, *BST.* 19, p. 8, p. 20; *Bbhū.*, Book I. ch. IX-XIV; *Laṅkāvātārasūtra*, trans. Suzuki, pp. 204-05.

[2]For example, *Mvy.*, section 34 which gives the list of ten *Pāramitās;* also *Dharma-Saṅgraha*, section 18; *Bbhū.*, ch. IV of Book III '*Caryā-paṭala*'.

[3]See Govind Chandra Pande, *BDVI.*, p. 363. Thus, *Pramuditā* and *Dāna*; *Vimalā* and *Śīla; Prabhākarī* and *Kṣānti; Arciṣmatī* and *Vīrya; Sudurjayā* and *Dhyāna; Abhimukhī* and *Prajñā; Dūraṅgamā* and *Upāya-kauśalya; Acalā* and *Praṅidhāna; Sādhumatī* and *Bala;* and *Dharmamegha* and *Jñāna*.

[4]*MSL.*, ed. and trans. S. Lévi 101.12 ff; 115.16 ff.

[5]Har Dayal, op. cit., p. 171.

[6]*Laṅkāvatārasūtra*, trans. Suzuki, pp. 204-05.

tion in the religious as well as in the social context.[1] As such, various passages in the early Buddhist texts speak of the virtue of gift, about its great spiritual advantage and the modes and the motives involved therein.[2] Mahāyāna takes up this ancient tradition but exalts it further by making it a necessary ingredient of a *Bodhisattva's* personality and adducing to it 'a spirit of exaggerated sentimentality.' Śāntideva concludes his first chapter of *Śikṣāsamuccaya* on *Dāna-pāramitā* by quoting from the 'Ratnamegha-sutra' that 'Liberality constitutes, veritably, the Enlightenment of the Bodhisattva.'[3] It consists in the preparedness of giving everything (*sarvasvatyāga*) to others.[4] Inspired by the spirit of liberality, a *Bodhisattva* aspires to be medicine and a physician to the diseased and attend on them, make all arrangements for those who are thirsty and hungry and the famine-stricken people, and satisfy the needs of the destitute and the poor by giving them beds, clothes and food;[5] but, above all, apart from giving various material objects, a *Bodhisattva* is happily willing to grant even his merit—of past, present and future (*tryadhvagataṁ śubhaṁ*)—for the sake of others.[6] This belief in the possibility of transfer of one's merit to others clashes against the older and stricter doctrine of *Karman* which conceives of an identity between the doer and the experiencer of an action and disallows any kind of sharability by anyone in its fruits. But, the Mahāyāna is so much enamoured by the ideal of liberality that it does not mind sacrificing any other ideal for its sake—so much so that a certain *Bodhisattva*, Jyotirmāṇavaka by name, did not hesitate to do away with his long practised vow of chastity out of compassion for a woman.[7] A *Bodhisattva* should be ready to sacrifice

[1]G.S.P. Misra, 'A Study of Philanthropy in Early Buddhist Ethics', *Indica*, 18, no. 2, pp. 73 ff.

[2]See especially—*DN.*, 'Pāyāsi-sutta'; *AN.*, 'Dāna-vagga', 'Sumana-vagga', 'Mahāyañña-vagga', 'Sīhanāda-vagga'; *SN.*, 'Sotāpatti-saṁyutta'; *Dhammapada*, verse 354. *Itivuttaka*, section 26.

[3]*Śikṣā.*, p. 22: *Dānaṁ hi Bodhisattvasya bodhiriti.*

[4]*Bodhic.*, 5.10. [5]ibid., 3. 7-9.

[6]ibid. 3.10; *Śikṣā.*, 1.4. For the various types of gifts to be made by a *Bodhisattva* in order to attain perfection in *Dāna-pāramitā* see 'Dānapaṭala' in *Bbhū.* Book I. ch. IX, pp. 80 ff.

[7]*Śikṣā* (Ed. Vaidya), p. 93. The idea is foreshadowed in the *Kathāvatthu* which alludes to a certain school—Vaitulyakas as we know—the viewpoint that with a certain purpose even sexual intercourse or sleeping with other's wife is permissible—*ekādhippayena methuno dhammo paṭisevitabbo . . . paradāro gantabbo. Kathāvatthu* (Nālanda ed.), p. 535. According to Buddhaghosa, 'with a certain

for the sake of others his hand, foot, eye, flesh, blood, marrow, limbs great and small and his head.[1] This exaggerated sentimentality that the Mahāyānist authors adduced to this perfection led them to invent many stories such as that of King Śivi who offers a feast of his own limbs for the sake of other creatures and readily gives his eyes when asked by Śakra in disguise.[2] However, according to Mahāyāna, the best gift that a *Bodhisattva* can give to others is the gift of *Dharma*, other gifts considered of a lower category than this. A *sūtra* preserved in Chinese translation reads:

"What is a bad means (*anupāya*)? When, by the practice of the perfections the Bodhisattvas help others, but are content to supply them with merely material aid, without raising them from their misery or introducing them into beautitude, then they are using a bad means.

Why? Because material help is not sufficient. Whether a dunghill be large or small, it cannot possibly be made to smell sweet by any means whatsoever. In the same way, living beings are unhappy because of their acts, because of their nature; it is impossible to make them happy by supplying them with merely material aid. The best way of helping them is to establish them in goodness."[3]

2. *Śīla*. Sila may generally denote good conduct. In the early texts, it is the first in the triplet of *Śīla*, *Samādhi* and *Prajñā*. It has both negative (*vāritta sīla*) and positive (*cāritta sila*) aspects.[4] Self-preservation (*ātmabhāva-rakṣā*) with the aim of bringing benefit to others (*sattvāñaṁ paribhogāya*) is said to be the main purpose of morality.[5] The texts contain various lists of virtues which are sometimes overlapping. Attachment (*rāga*), malice (*dveṣa*) and delusion (*moha*) are the three 'Roots of Evil' and good conduct is difficult to conceive till these have their vestiges in human personality. The 'ten precepts' of morality as laid down in early Buddhism (*dasa-sīla*) have been discussed in an earlier chapter. The Mahāyāna texts also speak of ten

purpose' (*ekādhippaya*) here alludes to compassion. See G.C. Pande, *BDVI*, p. 298.

[1]*Śikṣā.*, p. 16.

[2]The story of Śivi occurs with some variations in the *Avadāna-śataka*, the *Jātaka-mālā* and the *Avadāna-Kalpalatā*. For other stories of similar nature see Har Dayal, op. cit., pp. 181 ff.

[3]Quoted by Henri de Lubac, *Aspects of Buddhism*, p. 24.

[4]*Viśuddhi Mārga*, trans. by Bhikshu Dharmarakshita, I, p. 13.

[5]*Śikṣā.*, p. 23.

'ways of action' (*Karma-pathāḥ*) in negative and positive forms.[1] In Mahāyāna, however, we come across the curious doctrine that a *Bodhisattva* can violate any or all of these precepts if he does so on the consideration of mercy and compassion for another being.[2] In the *Bodhisattvabhūmi* we find an enumeration of the circumstances under which a *Bodhisattva* may justifiably commit transgressions of the moral precepts; the governing factor, however, is always compassion and a desire to save others from sinful acts. Thus, a *Bodhisattva* may even kill a person who intends to kill other beings, *śrāvakas, pratyekabuddhas Bodhisattvas.* While committing the transgression he should feel in this way: 'Though this sinful act would lead me to purgatory, it does no matter for I would be saving the other person from suffering in purgatory.' In the like manner, he may take away the ill-gotten gains of cruel and unjust kings and ministers; he may steal from the thieves and smugglers to help monks; he may engage in sex with a woman in order to prevent her from entertaining thoughts of hatred and ill-will; he may use harsh language in order to warn and restrain a sinner; he may lie if that helps others; he may take part in various worldly amusement with a view to soothing the misery and anxiety of others, and so on and so forth.[3] Such a thesis suggests a keen observation on the part of the Mahāyānist thinkers that no ethical rule can be universally valid under all circumstances, but it may also point to a general state of degeneracy among the monks subsequent on which an alibi was sought for their moral lapses in the assumed motive of compassion for others. It clearly tends to give moral sanction to such violations of accepted ascetic and social norms which later developed in the Tantrayāna Buddhism.

3. *Kṣānti*. The third *Pāramitā—Kṣānti Pāramitā*—stands for forbearance and is generally opposed to hatred (*dveṣa*) and anger (*krodha*).[4]

[1]*Mahāvastu*, trans. J.J. Jones., I, p. 3; *MSL.*, ed. Lévi, 110.4; *Daśabhūmikasūtra*, 25.17; ibid., 23.6; *Śat. Pr.* 479.3; *Mvy.*, section 92.

[2]*Bodhic.*, V. 84.

Evaṁ buddhvā parārtheṣu bhavetsatatamutthitaḥ.
Niṣiddhamapyanujñātam kṛpālorarthadarśinaḥ.
Also *Śikṣā.*, pp. 93-94.

[3]*Bhū.*, 'Śilapaṭalam' pp. 112-16.

[4]Prajñākaramati defines *dveṣa* as the harsh and cruel state of mind and considers it the source of anger: *cittasya karkaśāvasthā dveṣaḥ. Tasyodbhūtavṛttistu krodhaḥ* . . . *Bodhic.* p., 82.

It is exalted as the most excellent type of penance.[1] It is said to be of three kinds: (1) forbearance of pain (*duḥkhādhivāsana-kṣānti*), (2) forbearance of seeing the Doctrine (*dharmanidhyāna-kṣānti*) and (3) forbearance of injuries and insults (*parāpakāra-marṣaṇo-kṣānti*).[2] Pain is something inherent in the very nature of human existence and, realizing this, one should be readily prepared to face it and bear it bravely. By practice of bearing small pains, one may prepare oneself for bearing great pains.[3] Moreover, pain helps us in many ways in the purification of our personality: it removes pride, generates compassionate feeling for others, strengthens devotion in the Buddha.[4] The primary connotation of this perfection is, however, brought about in its third type: it consists in that disposition of mind which enables one to endure and pardon the injuries and insults inflicted by others; the keynote is to love one's enemy. A *Bodhisattva* forgives others for all injuries and insults at all times and in all situations.[5] He does not bear any ill-will or anger even toward those who inflict all sorts of cruelties to his person.[6] Consideration of certain great principles helps a *Bodhisattva* in the making of such a mental disposition: an enemy of the present might have been a friend, a close relative or a teacher in past life; no man or woman has any permanent substantial individuality, from which it follows that there is really no one who insults or injures or could be reviled and injured; it is of no use to be angry with ephemeral and mortal beings who are all, without any exception, subject to three aspects of suffering.[7] The second type, viz., *dharmanidhyānakṣānti*, is the most difficult type of *kṣānti* and consists in the realization of the True Law and the true nature of the universe. Commenting on it Poussin writes: "The name of patience applied to 'insight into the law' is justified from a double point of view: (1) resistance and resignation of mind are necessary to the acceptance of the doctrine of the non-existence of the things: those who do not

[1] *Bodhic.*, VI. 2;. *Na ca dveṣasamaṁ pāpaṁ na ca kṣāntisamaṁ tapaḥ;* cf. *Dhammapada*, verse 184: *Khantī paramaṁ tapo titikhhā;* in the early texts, the 'Kakacūpamasutta' of the *MN.*, contains the best expression of this moral virtue.

[2] *Śikṣā.*, p. 100; Also *Bbhū.*, p. 130.

[3] *Bodhic.*, VI. 14; *Śikṣā.*, p. 101.

[4] ibid., VI, 21, p. 86.

[5] *Bbhū.*, p. 135: *sarvañcāpakāraṁ kṣamate. Sarvataśca kṣamate. Sarvatra ca deśe kṣamate. Rahasi vā mahājanasamakṣaṁ vā sarvakālañca kṣamate . . .*

[6] *Śiksa.*, p. 101.

[7] *Bbhū.*, 'Kṣāntipaṭalam', pp. 131 ff.

'uphold the profound teaching' (gambhīra-dharma-kṣānti) are numerous; (2) this estimate of the reality of things is an essential element of patience in the ordinary sense.''[1]

4. *Vīrya*. The fourth *Pāramitā* is *Vīrya Pāramitā*. Literally meaning 'prowess,' 'energy,' 'strength,' 'heroism' or 'manliness' it has been recognized in Buddhism from the beginning as an important object of aspiration. Realization is not possible without exertion, a lazy man can never attain the goal. The Mahāyānist writers praise it as a necessary concomitant of Enlightenment: *Vīrya* is the base of *bodhi*.[2] A *Bodhisattva* should cultivate enthusiasm for good actions (*Kuśalotsāha*)[3] and strenuously guard himself against all sins, small or great,[4] realizing that sensual pleasures are like honey on the edge of a razor (*Kṣuradhāramadhūpama*).[5] He gives a careful reflection before he is to undertake an enterprise but once he takes it up he carries it to its successful end.[6]

5. *Dhyāna*. The fifth *Pāramitā* is *Dhyāna* which is defined in one Mahāyāna text, *Bodhisattvabhūmi*, as 'concentration and fixity of mind.'[7] After having strengthened energy, a *Bodhisattva* should put his mind to trance for one with a distracted mind (*vikṣipatacittah*) is always in the clutches of *kleśas*.[8] This *Pāramitā* has an ascetic connotation. In order that mind does not get distracted, a *Bodhisattva* is required to develop *kāyaviveka* and *citta-viveka*, the former consisting in isolation of body from the worldly people (*janasamparkavivarjanatā*) and the latter consisting in the isolation of mind from sensual and worldly desires (*kāmādivitarka-vivarjanatā*).[9] *Śamatha* and *Vipaśyanā* are the two ingredients of *Dhyāna*.[10] It includes meditation on the evils of sensual pleasures, on various virtues that lead to wisdom, on the two truths (relative and absolute), on Four *Brahma-vihāras*, etc.

[1] *ERE.*, II, p. 751.

[2] *Bodhic*. VII. 1; *Bbhū.*, 'Vīryapaṭalam', p. 139: *Yataśca sarveṣāṁ bodhikārakāṇāṁ kuśalānām dharmāṇamevam samudāgamāya vīryameva pradhānaṁ śreṣṭham kāraṇam na tathānyat*.

[3] *Bodhic.*, VII. 2. [4] ibid., VII. 60-61.

[5] ibid., VII. 64. [6] ibid., VII. 47.

[7] *Bbhū.*, p. 150: *Cittaikāgrañcittasthitiḥ*.

[8] *Bodhic.*, VIII. 1.

[9] ibid., VIII. 2, p. 136.

[10] Prajñākaramati defines *Śamatha* as concentration of mind (*Śamathaḥ cittaikāgratālakṣṇaḥ samādhiḥ*) and *Vipaśyanā* as the knowledge which reveals the things as they are (*Vipaśyanā yathābhūtaparijñānasvabhāva prajñā*), *Bodhic.*, p. 137.

6. *Prajñā*. The sixth *Pāramitā* is *Prajñā-pāramitā*, the climax of wisdom, which is said to incorporate the other five *pāramitās* within it.[1] 'The perfection of wisdom gets its name from its supreme excellence (*paramatvāt*).'[2] It is from this that all-knowledge of the Tathāgatas has come forth; they owe their Enlightenment to this perfection of wisdom.[3] The acquisition of this perfection brings about great advantages: "Māra and his hosts will be unable to harm those who take up this perfection of wisdom... A person who is devoted to this perfection of wisdom will certainly experience no fear, he will certainly never be stiff with fright... The Bodhisattva, the great being, who is trained in this lore will reach full enlightenment, will gain the gnosis of the all-knowing...."[4] It is the supreme and perfect knowledge in all its aspects—'the unobscured knowledge of all that is knowable.'[5] It is the knowledge of the true nature of things which is the knowledge of the Void (*Śūnyatā*).

Some important points of ethical significance emerge from the above discussion of the *pāramitās*. All virtues are taken to centre round the primary virtue of compassion which has the feeling of friendliness as its natural corrolary. In them is found a much advanced awareness of social emotions, so much so that the Mahāyānist writers do not mind even the transgression of some such observances which would otherwise be considered fundamental and crucial in a spiritual community. The ascetic tenor and rigour of early Buddhism comes to be softened to a great extent. Though, theoretically, Friendliness (*Maitrī*) was regarded as a virtue even in early Buddhism, the socialization of this virtue was to some extent hampered by an opposite ideal which decried too much mingling of the spiritual seeker with the worldly people as it would give birth to attachment and, so, bind him. The Mahāyāna sought to remove this contradiction by giving a new orientation to the conception of *Saṁsāra* and *Nirvāṇa* and pointing to the fact that Friendliness only leads to true selflessness. To love others is also of great individual advantage. Removal of anger and hatred, which naturally goes with the feeling of love for others, makes life

[1]*Bodhic*., p. 169; *Aṣṭ. Pr*., ed. Conze, p. 31.
[2]*Aṣṭ. Pr*., ed. Conze, p. 31.
[3]ibid., p. 27, p. 37.
[4]ibid., pp. 22-24.
[5]*Bbhū*., p. 146: *Sarvajñeyānāvaraṇajñānāya ca paramaduṣkarā*. The 'Prajñā-paṭalam' of the text deals with its diverse aspects.

happy and tension-free and brings serenity and composure in personality. Mahāyāna gave a new impetus to the socialization of this virtue by assigning over-riding importance to compassion. The altruism of Mahāyāna is further reflected in its doctrine of 'transfer of merit' which goes to even transform the nature of *Karman* which, originally, advocated non-sharability in the fruits of one's action. By placing before itself the ideal of 'liberation for all' as the supreme ideal, the Mahāyāna left the ideal of individual liberation far behind as the goal of spiritual exertion. However, the ascetic and individualistic role was not completely lost in Mahāyāna. The last two *pāramitās* are clearly individualistic in their connotation and implicate the necessity of isolation from the world and some sort of introversion. Without bringing about much change in the original metaphysical system, the Mahāyāna could build up a new supra-structure which was necessary with the growth of the teachings of the Master in the form of a popular religion. Har Dayal has rightly pointed out that the Mahāyāna tried to 'bridge the gap' that apparently lay between the community of the householders and the community of ascetic monks. He has spelled out his understanding of the *pāramitās* in the following words: "The early Mahayanists were perhaps proud of having combined the social virtues of a righteous layman—householder with the ascetic ideals of a meditative monk in this formula of the pāramitās. They thus bridged the gap that yawned between popular and monastic Buddhism."[1]

[1]Har Dayal, *Bodhisattva Doctrine*, p. 170.

CHAPTER 6

Beyond Good and Evil

Notion of yet Another Dharma-cakra-pravartana

The Mahāyāna brought about radical change in the orientation and form of Buddhism. The desire to trace the emergent form to the Master himself prompted its followers to advocate the notion of not one but two *Dharma-cakra-pravartanas.* The first constituted the Hīnayāna while the second one gave birth to Mahāyāna. The latter theorized that their doctrines embodied the real spirit of the Tathāgata's teachings and were, in fact, directed to more enlightened, and spiritually advanced, among his disciples. The Mahāyānic philosophical and doctrinal tenets were imbued with serious implications which, when these were stretched further in due course of time, got crystallized into an entirely new form generally designated as the Vajrayāna or Tantrayāna phase of Buddhism.[1] Because of the mysterious and secret nature of its teachings, meant for only a few instructed or initiated individuals, the appellation of 'Esoteric Buddhism' or 'Buddhist Esoterism' is also used for it. In due course of time it evolved into a number of sub-schools. The new set of teachings had, apparently, such fundamental deviations from the original teachings of the Master, both in theory and practice, that some theorisation was needed if it were to be considered originally springing from Buddha himself. It was, therefore, proclaimed that this esoteric set of teachings (*mantranaya*) was imparted by Buddha, at his third *Dharma-cakra-pravartana*, to a separate band of disciples at Śrīdhānya, as he had earlier taught the Mahāyāna (*prajñāpāramitānaya*) at Gṛdhrakūṭa.[2]

[1]For a historical treatment of the origin and growth of the Buddhist Tantra see generally, Benoytosh Bhattacharya, *Introduction to Buddhist Esoterism*, chs. II, III-IV; S.B. Dasgupta, *An Introduction to Tantric Buddhism*, ch. III; Govind Chandra Pandey, *BDVI*, ch. XII; P.C. Bagchi, 'Evolution of the Tantras' in *The Cultural Heritage of India*, IV, ch. XII; L.M. Joshi, op. cit., ch. X; Alex Wayman, *The Buddhist Tantras*, Introduction.

[2]*Sekoddeśaṭīkā*, pp. 2-4: *Śrīdhānye niyatamantranaya deśanāsthāne* . . . It con-

The Buddhist Tantra texts, as a distinct class of literature and as an expression of a distinct mode of spiritual seeking (*sādhanā*), date from the seventh century. Henceforth, roughly speaking for three succeeding centuries, till its disappearance from the Indian scene, Buddhism prevailed in the Tantric form, growing into diverse sub-sects and developing within it complex rituals and imposing pantheon. Though it had a number of similarities with the Brahmanical Tantra, its distinctive character cannot be gainsaid. Its philosophical foundation was supplied by the doctrinal views of the Mādhyamika and Yogācāra systems of the Mahāyāna as influenced by the idealistic monism of the *Upaniṣads*. As Dasgupta has observed, '. . . the metaphysical fragments, found in the different Tantric literature, are nothing but indistinct echoes of these schools of Mahāyāna philosophy . . .'[1] To this were added a theology and ritualistic practices which constitute the common repertoire of Tantricism as a whole. In order that only the properly initiated individuals have an access to the subtle doctrine contained in them, the texts use a mystifying language which is traditionally called 'saṁdhā-bhāṣā.'[2]

tains a quotation from another Tantra text which states: *Gṛdhrakūṭe yathāśāstaḥ prajñāpāramitānaye, Tathā mantranaye proktā Śrīdhānye dharmadeśanā.*

This tradition is preserved in the Tibetan sources. Buston observes that Buddha preached the Kālacakra system (a sub-school of Tantrayāna) in the year of his Enlightenment; he rejects the view held by other Tibetan authors that he preached it in his 80th year i.e., the year of his *Parinirvāṇa*, see *Blue Annals*, II, p. 754, n. 1. Yet another Tibetan authority speaks of three *Dharma-cakra-pravartanas* by Buddha: the first in the year of Enlightenment at Ṛṣipattana, the second in the 13th year of Enlightenment at Gṛdhrakūṭa where he taught Mahāyāna, and the third in the 16th year of Enlightenment at Śrīdhānyakaṭaka where he imparted the tenets of Mantrayāna. See, Rahul Samkrityayan, *Purātattva Nibandhāvalī*, p. 113, n. 3.

[1]Dasgupta, op. cit., p. 16.

[2]Mahamabhopadhyaya H.P. Shastri rendered the term as 'Saṁdhyā-bhāṣā,' the twilight language' (*ālo-āndhāri bhāṣā*) *Bauddhagāna O Dohā* (Bengali), p. 8 i.e. a language which is slightly clear and slightly not clear and which has behind the apparent expression some hidden meaning. Writing in *Indian Historical Quarterly* (1928, pp. 287 ff) a Vidhusekhar Shastri put forth a large number of facts to suggest rejection of this interpretation. He sought to interpret the term as *abhiprāyika-vacana* or *neyārtha-vacana*, 'intentional speech,' 'intended to imply or suggest something different from what is expressed by the words.' P.C. Bagchi (*Studies in the Tantras*, p. 27) is in concordance with this view. L.M. Joshi (op. cit., p. 208, fn. 10) too takes 'Saṁdhyā bhāṣā' to be a wrong pronunciation and its translation as 'the twilight language' a wrong translation. F. Edgerton

Vajra and Sahaja

The Tantric Buddhism in general is called Vajrayāna, the 'adamantine path.' *Vajra* is the term used for the ultimate reality and so called because of its adamantine character. It can be clearly seen that *Vajra* stands for the same notion as was represented by the notion of of *Śūnyatā* under the Mahāyānic ideology. The *Advaya-vajra-saṁgraha* explicitly says that it is *Śūnyatā*, which is firm, substantial, indivisible and impenetrable, incapable of being burnt and indestructible, that is called *Vajra*.[1] Realisation of *Vajra* is, thus, the realisation of the void-nature of all things, both the self and not-self. It is the realisation of the highest wisdom (*prajñā*) which denotes the state of transcendence of all dualities, all distinctions of subjectivity and objectivity. The Yogācārins had already conceived it as pure consciousness (*vijñapti-mātratā*) which reduced all phenomena to mere illusion and considered Mind as the only reality. In Mahāyāna, the *Dharmakāya* of Buddha was considered to be constituted by *Śūnyatā*-essence and represented a monistic conception of Reality. In Tantric Buddhism, the same idea was concretized in the conception of *Vajra-sattva*. Apart from

(*Buddhist Hybrid Sanskrit Dictionary*) takes *saṁdhā* as "esoteric meaning" and, subsequently, *saṁdhābhāṣita* as "expressed with esoteric meaning." Alex Wayman has the following to say: "Of course, the words *saṁdhi*, *saṁdha* and *saṁdhyā* can all be used for "twilight." While the word *saṁdhyā* is especially used in this meaning, it is invalid to reject it in "*saṁdhā bhāṣā*" arguing that *saṁdhi* or *saṁdhā* are the forms rather than *saṁdhyā*. There is little doubt from Candrakirti's and Tson-kha-pa's remarks that Mahamahopadhyaya H.P. Sastri was right in translating the term as "twilight language" . . . The term *saṁdhā-bhāṣā* ("twilight language") aptly refers to the ambiguity, contradiction, or paradox of the moment between darkness and light . . . The twilights symbolized the sensitive points in the temporal flow when spiritual victory was possible. A special vocabulary was created to refer to these critical points and called in the Buddhist Tantras "twilight language." Alex Wayman, *The Buddhist Tantras*, pp. 129-30. For some illustrations of this language, see ibid., pp. 131-32. Prof. G.C. Pande, (*BDVI*, p. 465) too writes it as '*saṁdhyā-bhāṣā*' and draws attention to the reference of *abhisandhiviniścaya* (i.e. a meaning different from what is expressed in words) in the *Abhidharmasamuccaya* of Asaṅga where an example of such a language is also given. According to Pande, it clearly refers to the '*saṁdhyā-bhāṣā*' of the later day Tantrikas and *Siddhas*. For a detailed discussion of *Sandhabhāṣā* see also Agehananda Bharati, *The Tantric Tradition*, ch. 6.

[1]*Advaya-vajra-saṁgraha*, p. 37.
Dṛḍhaṁ sāraṁ asauśīryam acchedyābhedalakṣaṇam
Adāhi avināśi ca śūnyatā vajramucyate

Nirmāṇakāya, *Saṁbhogakāya* and *Dharmakāya*, another body of Buddha came to be conceived which was called *Vajrakāya*, his adamantine body. *Vajrasattva* is understood as embodying the identity of *Śūnyatā* and *Jñānamātratā* (pure consciousness).[1] It is the *Śūnyatā*-essence, transcends all imagination, is omniscient and embodies pure wisdom.[2] The Being, which has no origination and destruction, is all-good, the soul-substance of all, *Vajrasattva* includes in him all the static and the dynamic.[3]

The *Vajrasattva* embodies not only *Śūnyatā* or *Prajñā* but *Karuṇā* also. In Vajrayāna, Reality is non-dual (*advaya*), constituted of *Śūnyatā* and *Karuṇā* in unity. Together they constitute what is called *Bodhicitta* or Bodhi-mind.[4] *Karuṇā* is called *Upāya* (Means) and, following the general Tantric ideology, *Prajñā* (wisdom) and *Upāya* (Means) are symbolized as the female and male energy respectively—which are inseparable (whence Reality called *Advaya* and *Yuganaddha*). The Mahāyāna had laid equal emphasis on *Śūnyatā* or *Prajñā* and *Karuṇā*; they are the two legs on which Mahāyāna stands. The same spirit or unity of the two is expressed in one of the *dohās* of Sarahapāda wherein he declares: "He who casts aside *Karuṇā* and adheres to *Śūnyatā* alone can never have access to the right path; likewise, he who concentrates on *Karuṇā* alone cannot attain salvation even in thousand births; but, he who is able to mingle *Śūnyatā* with *Karuṇā* remains neither in *bhava* (*saṁsāra*) nor in *nirvāṇa*."[5] *Prajñopāya* stands for complete mixture of wisdom and compassion like the mixture of water and milk, thus meaning state of non-duality.[6] The *Siddhas* use

[1]ibid., p. 24:
Vajreṇa śūnyatā proktā sattvena jñānamātratā
Tādātmyam anayoḥ siddhaṁ vajra-sattva svabhāvataḥ.
[2]*Prajñopāyaviniścayasiddhi*, ch. III, verse 9.
[3]*Jñāna-siddhi*, p. 84.
[4]*Guhyasamāja Tantra*, p. 153:
Anādinidhanaṁ śāntaṁ bhāvābhāvakṣayaṁ vibhum
Śūnyatākaruṇābhinnaṁ bodhicittaṁ iti smṛtam
[5]*Dohā* of Sarahapāda P.C. Bagchi's edition, p. 29:
Karuṇā chhaḍḍi jo suṇṇahi laggu
Naū so pāvai uttima maggu
Ahavā karuṇā kevala bhāvaī
Jamma-sahassahi mokkha na pāvaī
Suṇṇa karuṇā jai jouṇa sakkai
Nau bhave ṇau ṇivvāṇe thakkai
[6]See *Prajñopāya-viniścaya-siddhi*, p. 5.

the boat-analogy to express compassion, which carries all beings to the other shore.[1] This *Bodhicitta* is said to be 'without beginning, without death, quiescent, free from the notions of 'is' and 'is not', free from thought construction, without support and immutable.'[2] Because of its two constituents, *Prajñā* (= *Śūnyatā*) and *Upāya* (=*Karuṇā*), it is called *Prajñopāya*; both these are absolute and without support and are merged into one another so inseparably, as one sky merges into another sky.[3] The *Bodhicitta*, 'non-dual' and 'supreme', is the same as *Śrī Vajrasattva* and *Saṁbuddha.*[4] As Absolute it is neither dual nor non-dual and is self-experienceable (*pratyātmavedya*).[5]

In Sahajayāna, which is an offshoot of *Vajrayāna*, the *advaya* or *yuganadha* is expressad by the *Siddhas* as *sahaja* (the innate) or *samarasa* (the sameness). It is the commingling of the *Prajñā* and *Upāya.* In this state all positive and negative aspects of mind vanish, mind becomes entirely pure and free from both *bhāva* (existence) and *abhāva* (non-existence).[6] In this *samarasa* or *sahaja* state, all bondage is completely annihilated and everything becomes the same; there remains neither the Śūdra nor the Brāhmaṇa.[7] One who has steadied his mind in *samarasa* or *sahaja*, says a *dohā* of Kāṇa-pāda, becomes at once perfect and free from disease and death.[8] With the rise of wonderful *sahaja*-realisation in the sky of mind, says Bhusuka-pāda, all illusions

[1]*Caryā* no. 8.
[2]*Citta-viśuddhi-prakaraṇa*, verse 1.
[3]*Prajñopāya-viniścaya-siddhi*, ch. IV, verse 11:
Nirālambapade prajñā nirālambha mahākṛpā
Ekībhūta dhiyā sārdhaṁ gagane gaganaṁ yathā
[4]ibid., ch. IV, verse 17:
Etadvyamityuktaṁ bodhicittaṁ idaṁ param
Vajraṁ Śrīvajrasattvaṁ ca Saṁbuddha bodhireva ca.
[5]ibid. ch. I, verse 20:
Na dvayaṁ nādvayaṁ śāntaṁ śivaṁ sarvatra saṁsthitaṁ
Pratyātmavedyamacalaṁ prajñopāyamanākulam
[6]*Dohā* of Tillopada, no. 11 Bagchi's edition:
jahi jāi citta tahi suṇahu acitta
samarasa (ṇimmala bhāvābhāva-rahia)
[7]*Dohā* of Saraha, no. 46:
javve maṇa atthamaṇa jāi taṇu tuṭṭai vandhana
tavve samarasa sahaje vajjai ṇau sudda na vamhaṇa.
[8]*Dohā* no. 19:
sahaje ṇiccala jeṇa kia samarase ṇiamaṇa rāa
siddha so puṇa takkhaṇe ṇau jarāmaraṇa sa bhāa

disappear and mind gets flooded with the feeling of bliss; one becomes what one naturally is.[1]

Mahāsukha as the Final Goal

From the very beginning, the Buddhists had conceived *Nirvāṇa*, the term for the ultimate goal of realization, both as negative and positive entity.[2] A realized individual was supposed to be enjoying the 'Bliss of Liberation' (*vimuttisukha*).[3] It is this aspect of *Nirvāṇa* that is emphasized in the *Vajrayāna;* the ultimate Reality is taken to be of the nature of Great Bliss (*mahāsukha*), as perfect wisdom without bliss is considered an impossibility.[4] *Mahāsukha* is the same as the Lord *Vajrasattva;* it is the same as the non-dual state of *Prajñā* and *Upāya* (*Prajñopāya*).[5] As such, in the Tantric theology Vārāhī, the Supreme Goddess, representing Śūnyatā, is represented as being in close embracement of the Lord Mahāsaukhya; similarly, the Goddess Nairātmā is represented as tightly embracing the Lord Heruka.[6] However, as Ultimate Reality or the Absolute, *Mahāsukha* has the essential nature of transcendence; it lies beyond the grasp of all thought-constructions (*vikalpa*), both negative and positive, and is indescribable and self-experienceable.[7]

[1]*Caryā* 30:
uittā gaaṇa mānjhe adabhūā
pekhare Bhusuka sahaja sarūā
jāsu sunante tuṭṭai indiāla
nihue ṇia mana dea ulāla
Caryā 37:
anubhava sahaja mā bhola re jāi
caukoṭṭivimukā jaiso taiso hoi
jaisaṇe ichalesi taisana ācha
sahaja pathaka joi bhānti nahi vāsa.

[2]Misra, *The Age of Vinaya*, pp. 73-74.

[3]See *Mv.*, p.3: *Tena samayena Buddho bhagavā Uruvelāyaṁ viharati . . . vimutti-sukhapaṭisaṁvedī.*

[4]*Advaya-vajra-saṁgraha*, p. 50:
Sukhābhāve na bodhiḥ syāt matā yā sukharūpiṇī.
Prajñopāya-viniścaya-siddhi, p. 6:
Anantasukharūpatvāt Śrī Mahāsukhasaṁjñitam.

[5]ibid.: *Vajrasattvaṁ namaskṛtya prajñopāya-svarūpiṇam*
Mahāsukhadvayam vakṣye vastu-tattvaṁ samāsataḥ

[6]*Sādhanamālā*, II, p. 491: *Hevajra Tantra*, pt. I, p. 110.

[7]See *Jñāna-siddhi*, VII. 1; ibid., VII 3; *Dohā* of Sarahapada, no. 32; in one of

Theory and Practice

Based primarily on Mahāyānic ideological and philosophical tenets, the Buddhist Tantra seeks to present a non-dualistic view of cosmos and life. The final aim of the spiritual seeker is to realise the unity of all life and free his mind from all thought-constructions which derive from a dualistic approach to things. The Ultimate Reality was conceived as entire and complete, and so inseparable, union of wisdom (*Prajñā* or *Śūnyatā*) and compassion (*Karuṇā*) which, as Lord Supreme, was concretized in the form of *Vajrasattva*. The idea of *Śūnyatā* amounted to seeing the true nature of all the things 'as they are' (*Yathābhūtam*) and terminated all distinctions between *Saṁsāra* and *Nirvāṇa*. As external objects are nothing but projections of mind, the real task is to place it in its original nature which is a state of transcendence of all distinctions, dualities and discriminations. *Karuṇā* was equally emphasized and was conceived as *Upāya* (Means) through which the seeker could reach the other shore. We have discussed earlier how in Mahāyāna all activities of a Bodhisattva were supposed to bear the stamp of *Karuṇā*, to the extent of even allowing him to deviate from the normal ethical path. The doctrine was adopted by the Tantra in its entirety. A *sādhaka* is ordained to be compassionate; he prays to the Buddhas and Bodhisattvas to postpone the attainment of their own *Nirvāṇa* for the benefit of all beings.[1] The *Ḍākārṇava* injuncts the *sādhaka* to meditate on compassion for beings who are in the bondage of the world[2] and Sarahapāda declares life to be absolutely meaningless if no good is done to others.[3] The importance of compassion is manifested even in the conception of the divinities of the

his *Dohās* (See *Dohakosa* of Saraha, ed. by Rahula Saṁkrityayana, p. 12) Saraha says the following:

Jahiṁ maṇa pavaṇa na sañcarai, ravi-sasi nāhi pavesa
Tahiṁ baḍha citta visama karu, Saraheṁ kahia uesa

and further:

Āi ṇa anta ṇa majjhatahi, ṇau bhava ṇau ṇivvāṇa
Ehu so paramamahāsuha, ṇau para ṇau appāṇa

[1]*Sādhanamālā*, II, p. 334.

[2]*Ḍākārṇava* ed. N.N. Chaudhari, p. 122:
loaṇa karuṇa bhavahu tumma
saala surāsura buddhahu jimma

[3]*Dohākośa*, ed. P.C. Bagchi, p. 23:
Para ūāra ṇa kiaū atthi ṇa dīau dāna
Ehu saṁsāre kavaṇa phalu varu chuḍḍahu appāṇa

Tantric pantheon who possess it as an inherent attribute. Thus, Mañjuśrī is depicted as having compassion for the whole world and being intent on doing good to all beings and the goddess Vārāhī as engrossed in the emotion of universal compassion.[1] *Prajñā* and *Karuṇā*, however, constitute a single entity (*advaya*; *yuganaddha*), whence *prajñopāya* is used as the term expressing the Ultimate Reality.

In accordance with the general Tantric ideology, the Buddhist Tantras, too, symbolically express the union of *Prajñā* and *Karuṇā* as sexual union, the former representing the female element and the latter male element. The worship of female energy (*śakti*) constitutes an essential part in Tantricism as a whole including the Buddhist Tantra.[2] Symbolically, the female energy is also called '*Yoginī*', and '*Mudrā*' '*Vajrī*', '*Bhagavatī*', '*Vidyā*', etc. Both the elements have to be given equal emphasis in *sādhanā* as the one does not exist separately from the other; in *Mahāsukha*, each is the co-efficient of the other. The sex-analogy of the union of *Prajñā* and *Karuṇā* led to the idea that the *sādhaka* can realise the goal only with the help of a female partner or *yoginī;* liberation cannot be attained without a female partner.[3] It is in the blissful embrace of a young girl that a Vajrayānist *yogin* finds *Nirvāṇa.*[4] The Buddhist *Siddhas* generally mention *Ḍombī*, a low caste woman, as the female partner with a view to underlining their transcendence of class and caste distinctions. In one of the songs Kāṇhapāda declares that he has married a *Ḍombī* and has stopped further birth and goes on to add that whoever has once lived with her can never leave her even for a moment and is maddened by the bliss of *Sahaja.*[5]

[1]See S.B. Dasgupta, op. cit., p. 56 and ibid., fn. 2-3.

[2]Some scholars think that the use of the term *śakti* in the sense in which it is used in the Brahmanical Tantra is not correct. See, for example, D.L. Snellgrove (ed. and tr.) *Hevajra Tantra*, pt. I, p. 44 and Lama Anagarika Govind, *Foundations of Tibetan Mysticism*, pp. 96-98. The latter concludes his account by saying that 'the concept of Śakti has no place in Buddhism.'

The majority of scholars, however, takes it to be a common characteristic of all versions of Tantra. See Poussin in *ERE*, XII, p. 193; B. Bhattacharya, op. cit., p. 53; S.B. Dasgupta, op. cit., pp. 3-4; Gopinath Kaviraj, *Bhāratīya Saṁskriti Aur Sādhanā*, pt. I, p. 534; Agehananda Bharati, *The Tantric Tradition*, pp. 200ff. L.M. Joshi, op. cit., pp. 353ff: G.C. Pande, *BDVI*, p. 466.

[3]*Guhyasamāja Tantra*, pp. 161ff: *Hevajra Tantra*, pt. I, p. 94.

[4]*Hevajra Tantra*, pt. I, pp. 90, 96.

[5]*Caryā* no. 19:
Ḍombi vivahiā ahāriu jāma
Jautuke kia āṇutu dhāma

In such a worship of female energy, all social norms are done away with and very often the texts use a language which is filthy and vulgar. The fact has evoked very harsh and hostile comments on Tantrism by several scholars. While Kern characterizes Tantrism, both Brahmanical and Buddhist, as 'a popularised and, at the same time, degraded form of yoga' in which 'the objects are commonly of a coarser character, and the practices partly more childish, partly more revolting',[1] Dr. Bhattacharya condemns the Tantras as examples of 'the worst immorality and sin'.[2] But, as has been maintained by several competent scholars of Tantra, the Tantra texts are not to be read literally as they are written in esoteric language, the real import of which is revealed only to the properly initiated ones. Commenting on the language of the Tantras, Lama Govind observes the following: "This symbolic language is not only a protection against the profanation of the sacred through intellectual curiosity and misuse of yogic methods and psychic forces by the ignorant or uninitiated, but has its origin mainly in the fact that everyday language is incapable of expressing the highest experiences of the spirit . . ."[3] According to Eliade *sandhābhāṣā* has a double purpose: to camouflage the doctrine against the non-initiate, and to 'project the yogi into the "paradoxical situation" indispensable for his spiritual training.'[4] The Tantra is a practical religion which is based on a mystical philosophy. It is because of this that Tantrism underlines the necessity of a competent *guru*, who alone can reveal to the *sādhaka* the hidden meaning of the apparently revolting and vulgar words. When Tantra says that lust can be crushed by lust,[5] it does not

Ahaṇisi surata-pasaṅge jāa
Joiṇiajāle raaṇi pohāa
Ḍombiera saṅge jo joi ratto
Khaṇai na chāṇaa sahaja unmatto
Also Kāṇha-pāda in *Caryā* no. 10:
Ālo ḍombi toe sama karibo saṅga
Nighina Kāṇha kāpāli joi laṅga

[1]H. Kern, *Manual of Indian Buddhism*, p. 133.

[2]B. Bhattacharya in *Sādhanamālā*, II, Introduction, p. XXII: See also his *Introduction to Esoteric Buddhism*, Preface where he calls Tantrism a 'disease.' For similar harsh views see also, Elliot, *Hinduism and Buddhism*, II, p. 124; M. Winternitz, *History of Indian Literature*, II, pp. 330-39.

[3]*Foundations of Tibetan Mysticism*, p. 53.

[4]Quoted by Agehananda Bharati in The *Tantric Tradition*, pp. 172-73.

[5]*Guhyasamāja Tantra*, pp. 26-27; *Citta-viśuddhi-prakaraṇa*, verses 36, 37, 38.

advocate the philosophy of sex-indulgence. Not only that these sex-practices were not intended for the untrained novices, the Tantric texts have given symbolic meanings to all the objects involved in the act. They have constructed a distinct system of *yoga* which is simultaneously mystical yet practical.[1] According to Dr. Giuseppe Tucci, 'the Tantras contain one of the highest expressions of Indian mysticism, which may appear to us rather strange in its outward form because we do not understand the symbolical language in which they are written.'[2] It is, however, not gainsaying the fact that these practices brought about a lot of degeneration and corruption in Buddhism and made it liable to a general attack and criticism by the people.

The significance that is assigned to *mantras* and various practical means[3] is well known. In Tantra, the body is considered the locus of all truth.[4] Body is the microcosm which contains within it the whole universe; all the elements of the universe are present in it. As such, body itself has to be converted into the medium through which the truth has to be realized. This notion led the Tantric thinkers to do a physiological analysis of the nerves etc., and formulate the theory of different *cakras* or 'lotuses' as present in the body. On the basis of this analysis a practical *yoga* system was evolved, the nature or which was essentially esoteric and understandable only under the guidance of a competent teacher (*guru*), well adept in the secrets of the Tantric path. For the pupil, having a desire to delve deep into the mysteries of the Tantra *yoga*, *guru* is Lord himself, an embodiment of wisdom and Great Bliss, the ultimate refuge.[5] A reviler of his preceptor, says the *Guhyasamāja-tantra*, can never be successful in his spiritual efforts.[6] A new importance came to be attached to body under the theory that it is the medium of realisation. Starting with the conviction that any

[1]See Dasgupta, op. cit., pp. 160ff; G.C. Pande, *BDVI*, pp. 469ff; Alex Wayman, *The Buddhist Tantras*, Section II and III; F.D. Lessing and A. Wayman, *Introduction to the Buddhist Tantric Systems*, chs. IV-VIII.

[2]*Journal of the Asiatic Society of Bengal*, XXVI, 1930, p. 128.

[3]Ch. 18 of the *Guhyasamāja Tantra* gives a four-fold classification of *Vajra-yoga*, viz., *Sevā*, *Upasādhana*, *Sādhana* and *Mahāsādhana*.

[4]Sarahapāda says:
Paṇḍia saala sattha bakhāṇia
Dehahiṁ Buddha basanta ṇa jāṇia

[5]*Sekoddeśa-ṭīkā*, p. 24.

[6]*Guhyasamāja-tantra*, p. 20:
Ācāryanindanaparā naiva siddhyanti sādhane.

action done in conformity with *Prajñā* and *Upāya* would always be a wholesome action and that it is motive which determines the ethical or unethical nature of an action, the Tantra went on to advocate that no desires should be suppressed and all the wants of body need be fully satisfied without fear of accruing any sin.[1] Apparently, in complete disregard of accepted social and moral norms the injunction is given to indulge into grossly immoral acts.[2]

Essence of Tantric Ethics

Tantra expounds an extreme form of idealism which takes phenomena having no independent existence of their own and all things as mere projections of mind. It was derived therefrom that objects of the world *per se* are value—neutral and their moral or immoral nature depends on mind only. Even early Buddhist ethics was essentially intuitional wherein goodness or badness of an action was considered to be determined primarily by the motive behind it.[3] This notion was carried to its farthest extreme in Tantric ideology. The *citta-viśuddhi-prakaraṇa* states that since mind (*citta*) is the antecedent factor of all the *dharmas* and all physical actions follow from it, as such, mind (*citta*) alone can be considered the determinant of the ethical nature of an action;[4] a perfect individual, with his mind rooted in *Prajnā* and *Upāya*, can, therefore, never act unethically.[5] Actions of a perfect man transcend the scope of all popular norms of morality.

On the issue of virtue and vice, the *Jñāna-siddhi* of Indrabhūti seeks to present the Tantric viewpoint by doing an analysis of action as such.

[1]See *Guhyasamāja-tantra*, p. 27.

[2]For example, *Guhyasamāja-tantra*, pp. 20, 26, 102:
Prajñopāyaviniścaya-siddhi, p. 23.
It has been argued that such passages are meant to be a paradox and should not be taken literally. See Lama Angarika Govinda, *Foundations of Tibetan Mysticism*, pp. 100-102.

[3]See ch. II.

[4]*Citta-viśuddhi-prakaraṇa*, verse 10:
Manapūrvaṅgamā dharmā manaḥśreṣṭhā manojabāḥ.
Manasā hi prasannena bhāṣate vā karoti vā

[5]ibid., verses 11-13: The point is illustrated with the help of an example. An old man is directed by a slumbering monk to go to a place quickly who, so directed, because of rapidity of motion, has a fall and dies. Apparently, the monk is the cause of his death but since he had asked the old monk to go quickly to the particular place with a good motive, he has committed no sin. Compare similar examples in earlier texts. See Miśra, *The Age of Vinaya*, p. 83.

It points to the existence of three elements, *kāya* (body), *vāk* (speech) and *citta* (mind), in an action and further states that without mind neither body nor speech has the power to operate; therefore, mind alone is responsible for the goodness or badness of an action.[1] What, then, can be taken as the measuring-yard for the assessment of the nature of an action? The criterion that is recommended is that an action done with the motive of doing good to the world would be a good action and action propelled by a contrary motive would be a bad action.[2]

The worldly objects are nothing but thought-constructs. In reality, the world is void. The concepts of virtue (*puṇya*) or sin (*pāpa*), therefore, are artificially constructed concepts having no real basis. Tillopāda declares, "I am void, the world is void, all the three worlds are void; as such in pure *Sahaja* there is neither sin nor virtue."[3]

In the journey of Buddhism from its early phase upto the Tantrayānic phase, the changes in ethical outlook can be, to some extent, accounted by the changes in the conception of relationship between mind and the world. In early Buddhism the focus of attention is an individuating and activating mind which is also conceived as different from matter. There, the material world is taken to be a corrupting force and, therefore, stress is laid on practice of the detachment of mind from the worldly objects. In this process, negative virtues become an aid in spiritual seeking; not-wishing, not-acting, not-wanting become the goals to be pursued. But, when Mahāyāna came to conceive the world itself to be projection of mind, such negative virtues ceased to be adequate. In the new framework, positive virtues became essential which were required to strengthen mind so that it could interfere in the world in an effective manner. The ultimate goal was conceived both ways: on the one hand, the ultimate goal was considered to be the attainment of mental quietude; on the other hand, it was propounded that everything remains as it is but understanding of it changes. The popular version, however, was that it resulted in the

[1] *Jñāna-siddhi*, ch. IX, verses 6-7.
[2] *Jñāna-siddhi*, ch. IX, verse 8:
Hitārthaṁ yad bhavet karma sarvaṁ saccaritaṁ bhavet
Viparyātapuṇyam tat pravadanti jinottamāḥ.
[3] *Dohā* no. 34:
Hau suṇṇa jagu suṇṇa tihu (na) suṇṇa
(Nimmala sahaja ṇa pāpa na puṇṇa).

creation of a blissful world. Vajrayāna takes one step further from the Mahāyānic standpoint. Once it is accepted that mind is an active power, and original power, how is it possible that there can be evil in mind? If world is the projection of mind, obviously it can only be an illusion. The goal is to make this power (mind) full and free. It can be achieved only when the *sādhaka* has learnt to leave the habit of looking outwards and has replaced his empirical-individual consciousness by universal consciousness. In the latter state of consciousness, his mind becomes one with reality and is freed from all arbitrary discriminations.

This understanding of mind led to the difference in method that was to be observed for spiritual attainment. Mahāyāna had emphasized the observance of *pàramitās* which stand for various positive virtues which bring about perfection in the seeker. Vajrayāna changed the shift and stated that evil is not removed by merely neglecting the desires for various pleasures or by suppressing them. What we call evil is only a perverted form of the original nature of mind. What is, therefore, required is only the transmutation of mind-*parāvṛtti* as the *Mahāyānasūtrālaṅkāra* of Asaṅga had advocated. With the transmutation of mind the colouring of the external object gets transformed; for example, the erotic thing become aesthetic and so on. According to Vajrayāna, morality lies not in what things you look at but how you look at them.

Mind generally appears to be contaniing within it the duality of knowledge and action. Vajrayāna seeks to erase completely all duality in mind. All symbols in Vajrayāna pertain to the seeking of getting unity in duality. *Mantra*-energy or female-energy all lead to it. The ultimate ethico-spiritual goal is to go beyond both good and evil. The attempt of Sahajayāna is to catch the original spontaneity of mind; that is why it becomes antinomian in its degenerated form.

APPENDIX I

Logical and Scientific Method in Early Buddhist Texts*

By rejecting animism and ritualism and emphasizing a rational outlook which treats reality as a causally and functionally determined system of plural synergies (*saṁskāras*), the emergence of Buddhism marks an important event in the history of Indian thought. The most distinctive feature of Buddhist ethics is its freedom from theism, which leaves room for rationalism and rules out submission to some superhuman power controlling the world-process. Prior to the advent of Buddhism even the *Upaniṣads* were not completely free from theistic influence in their speculations. It is proposed here to point to the Buddhist contribution to the growth of scientific outlook and methodology in India.

Buddha laid much emphasis on experience. He declares that like a friend and well-wisher he can show one only the path leading to the *summum bonum*; the probability of its attainment is entirely dependent upon the personal capacity of the way-farer.[1] Buddha refuses to accept anything which is beyond experience.[2] But what is amenable to experience has, according to him, two aspects—that which can be objectively experienced and that which can only be "transcendentally" experienced. In other words, reality has two aspects, phenomenal and absolute. Phenomenal reality can be objectively experienced and verbally communicated. Ultimate or absolute reality, on the other hand, cannot be so communicated. *Paññā* or knowledge of a Buddha

*Published earlier in the *Journal of the Royal Asiatic Society*, 1968, 1 & 2.

[1]In the Cūlahatthipadopamasutta of the *Majjhima Nikāya* Buddha compares the way-farer with a clever elephant-tracker who for himself treads the path and knows the truth: *The middle length sayings* trans. of the *Majjhima Nikāya PTS* edition, I, p. 47: "Dhamma is well-taught by Lord . . . it is a come-and-see thing . . . to be understood individually by the wise."

[2]This attitude is well exemplified in regard to what have been termed "avyā-kata" questions.

is intuitive and synoptic, as he himself practically realizes (*sayaṁ abhiññā*), for the ultimate truth is beyond logic (*atakko*).[1] It is in view of the two divisions of reality that Buddhism is at once positivistic and mystical. In a sense, Wittgenstein was only repeating Buddha when he wrote the famous last sentence of the *Tractatus*: "Whereof one cannot speak, thereof one must be silent."[2]

Let us see how the Buddhist scriptures reason and view logical reasoning. From the Buddhist scriptures it is quite apparent that the use of an intellectual and logical method was already known for some time. Two very old terms for logic, *hetu* (condition) and *naya* (method), which practically stand for all reasoned thinking in the Buddhist and Jaina scriptures,[3] occur in the *Nikāyas*. For example, in a passage of the *Dīgha Nikāya* certain matters are said to be "not in the sphere of 'takka'."[4] In a passage of the *Aṅguttara Nikāya*, Buddha is said to have considered tradition, reasoning, and fancy not to be any criteria for the assessment of a religious doctrine.[5] K.N. Jayatilleke believes[6] that in this context the term *hetu* has not only the earlier Upaniṣadic meaning of just "ground" but "epistemological ground" (*pramāṇa*). *Takkapariyāhataṁ* (overcome by reasoning) and *vīmaṁsānucaritaṁ* (addicted to investigation) are two terms often used to disqualify a religious preacher or thinker.[7] These passages would suggest a Buddhist disbelief in logical reasoning and its validity as a means of knowledge.[8]

This, however, does not appear to be a correct conclusion. What is rejected here is certainly not the logical method or its validity but a vicious and unnecessary dialectic and an extreme application of it to transcendental matters. Such a conclusion is corroborated by the

[1]*Mahāvagga*, Nālandā ed., Nālandā-Devanāgarī-Pāli series, Pāli Publication Board, Bihar Government; henceforth abbreviated as Nālanda ed., p. 11.

[2]Ludwig, Wittgenstein, *Tractatus logico-philosophicus*, sixth impression, 1955, p. 189.

[3]S.C. Vidyabhusana, *History of the Mediaeval School of Indian Logic*, p. 4.

[4]*Dīgha Nikāya* Nālanda ed., I, p. 16; also pp. 20, 22, 27. Prof. Rhys Davids translates *takka* as "logic," see *Dialogues of the Buddha*, trans. of the *Dīgha Nikāya*, *SBB*, Series, I, pp. 28-29.

[5]*Aṅguttara Nikāya*, Nālanda ed., I, p. 176.

[6]K.N. Jayatilleke, *Early Buddhist Theory of Knowledge*, p. 206.

[7]See e.g. *Dīgha Nikāya*, Nālanda ed., I. 16; *Majjhima Nikāya*, Nālanda, ed., I, 96; ibid., II, p. 219.

[8]See e.g. S.C. Vidyabhusana, op. cit., p. 59.

general prevalence of the logical and intellectual method in the Suttas. "In the Suttas no sentence occurs oftener than 'Taṁ kissa hetu?' 'What is the reason of that?'."[1] This spirit of reasoned inquiry is often seen in many instances from Buddha's own conduct and admonitions to his followers. In the Brahmajālasutta of the *Dīgha Nikāyā*, for example, he advises monks not to get angry or pleased if others belittle or applaud the Buddha, the Dhamma, or the Saṅgha; else they would not be able to judge the truth of what the others say. They should, however, comment critically on such statements by saying, "For this or that reason, this is not the fact, that is not so, such a thing does not exist among us, is not in us" or "For this or that reason this is the fact . . .," etc.[2] It is noteworthy in this connection that the word *pramāṇa* which is so frequent in the later logical texts of India occurs in the *Piṭakas* only in the sense of "measurements"[3] and not as an indispensable logical term.

Buddhism is a pragmatic religion. De la Vallée Poussin says "nous avons défini l'ancienne dogmatique comme une doctrine essentiellement 'Pragmatique . . .' ".[4] It is at the same time empirical and rational. This has led the Buddhists to found a system of psychology and logic with a view to understanding experience through analysis and objectification.

The method of reasoning is obviously analytical. The atmosphere of the age required the preacher of a doctrine to be critical and only then could he hope to make any impact on the audience. In a passage of the *Majjhima Nikāya* Buddha himself claims to be an "analyst" and not a dogmatist who gives categorical statements (*Vibhajjavādo . . . ahaṁ . . . nāhaṁ . . . ekaṁsavādo*).[5] It is because of the prominence of this method in the texts that in the Third Council the philosophy of Buddha was agreed to be nothing but *Vibhajjavāda* (analytical method); the word, however, does not occur in the *Tripiṭaka* itself. We quote below two passages from the *Vinaya* to illustrate the analytical method in the early Buddhist texts, which very often takes the form of a cate-

[1]*Encyclopedia of Religion and Ethics*, ed. Hastings, VIII, p. 132,

[2]*Dialogues of the Buddha*, trans. of the *Dīgha Nikāya* by T.W. Rhys Davids, I, p. 3.

[3]See e.g. *Pārājika*, Nālanda ed., 220; *Pācittiya*, Nālanda ed., p. 380; *The Book of the Discipline*, trans. of the *Vinaya Piṭaka* by I.B. Horner, I, p. 254; III, p. 286.

[4]De la Vallée Poussin, *Le Bouddhisme*, p. 129.

[5]*Majjhima*, Nālanda ed., II, p. 469.

chism; in the "Anattapariyāya" of the *Mahāvagga*, Buddha is said to have argued like this to show *anattā* in all the five *khandhas*:

"Body, monks, is not self. Now were this body self, monks, this body would not tend to sickness and one might get chance of saying in regard to body, 'Let body become thus for me, let body not become thus for me.' But, inasmuch, monks, as body is not self, therefore, body tends to sickness, and one does not get the chance of saying in regard to body, 'Let body become thus for me, let body not become thus for me;' " and so with the other khandhas.[1]

In the same context, the doctrine has been further argued like this:

"What do you think about this, monks? Is body permanent or impermanent?"

"Impermanent, Lord."

"But is that which is impermanent painful or pleasurable?"

"Painful, Lord."

"But, is it fit to consider that which is impermanent, painful, of a nature to change, as 'This is mine, this am I, this is myself'?".

"It is not, Lord."[2]

However, to be logical requires a number of things. For the first time in the history of Indian thought Buddhist texts reveal an explicit awareness of the concept of definition (*lakṣaṇa*), which is so necessary in the realm of logical studies. In logical formulation and discussions it is an essential thing that the exact meaning of each and every word used should be laid down in a precise manner. The authors of these early Buddhist texts made sincere efforts toward giving dictionary-type definitions of words. The Vibhaṅga of the *Vinaya* is replete with definitions which are in nature not very different from those given in modern dictionaries. In the Vibhaṅga of the seventy-ninth Pācittiya for the *bhikkhunīs* there occur two very interesting definitions: *Puriso nāma pattavīsativasso. Kumārako nāma appattavīsativasso.*[3] That is, a *purisa* is one who has passed the age of 20 while a *kumāraka* is one who has not passed this age-limit. It is as if here are being given the definitions of a "major" and a "minor" person. It would be interesting to note that in *Chamber's Twentieth Century Dictionary* one of the meanings of the word *major* is given as "a person of full age (21 years)." While giving the meaning of "crops" it has been said that

[1]*The Book of the Discipline*, trans. of the *Vinaya* by I.B. Horner, IV, p. 20.
[2]ibid. [3]*Pacittiya*, Nālanda ed., p. 463.

grains and pulses planted as food for the use of human being can be termed crops (*haritaṁ nāma pubbaṇṇaṁ aparaṇṇaṁ yaṁ manussānaṁ upabhogaparibhogaṁ ropimaṁ*).[1] Likewise, the definition of "kings" is given as those who are ruling heads over a certain territory along with the officers who govern the administration on behalf of them (*Rājāno nāma pathavyā rājā, padesarājā, maṇḍalikā antarabhogikā akkhadassā mahāmattā yo vā pana chejjabhejjaṁ karonta anusāsanti. Ete rājāno*).[2] It is needless to quote any more, for such quotations can be cited *ad lib.*

Another important feature of these texts is a tendency to classify the objects and topics under discussion. This tendency is prominent in the *Abhidhamma Piṭaka*. The antiquity of classification can be traced as far back as Vedic times[3] and its abundance in the first two *Piṭakas* also shows its prevalence even in the earliest stratum of the canon. This is to be observed not only with regard to the topics of abstract ideas; but also, when the material objects are discussed, their types have been enumerated in great detail to the full extent of available knowledge about them. The threefold classification of suffering (*dukkhatā*) into *dukkhadukkhatā*, *pariṇāmadukkhatā*, and *saṅkhāradukkhatā* touches all the conceivable aspects of it: suffering as a result of a direct contact of the senses with the sense-objects, that occasioned after the exhaustion of what is called pleasure, and that which comes into existence as the result of one's *saṁskāras*;[4] *taṇhā* or desire has also got a threefold classification, into *kāmataṇhā*, *bhavataṇhā*, and *vibhavataṇhā*.[5] The doctrine of *karman* is very important in Buddhism. *karman* reflects the impression of one's deeds due to produce some effect at a future date. The most frequent classification of action in the *Nikāyas* is into *kusala*, *akusala*, and *avyākata*, which lead one to *sukha*, *dukkha*, and "neither-*sukha*-nor-*dukkha*" respectively. One not less frequent classification is into four types.[6] Sometimes it is categorized as "good" and "bad" only.[7] A comprehensive enumeration of

[1]ibid., p. 363. [2]*Pārājika*, Nālanda ed., p. 57.

[3]cf. G.C. Pande, *Studies in the Origins of Buddhism*, p. 25ff.

[4]*The Book of the Kindred Sayings*, trans. of *Saṁyutta Nikāya*, *PTS* ed., IV, p. 173.

[5]*Mahāvagga*, Nālanda ed., p. 13.

[6]*Majjhima Nikāya*, Nālanda ed., II, p. 63; also *Gradual Sayings*, trans. of the *Aṅguttara Nikāya*, *PTS*, II, p. 238; *Dialogues of the Buddha*, trans. of the *Dīgha Nikāya*, III, p. 221.

[7]*Majjhima*, Nālanda ed., II, p. 375, III, p. 17, etc.

the types of different material objects is to be seen in a like manner. An immense increase in the knowledge of seed-stock and a careful study of the variation in the method of sowing had brought in a division of plants and agricultural products into five, those propagated from roots (*mūlabījaṁ*), propagated from stems (*khandhabījaṁ*), propagated from joints (*phaḷubījaṁ*), propagated from cuttings (*aggabījaṁ*), and lastly those propagated from seeds (*bījabījaṁ*). Among the agricultural products, turmeric, ginger, and garlic are listed in the *mūlabījaṁ* class, sugar-cane in the *phaḷubījaṁ* class, and grains and pulses under the last category; the other two classes of the five include different types of trees and grass.[1] Not only this, the Vibhaṅga of the second Pācittiya presents a classification of some social and economical notions and institutions (of *jāti*, *nāma*, *gotta*, *kamma*, and *sippa*) and of the "sex" (*liṅga*) of each into *hīna* ("low" or "bad") and *ukkaṭṭha* ("high" or "good"). Examples have also been given of each of the types.[2] One plainly discerns a treatment of the terms of the sort to be observed in modern dictionaries and encyclopaedias.

An obvious development of the logical method is demonstrated in the *Abhidhamma Piṭaka*, where it is more systematic and advanced. From the account of the Second Council in the 11th chapter of the *Cullavagga*, which refers to the first two *Piṭakas* but not to the third,[3] it is clear that in the beginning the *Abhidhamma Piṭaka* did not exist in the form of a text. This text seems to have come into existence on account of an advancement and refinement in the manner of expression of the doctrine. According to Buddhaghosa, the famous commentator, the prefix *abhi*-in the term *Abhidhamma* stands for "higher," giving it the meaning of "higher religion." Thus it does not refer to the contents of the text but only to the logical and more detailed mode of expression adopted here for the exposition of the doctrine.[4] The *Abhidhamma* is a text of scholastic reasoning, an outcome of incursive and profound discussions on various minute and technical issues of the preachings of the Master.

The *Abhidhamma Piṭaka* may be summarized as an attempt at dealing in an exhaustive manner with the following subjects: (*a*) terms

[1] *Pācittiya*, Nālanda ed., p. 55. cf. I.B. Horner, *The Book of the Discipline*, II, pp. 27-29.

[2] *Pācittiya*, Nālanda ed., pp. 10-12; *The Book of the Discipline*, II, pp. 173-78.

[3] *Cullavagga*, Nālanda ed., pp. 408-10.

[4] cf. A.C. Taylor in *JRAS*, 1894, pp. 560-66, and Rhys Davids, *SBE.*, pp. 36, 237; Winternitz, *History of Indian Literature*, II, p. 165, n. 1.

and their meaning, (*b*) propositions and their inter-relations, and (*c*) debates in a formalized manner.[1] Under (*a*) come *Dhamma-saṅgaṇi*, *Vibhaṅga*, and *Puggala-Paññatti*, i.e. the first two books and the fourth book of the *Abhidhamma Piṭaka*. Under (*b*) come an older set of sentences called *Mātikā* which, according to Mrs. Rhys Davids, "may be all we have left of what, in the first Piṭakas, is always put where we might put Abhidhamma, namely, after Vinaya and Sutta (or Dhamma, doctrine),"[2] *Yamaka*, *Dhātukathā*, and *Paṭṭhāna*. The section (*c*) is represented by the fifth book of the *Abhidhamma Piṭaka*, the *Kaṭhāvatthu*.

The first book of the *Abhidhamma Piṭaka*, *Dhammasaṅgaṇi*, presents an abundance of classification pertaining to body and mind. The very title of the book means "the enumeration of the Dhammas by way of questions and answers."[3] In the book is to be found a question like "katame dhammā kusala?" which is to be followed by a detailed answer to the question. The answer concludes with the expression "ime dhammā kusalā." This style has such a deep root in the mind of the author or the authors of the book that even when the answer speaks of only one factor, the concluding expression is the same as if it referred to more than one factor.[4] In the first division of the book, *Cittupādakaṇḍa*, are given the various classifications of consciousness.

The *Vibhaṅga* is a supplement to the first book, *Dhammasaṅgaṇi*. While *Dhammasaṅgaṇi* goes on to enumerate the *dhammas* and point out how many *khandhas*, *āyatanas*, *indriyas*, *jhānaṅgas*, etc., are contained in them, the *Vibhaṅga* seeks to probe into the exact limits of each of them in a way designed to facilitate the understanding of their mutual relationship with the *dhammas*. An example is quoted here dealing with the *vedanākkhandha* from among the five *khandhas*.[5]

Tattha katamo vedanākkhandha?

Yā Kāci vedanā atītānāgatāpaccuppannā ajjhattā vā bahiddhā vā oḷārikā vā sukhumā vā hīnā vā paṇītā vā yā dūre santike vā, tadekajjhaṁ abhisaññūhitvā abhisaṅkhipitvā—ayaṁ vuccati vedanākkhandho.

"What is *vedanākkhandha*? Whatever feeling is there, past, future,

[1]See Mrs. Rhys Davids, *The Birth of Indian Psychology and its Development in Buddhism*, pp. 356-57.

[2]ibid., 356.

[3]*Dhammasaṅgaṇi*, ed. P.V. Bapat and R.D. Vadekar, xi.

[4]e.g. 1050, 1084, 1087, 1421, 1437, 1440.

[5]*Vibhaṅga*, Nālanda ed., pp. 5-8.

present, belonging to the person or existing externally, gross or subtle, bad or good, distant or near, all of them taken together as a whole is called *vedanā*—the aggregate of matter."

Now, here past, future, and present are associated with the *khandha* under discussion. Feeling of one's own are called *ajjhattikā vedanā* and those belonging to others *bahiddhā vedanā*. A gradation of gross and subtle feelings is drawn in the following manner.[1]

(*Oḷārikā sukhumā vedanā.*) *Tattha katamā vedanā oḷārikā sukhumā? Akusalā vedanā oḷārikā, kusalāvyākatā vedanā sukhumā. Kusalākusalā vedanā oḷārikā, avyākatā vedanā sukhumā. Dukkha vedanā oḷārikā, sukhā ca adukkhamasukhā ca vedanā sukhumā. Sukhadukkhā vedanā oḷārikā, adukkhamasukhā vedanā sukhumā. Asamāpannassa vedanā oḷārikā, samāpannassa vedanā sukhumā. Sāsavā vedanā oḷārikā, anāsavā vedanā sukhumā. Taṁ taṁ vā pana vedanaṁ upādāyupādāya vedanā oḷārikā sukhumā daṭṭhabā.*

"What feelings are gross and what feelings are subtle? Immoral feelings are gross, moral and non-moral feelings are subtle. Moral and immoral feelings also may be considered as gross, and non-moral feelings as subtle. Painful feelings are gross, pleasurable and neutral feelings are subtle. Painful and pleasurable feelings also may be considered gross, and neutral as subtle. The feelings of one who has not attained *jhāna* are gross and of one who has attained it are subtle. The feelings contaminated with *āsavas* are gross while those without it are subtle."

The next pair, *hīna* and *paṇīta*, are explained in identical terms with the difference that *oḷārika* is replaced by *hīna* and *sukhuma* by *paṇīta*. For "distant" (*dure*) and "near" (*santike*), the same kinds of pairs of *vedanā* are given and are presented as mutually distant one from the other.

The *Puggalapaññatti* is another book which manifests a tendency towards classification and definition, but unlike the above two, it is devoted to the study of human types and not to the study of the *dhammas*. For this it applies various measuring-yards. In the fashion of the *Aṅguttara Nikāya*, it groups its classifications in ascending numerical orders of ten. We quote here two examples as illustrating the classification of human types into single and joint classes:

(a) *Katamo ca puggalo puthujjano?*

[1] *Vibhaṅga*, pp. 6-7.

"What sort of person is said to be a worldling?"

Yassa puggalassa tīṇi saṁyojanāni appahīnāni, na ca tesaṁ dhammānaṁ pahāṇāya paṭipanno. Ayaṁ vuccati puggalo "puthujjano".

"The person whose three fetters have not been put away and who is not proceeding to put these away—such a person is said to be a worldling."[1]

(b) *Katame dve puggalā dullabhā lokasmiṁ?*

"Which two sorts of persons are rare in the world?"

Yo ca pubbakārī, yo ca kataññū katavedī-ime dve puggalā dullabhā lokasmiṁ.

"One who does good and one who knows it—these two persons are rare in this world."[2]

For an assessment of the definitions occurring in these *Abhidhamma* books we cannot do better than quote Mrs. Rhys Davids:

"Abhidhamma definitions, while they are certainly a notable psychological advance over anything achieved in earlier or contemporary Indian literature, may not be satisfying to our own logical tradition. They consist very largely of enumerating synonymous, or partly synonymous, terms, such as we might call overlapping circles. But, they reveal to us much useful information concerning the term described, the terms describing this term, and the terms which we may have expected to find, but find not. And they show the Socratic earnestness with which these early Schoolmen strove to clarify their concepts, so as to guard their doctrines from the heretical innovations, to which ambiguity in terms would yield cheap foothold."[3]

The three *Abhidhamma* books *Dhātukathā*, *Yamaka*, and *Paṭṭhāna* are concerned with determining mutual relationships among the various doctrinal constituents in a logical form. The *Dhātukathā* makes a study of the *dhammas* in relation, as suggested by the name of the book, not only to *dhātu* but also to *khandha* and *āyatana;* for example, to what extent the *dhammas* are included in the *dhātu*, *khandha*, and *āyatana* divisions and to what extent they are not, or to what extent the *dhammas* are associated with the contents of these and to what extent they are not. All possible questions have been raised in this connexion and sometimes they become very complicated. According

[1] *Puggalapaññatti*, Nālanda ed., p. 21.

[2] ibid., 42.

[3] Mrs. Rhys Davids, *The Birth of Indian Psychology and its Development in Buddhism*, p. 369.

to Mrs. Rhys Davids[1] and following her Keith,[2] the *Yamaka* contains a study in the applied logic of conversion. Jayatilleke criticizes this view and believes that the book simply seeks to define and delimit the use of terms by means of pairs statements.[3] The very name of the book, *Yamaka*, means "The book of pairs" and in adherence to this is found, throughout the book, a dual grouping of questions. For the framing of the second question is applied the method of conversion i.e. the subject and predicate of the first question are just transposed, for example.

(*a*) *Ye keci kusalā dhammā, sabbe te kusalamūlā?*

(*b*) *Ye vā pana kusalamūlā, sabbe te dhammā kusalā?*

or

(*a*) *Ye keci kusalā dhammā, sabbe te kusalamūlena ekamūlā?*

(*b*) *Ye vā pana kusalamūlena ekamūlā, sabbe te dhammā kusalā?*[4]

In a logical form these statements may be put as:

(*a*) If any x is A, is any x B?

(*b*) If any x is B, is any x A?

Sometimes, we find a case of complete inversion like:

(*a*) Is not-A not-B?

(*b*) Is not-B not-A?

This book attempts to give the true meaning and significance of a term in its relationship with the others and for this it gives also the other meanings of the term if it is equivocal in nature. To illustrate the point we quote below one example from the Paññattivāra of the *Yamaka:*

(a) *Rūpaṁ Rūpakkhandho ti?*
Piyarūpaṁ sātarupaṁ rūpaṁ, na Rūpakkhandho.
Rūpaṁ ceva Rūpakkhandho ca.

(b) *Rūpakkhandho Rūpaṁ ti?*
Āmantā.[5]

Now, here, since the word *rūpa* is equivocal in nature and may be used conjoined with some other word (for example *piya-rūpa*, meaning "it is lovable by nature" or *eva-rupa* "of this nature", etc.), the answer to the first question (viz. "May all *rūpa* be called *rūpakkhandha*?") is

[1] *Yamaka, PTS.*, ed., p. xvi.
[2] Keith, *Buddhist Philosophy*, p. 304.
[3] op. cit., pp. 306-10.
[4] *Yamaka*, Nālanda ed., I, p. 3.
[5] ibid., p. 30.

given like this: "*Rupa* is also used in such words as *piya-rūpa* or *sāta-rupa* but there it does not mean *rūpakkhandha*". It is made clear that the proper import of the term here is "matter". The second question is just the converse form of the first: "may all *rūpakkhandha* be called *rūpa?*" Since *rūpakkhandha* is a very wide term and includes all modes of matter including *piya-rūpa* and *sāta-rūpa*, the second question is answered by a simple "yes".

Some scholars question the very utility of this book and argue that it does not contribute to an advancement of our knowledge about the universe of the *dhammas*. As against this Bhikkhu J. Kashyap has rightly said, "It may, therefore, be repeated and stressed that the Yamaka makes many things of Abhidhamma explicit that would have remained otherwise without it. It gives precision in the understanding of the Abhidhammika concepts and their behaviour . . .", which would, according to him, help in the understanding of the *Paṭṭhānappa-karaṇa*. *Paṭṭhāna* or *paccaya ṭhāna* represents a system of the *paccayas* or "relations" which exist between two *dhammas*, viz. the *paccaya-dhamma* and the *paccayuppanna-dhamma*. *Paccaya-dhamma* forms the basis for the emergence of the *paccayuppana-dhamma* and the relation between the two *dhammas* is named after the nature of the *paccaya-dhamma*. The object-subject relation, for example, is called *ārammaṇa-paccaya* since the *paccaya-dhamma* in this case is an *ārammaṇa* or an "object". As regards the significance of the book, Bhikkhu Jagadish Kashyap says that "the Paṭṭānappa karaṇa shows that the Dhammas are not isolated entities, but, in reality, *constitute a cosmos*, in which the smallest unity conditions the rest of it, and is also being conditioned in return."[1]

Among all the books of the *Abhidhamma*, the *Kathāvatthu* is intended to fulfil a very important task and that is to apply reasoning and logic to reduce all possible heterodox positions to an absurd footing. This book deals with about 200 questions on diverse issues, for example, on the personality of Buddha, characteristics of an Arhat, nature of the Saṅgha, cosmology, psychology, ethics, etc. The book is an evidence of the liberty of thought allowed in the order. All these discussions are in the form of questions and answers in the manner of a catechism with an imaginary opponent to argue with. Many passages from the *Vinaya Piṭaka* and the *Sutta Piṭaka* have been quoted to refute the false doctrines.

[1]Bhikkhu J. Kashyap ed., *Paṭṭhāna* I, Nālanda ed., Intro., p. x.

The *Kathāvatthu* makes an attempt to show the dialectical advantage of the Theravādins over other sects of the *sāsana* of the Buddha. In every thesis put forward by his opponent, the Theravādin would point out the implication of other theses which would not be acceptable to the opposite party. Putting his opponent in a position of dilemma, the Theravādin would refute the original thesis. As an example of the logic of the *Kathāvatthu*, here is quoted its very first discussion:

Controverted point: That the "person" is known in the sense of a real ultimate fact.

Theravādin: Is the "person" known in the sense of a real and ultimate fact?

Puggalavādin: Yes

Theravādin: Is the person known in the same way as a real and ultimate fact is known?

Puggalavādin: Nay, that cannot truly be said.

Theravādin: Acknowledge your refutation:

(i) If the person be known in the sense of a real and ultimate fact, then, indeed, good sir, you should also say, the person is known in the same way as (any other) real and ultimate fact (is known).

(ii) That you say here is wrong, namely, (i) we ought to say the person is known in the sense of a real and ultimate fact but (ii) we ought not to say the person is known in the same way as (any other) real and ultimate fact (is known).

(iii) If the latter statement (ii) cannot be admitted then indeed the former statement (i) should not be admitted.

(iv) In affirming the former statement (i) while denying the latter (ii) you are wrong.[1]

This logic can be symbolically represented like this:

Adherent—Is it true that A is B?

Opponent—Yes.

Adherent—Is it true that C is D?

Opponent—No.

Adherent—But if A be B—then (you should have said) C is D.

That B can be affirmed of A, but not D of C is false.

Hence your first answer is refuted.

or according to European logic:

If A is B, then C is D.

(But C is not D).

[1]*The Points of Controversy*, trans. of the *Kathāvatthu, PTS.*, pp. 8ff.

Therefore A is not B.

Next, the whole thing in inverse or indirect (*pratiloma*) method:

If D be denied of C,
then B should have been denied of A.
(But you affirmed B of A),
(therefore) that B can be affirmed of A, but not
D of C is wrong.

or according to European logic:

If C is not D, then A is not B.
(But A is B.)
Therefore C is D.[1]

The *Milindapañho* or the *Questions of Milinda* is another text of importance which, though non-canonical, belongs to the early Buddhists. Apart from its being, like the above-mentioned texts, analytical in the method of reasoning, another chief characteristic of this book lies in its attempt to answer a number of dilemmas observable in the Buddhist scheme of culture (and seeing dilemmas in the scripture itself attests a remarkable logical and scientific attitude). The dilemmas very frequently turn to various topics of dogmatics but they are mainly concerned with the different aspects of the personality of Buddha. The dilemmas are like the following: why should there be a veneration of relics if it is said that Buddha has utterly passed away? how can the Buddha be held as omniscient when at the same time it is also said that he pondered? why was Devadatta received in the Order when the Buddha knew that he would create a schism? and so on. The dilemmas are attempted to be solved with the help of suitable examples and illustrations. To offer a solution to the second dilemma, how the Buddha can be omniscient if he at the same time reflected, Nāgasena gives many examples and speaks of seven types of mind,[2] and finally concludes: "Just so, great king, though reflection is a necessary condition of the knowledge of the Tathāgata, yet on reflection it perceives whether he wants to know . . . Just as when the mighty king of kings (*cakkavattī*) calling to mind his glorious wheel of victory wishes it to appear and no sooner is it thought of than it appears—so does the knowledge of the Tathāgata follow continually on reflection." As regards the issue concerning the admission of Devadatta to the Order,

[1]See *The Points of Controversy*, Introduction, pp. xlviii ff.

[2]*Questions of King Milinda*, trans. of the *Millindapañho, SBE.*, XXXV, pp. 155-62.

many examples are given to show that Buddha admitted him to the Order out of mercy to release him of his pain. "If he had not done so Devadatta would have suffered torment in purgatory through a succession of existences, through hundreds and thousands of kalpas."[1] Even if the explanation offered for these dilemmas might not stand up to a scientific and logical test, one is tempted to believe that the monk-author (authors) had a questioning and reasoning mind and took trouble to seek explanations of two statements, attributed to Buddha, which appeared contradictory.

The scientific and logical attitude of the early Buddhists is seen at its best in their concept of law (*dhammatā*) and the concept of cause (*hetu*). In opposition to theories like "sassatavāda" (eternalism) and "adhiccasamuppāda" (accidental origin) held by some contemporary thinkers to explain the nature of the phenomena, Buddha believed in the doctrine of correlated action, which goes to suggest an existence of law and order in the progress of cause and effect. In Buddhist terminology the doctrine is known as *paṭicca-samuppāda*, which is meant to illustrate the law of *idappaccayatā* or the dependent origination of things. A short formula of this doctrine is given like this: *Imasmiṁ sati idaṁ hoti, imass uppādā idaṁ uppajjati; imasmiṁ asati idaṁ na hoti, imassa nirodhā idaṁ nirujjhatti*: "If this is, that comes to be, from the arising of this that arises; if this is not that does not come to be, from the ceasing of this that ceases."[2] In the context of Buddha's Enlightenment is given the larger formula of *paṭiccasamuppāda* which consists of twelve *nidānas* in the direct and indirect order (*anulomapaṭilomaṁ*). The formula is worth quoting for a proper understanding of it:

"Conditioned by ignorance are the habitual tendencies; conditioned by the habitual tendencies is consciousness; conditioned by consciousness is psycho-physicality; conditioned by psycho-physicality are the six (sense) spheres; conditioned by the six (sense) spheres is awareness; conditioned by awareness is feeling; conditioned by feeling is craving; conditioned by craving is grasping; conditioned by grasping is becoming; conditioned by becoming is birth; conditioned by birth, old age and dying, grief, sorrow and lamentation, suffering, dejection and despair come into being. Such is the arising of this entire mass of ill.

[1]*Questions of King Milinda*, trans. of the *Milindapañho.*, *SBE.*, XXXV, p. 169.
[2]See e.g. *Majjhima*, Nālanda ed., I, pp. 323, 325; *The Book of the Kindred Sayings*, trans. of the *Saṁyutta Nikāya*, *PTS.*, II, p. 66.

But from the utter fading away of this very ignorance (comes) the stopping of habitual tendencies; from the stopping of habitual tendencies the stopping of consciousness (and so on). Such is the stopping of this entire mass of ill."[1]

The root of all human suffering is thus traced to *avijjā* or ignorance, from which others follow, each of them constituting a cause for the following one. Very logically, the destruction of each cause has been said to annul its effect, whence the cessation of suffering.

The axioms "All is impermanent" (*sabbaṁ aniccaṁ*) and "All (things) in the world are devoid of a self" (*sabbe dhammā anattā*) are meant as corollaries of the doctrine of *paṭiccasamuppāda*. According to Buddhism, the elements of existence exist only for a moment. The world is in a process of continuous change, nothing remaining the same for two moments. As there is changeability in all the objects of phenomena, so is the "un-self-ness" (*anattā*) without any exception. The procedure adopted to explain this is purely analytical and it is because of the prominence of this method in the explanation of the phenomena that in the Third Council the philosophy of Buddha was agreed to be nothing but *Vibhajjavāda* (analytical method); the word, however, does not occur in the *Tripiṭaka* itself. In the doctrine of Anattā "The repudiation is of what would now-a-days be described as 'Animism'; the psycho-physical behaving mechanism is not a 'self' and is devoid (*suñña*) of any Self-like property."[2] An individual is not a unity but an aggregate of the five *khandhas* (*rūpa, vedanā, saññā, saṅkhāra*, and *viññāṇa*), each of which has no substance of itself. Had they not been devoid of *attā*, it would be possible for one to say "let my *rūpa* be thus, let my *vedanā* be thus" and so on.[3] All of these are impermanent (*aniccaṁ*) and that which is impermanent is *dukkha;* we will have to conclude in each case, "Netaṁ mam, nesohamasmi, na meso attā ti" (that is not mine, I'm not that, that's not my self).[4] It is, hereby, suggested that "one" can be expressed only in the terms of "many" in the same way—the *Milindapañho* cites the example—as a chariot can be explained only as a combination of the wheels, the framework, the flagstaff, the yoke, the reins, and the other constituent

[1]*Mahāvagga*, Nālanda ed., 3. For the translation, see *Book of the Discipline* trans. of the *Vinaya* by I.B. Horner, IV, 1-2.

[2]Ananda K. Coomaraswamy and I.B. Horner comp. and trans., *The Living Thoughts of Gotama the Buddha*, Intro., 29.

[3]*Mahāvagga*, Nālanda ed., 16-17. [4]ibid.

parts, and not as any of its constituent parts in its independent capacity.[1]

The point which should be discussed in this context concerns recognition of identity between the doer and experiencer of an act "for responsibility ceases where identity of character ceases."[2] The incongruity between a notion of moral responsibility and Buddhist doctrine of *anattā* (no-self) and *aniccatā* (impermanence) is a superficial one. Buddha's clear enunciation that "Karma is one's own", etc., goes to suggest that an individual is a pure product of his deeds and it is in his own hands to allow his miseries to continue or to stop them. Buddha believed all the phenomenal objects to be not-self and devoid of permanence, resulting in consequential denial of sameness between the same individual at two consecutive moments. But he believed in the principle of continuity, and though there is an absolute absence of sameness, there is similarity. The individual of a particular moment cannot be independent of one immediately preceding it inasmuch as the one is caused and conditioned by the other. The *Milindapañho*[3] gives several examples to explain it, one of which is that of a girl married to somebody in her childhood who when she is grown up is carried away by someone else. The latter cannot refuse to return her to her former husband on the ground that she is not the same girl as she was on the occasion of her marriage. She is, no doubt, not the same girl, but definitely not a different one.

Thus, it can be truly said that Buddhism appeared in the intellectual arena as a harbinger of a new trend in the realm of thinking. The empirical and analytical outlook of the Buddhists led them to found a system of psychology and logic which had great influence on Indian thought as a whole.

[1] *Milindapañho, SBE.*, XXXV, pp. 43-44.

[2] L.T. Hobhouse, *Morals in Evolution*, p. 504.

[3] *The Questions of King Milinda*, trans. of the *Milindapañho, SBE.*, XXXV, pp. 64-65, 74.

Bibliography*

I. Original Sources—Buddhist

Abhidhammatthasaṅgaho, Sarnath, 1941; translated as *Compendium of Philosophy* by Shwe Zan Aung, *PTS*, London, 1956.

Abhidharma-Kośa of Vasubandhu; *L' Abhidharmakośa de Vasubandhu*, traduit et annoté par Louis de la Vallée Poussin, vols. I-IX, Paris, 1923-26; *Abhidharma-Kośa*, translated in Hindi by Acharya Narendra Deva, part 1 and 2, Allahabad, 1958, 1973.

Advaya-vajra-saṅgraha, ed. H.P. Shastri, Gaekwad's Oriental Series (*GOS*), XL, Baroda, 1927.

Aṅguttara Nikāya, ed. Bhikshu Jagdish Kashyap, Nālandā-Devanāgarī Pāli Series, Pali Publication Board, Bihar Government (henceforth the texts of this series abbreviated as Nāl. edn.), 4 vols., 1960; translated as *The Book of the Gradual Sayings* in 5 vols. by *PTS*., (Vols. I, II and V by F.L. Woodward and vol. III, IV by E.M. Hare), London,

Aṣṭasāhasrikā-Prajñāpāramitā, ed. P.L. Vaidya, Buddhist Sanskrit Texts (henceforth the texts of this series abbreviated as *BST*), no. 4, Mithila Institute, Darbhanga, 1960; translated into English by E. Conze, *Bibliotheca Indica* (*BI*), Calcutta, 1958.

Aṭṭhasālinī, ed. P.V. Bapat and R.D. Vadekar, Poona, 1942; translated as *The Expositor* by Pe Maung Tin, edited and revised by Mrs. Rhys Davids, *PTS*., translation Series no. 8 and 9, London, 1958.

Avadāna-śataka, ed P.L. Vaidya, *BST*, no. 19, Darbhanga, 1958.

Bauddhagāna O Dohā ed. H.P. Shastri, Sāhitya Parishad Granthāvalī no. 55, Calcutta. (in Bengali).

Blue Annals (or Deb-ther sṅon-po by Gos lo-tso-ba gzoṅ-nu-dpal), translated into English by G.N. Roerich, 2 parts, Calcutta, 1949, 1953.

*The particular edition or translation used at any place in the text is indicated either by the abbreviation used or by specification otherwise.

Bodhicaryāvatāra of Śāntideva, ed. P.L. Vaidya, *BST*, no. 12, Darbhanga, 1960.

Bodhisattvabhūmi (being the XVth Section of Asaṅgāpada's Yogācārabhūmi), ed. N. Dutt, K.P. Jayaswal Research Institute, Patna, 1966.

Caryāgītikośa of Buddhist Siddhas, ed. Prabodh Chandra Bagchi and Śānti Bhikṣu Śāstrī, Visvabharati, Santiniketan, 1956.

Citta-viśuddhi-prakaraṇa of Āryadeva, ed. P.B. Patel, Santiniketan, 1949.

Cullavagga, ed. Bhikshu Jagdish Kashyap, Nāl. edn., 1956; translated by I.B. Horner as *The Book of Discipline, Sacred Book of the Buddhists*, (*SBB*), XX, London.

Daśabhūmika-sūtra, Publié par J. Rahder, Paris, 1926.

Dhammapada, trans. Radhakrishnan, London, 1966.

Dhammasaṅgaṇi, ed. Bhikshu Jagdish Kashyap, Nāl. edn., 1960.

Dharma-saṅgraha, ed. F. Max Müller, H. Wenzel and K. Kassawara, Oxford, 1885.

Dohā-Kośa, ed. Prabodh Chandra Bagchi, 1938; ed. Rahul Sāṁkrityāyana, Bihar Rashṭrabhāṣā Pariṣad, Patna, 1957.

Gilgit Manuscripts (Vinaya of the Mūlasarvāstivādin) 8 vols., ed, N. Dutt, Srinagar, .

Guhyasamāja-tantra, ed. B. Bhattacharya, *GOS*, LIII, Baroda, 1931.

Hevajra-tantra, ed. D.L. Snellgrove, 2 vols., London, 1959.

Itivuttaka, ed. Bhikshu Jagdish Kashyap, Nāl. edn., 1959.

Jātaka-mālā of Āryāśūra, Ed. P.L. Vaidya, *BST* no. 21, Darbhanga, 1959; trans. by J.S. Speyar, *SBB.*, I, London.

Jñāna-siddhi of Indrabhūti, ed. B Bhattacharya, *GOS*, XLIX, Baroda, 1929.

Kathāvatthu, ed. Bhikshu Jagdish Kashyap, Nāl. edn., 1961; trans. as *Points of Controversy* by Shwe Zan Aung and Mrs. C.A.F. Rhys Davids, *PTS*, London, 1960.

Lalita-vistara, ed. P.L. Vaidya, *BST*, no. 1, Darbhanga, 1958.

Laṅkāvatāra-sūtra, trans. D.T. Suzuki, London, 1956.

Mahāvagga, ed. Bhikshu Jagdish Kashyap, Nāl. edn., 1956; trans. I.B. Horner as *The Book of Discipline*, *SBB.*, XIV. London.

Mahāvastu, tr. J.J. Jones, *SBB*, XV, XVIII, XIX, London.

Mahāvyutpatti, ed. Sakaki, Kyoto, 1928.

Mahāyāna-Sūtrālaṅkāra, ed. S. Bagchi, *BST.*, no. 13, Darbhanga, 1970; ed. and tr. by S. Lévi, Paris, 1907, 1911.

Mahāyānasūtrasaṁgrahaḥ, I, ed. P.L. Vaidya, *BST*, no. 1, Darbhanga, 1961.

Majjhima Nikāya, ed. Bhikshu Jagdish Kashyap, Nāl. edn., 3 vols. 1958; trans. as *The Middle Length Sayings* by I.B. Horner, *PTS*, 3 vols., London.

Milindapañho, ed. R.D. Vadekar, Bombay University Publications, Devanagari *PTS*., *7*, Bombay, 1940; trans. as *The Questions of King Milinda*, Sacred Books of the East (*SBE*), XXXV-XXXVI, London, 1890-1894.

Mūlamadhyamakārikāḥ of Nāgārjuna, ed. J.W. De Jong., The Adyar Library and Research Centre, Madras, 1977.

Pācittiya, ed. Bhikshu Jagdish Kashyap, Nāl. ed., 1958.

Pārājika, ed. Bhikshu Jagdish Kashyap, Nāl. ed., 1958.

Paṭṭhāna, ed. Bhikshu Jagdish Kashyap, 6 vols., Nāl. edn , 1958-61.

Prajñopāya-viniścaya-siddhi of Anaṅgavajra, ed. B. Bhattacharya, *GOS*, XLIX, Baroda, 1929.

Puggala-paññatti, ed. Bhikshu Jagdish Kashyap, Nāl. edn., 1960; trans. Bimal Charan Law as *Designation of Human Types PTS*, London.

Saddharma-Puṇḍarīka, ed. P.L. Vaidya, *BST*. no. 6, Darbhanga, 1960. trans.H. Kern in *SBE*, XXI. London.

Sādhanamālā, ed. B. Bhattacharya, 2 vols., *GOS*, XXVI, XLI, Baroda, 1925, 1928.

Saṁyutta Nikāya, ed. Bhikshu Jagdish Kashyap, Nāl. ed., 4 vols., 1959; translated as *The Book of the Kindred Sayings* in 5 vols., *PTS*, London,

Śatasāhasrikā-Prajñāpāramitā (chs. i-xii), ed. P. Ghosa, *BI*, Calcutta, 1902-13.

Sekoddeśaṭīkā of Naropa (Naḍapāda), ed. M.E Carelli, *GOS*, XC, Baroda, 1941.

Śikṣāsamuccaya of Śāntideva, ed. P.L. Vaidya, *BST*. no. 11, Darbhanga, 1960.

Sutta-Nipāta, *Harvard Oriental Series* (*HOS*), XXXVII. Cambridge (Mass.),

Theragāthā, translated as *Psalms of the Brethren* by Mrs. Rhys Davids, Psalms of the Early Buddhists II, *PTS*, London, 1913.

Therīgāthā, translated as *Psalms of the Sisters* by Mrs. Rhys Davids, *Psalms of the Early Buddhists*, I, *PTS*, London, 1909.

Vibhaṅga, ed. Bhikshu Jagdish Kashyap, Nāl. edn , 1960.

Visuddhimagga of Buddhaghosa, ed., D.D. Kosambi, Bharatiya Vidya Bhawan Series, no. 1, Bombay, 1940; *Viśuddhi-Mārga*, trans. Bhiksu Dharmarakṣita 2 vols., Sarnath, 1956-57; trans. as the *Path of Purification* I & II by Bhikshu Nyāṇamali, Berkeley & London, 1976.

Yamaka, ed. Bhikshu Jagdish Kashyap, 2 vols., Nāl. edn., 1961.

II. Original Sources—Non-Buddhist

Aitareya Brāhmaṇa, Ānandāśrama Sanskrit Series Poona.

Āpastamba Gṛhyasūtra, SBE., XXX, London, 1886.

Āśvalāyana Gṛhyasūtra, SBE., XXIX, London, 1886.

Atharvavedasaṁhitā, ed. by S.D. Satwalekar, Aundh, 1938.

Bhagavadgītā, Gita Press, Gorakhpur.

Bṛhadāraṇyaka Upaniṣad (As in *Aṣṭāviṁśatyupaniṣadaḥ*). ed. Wasudev Laxman Sastri Pansikar, 7th ed., Bombay, 1930.

Chāndogya Upaniṣad, as in *Aṣṭāviṁśatyupaniṣadaḥ*.

Gṛhyasūtra of Hiraṇyakeśin, SBE., XXX.

Īśa Upaniṣad, as in *Aṣṭāviṁśatyupaniṣadaḥ*.

Jaina Sutras, pt. I, translation of *Ācārāṅga Sūtra* and *Kalpasūtra* by H. Jacobi, *SBE.*, XXII, London, 1884.

Jaina Sutrās, pt. II, translation of *Uttarādhyayana Sūtra* and *Sūtra Kṛtāṅga* by H. Jacobi, *SBE.*, XLV, London, 1890.

Kāṭhaka Saṁhitā, ed. by S.D. Satwalekar, Aundh.

Kaṭha Upaniṣad, as in *Aṣṭāviṁśatyupaniṣadaḥ*.

Mahābhāṣya of Patañjali, Gurukula Jhajjar (Rohtak), 1963.

Manu-Smṛti, Chowkhamba Sanskrit Series Office, Varanasi, 1970; trans. G. Bühler as *Laws of Manu, SBE.*, XXV.

Muṇḍaka Upaniṣad, as in *Aṣṭāviṁśatyupaniṣadaḥ*.

Nichomachean Ethics of Aristotle, A Commentary by H.H. Joachim, Oxford, 1951.

Pañcaviṁśa Brāhmaṇa, ed. A. Vedāntavāgīśa, Calcutta, 1869-74.

Pāraskara Gṛhyasūtra, SBE., XXIX.

Ṛgvedasaṁhitā, ed. by S.D. Satwalekar, Aundh.

Śatapatha Brāhmaṇa, ed. by Julius Eggeling, in 5 vols. *SBE*, XII, XXVI, XLI, XLIII, XIIV London, 1882-1900.

Śvetāśvatara Upaniṣad, as in *Aṣṭāviṁśatyupaniṣadaḥ*.

Taittiriya Brāhmaṇa, Ānandāśrama Sanskrit Series, Poona,

Taittirīya Saṁhitā, Ānandāśrama Sanskrit Series, Poona,

Taittirīya Upaniṣad, as in *Aṣṭāviṁśatyupaniṣadaḥ*.

Vājasaneyī Saṁhitā, ed. by S.D. Satwalekar, Aundh, 1927.

III. Secondary Sources

Bagchi, P.C., *Studies in the Tantras*, Calcutta, 1939.

Bareau, A., *Les Sectes Boudhiques du Petit Véhicule*, Saigon, 1955.

Barua, B.M., *History of Pre-Buddhist Indian Philosophy*, Calcutta, 1921.

Basham, A.L., *History and Doctrine of the Ājīvakas*, London, 1951.

Bharati, Agehananda, *The Tantric Tradition*, New Delhi, 1976.

Bhattacharya, Benoytosh, *An Introduction to Buddhist Esoterism*, Oxford, 1932.

Bhattacharya, Haridas, ed., *The Cultural Heritage of India*, IV, Calcutta, 1969.

Bose, A.C., *Hymns from the Ṛgveda*, Bombay, 1966.

Bouquet, A.C., *Comparative Religion*, Seventh edition, Hammonsworth, 1967.

Bradley, F.H., *Ethical Studies*, sec. edn., Oxford, 1952.

Brewster, E.J., *The Life of Gotama, the Buddha*, London, 1926.

Carus, Paul, *The Gospel of Buddha*, Delhi, 1961.

Chanda, R.P., *Indo-Aryan Races*, Rajashahi, 1916.

Conze, E., *Buddhist Meditation*, London, 1956.

——, *Buddhist Thought in India*, London, 1962.

——, *Buddhist Texts Through the Ages*, Oxford, 1953.

——, *The Prajñāpāramitā Literature*, The Hague, 1960.

Coomaraswamy, A.K., *Buddha and the Gospel of Buddhism*, New Delhi, 1975.

——, *Hinduism and Buddhism*, New Delhi, 1975.

——, and Horner, I.B., *La Pensée de Gotama le Buddha*, tr. J. Buhot, Paris.

——, *The Living Thoughts of Gotama the Buddha*, compiled and translated, New Delhi, 1970.

Copleston, Reginald Stephen, *Buddhism, Primitive and Present in Magadha and Ceylon*, London, 1892.

Crawford, S. Cromwell, *Hindu Ethical Ideas*, Calcutta, 1974.

Dandekar, R.N., *Some Aspects of the History of Hinduism*, Poona, 1967.

Dasgupta, S.B., *An Introduction to Tantric Buddhism*, Calcutta, 1950.

Dasgupta, S.N., *Indian Idealism*, Cambridge, 1962.

Dasgupta, Surama, *Development of Moral Philosophy in India*,

Calcutta, 1961.
De, Gokul Das, *Democracy in Early Buddhist Sangha*, Calcutta, 1951.
Deo, S.B., *History of Jaina Monachism*, Poona, 1956.
Dewey, John & James H. Tufts, *Ethics*, New York, 1956.
Ducasse, C.T., *Determinism, Freedom and Responsibility*, New York, 1958.
Dutt, N., *Aspects of Mahayana Buddhism and its Relation to Hinayana*, London, 1930.
——, *Early Monastic Buddhism*, I & II, Calcutta, 1941-45.
——, *Mahayana Buddhism*, rev. edn, Delhi, 1978.
Dutt, N.K., *The Origin and Growth of Caste in India*, I, Calcutta, 1931.
Dutt, Sukumar, *Early Buddhist Monachism*, New Delhi, 1984.
Elliot, Charles, *Hinduism and Buddhism*, 3 vols., London, 1954.
Ergardt, Jan T., *Faith and Knowledge in Early Buddhism*, Leiden, 1977.
Gard, A., *Buddhism*, New York, 1967.
Glasenapp, H. Von., *Doctrine of Karman in Jaina Philosophy*, trans. G. Berry Gifford, Bombay, 1942.
Gokhale, B.G., *Ashoka Maurya*, New York, 1966.
Govinda, A.B., *The Psychological Attitude of the Early Buddhist Philosophy*, London, 1975.
Govinda, Lama Anagarika, *Foundations of Tibetan Mysticism*, New Delhi, 1977.
Gopalan, S., *Outlines of Jainism*, New Delhi, 1975.
Guenther, Herbert V., *Philosophy and Psychology in the Abhidharma*, Delhi.
Har Dayal, *The Bodhisattva Doctrine in Buddhist Sanskrit Literature*, London, 1932.
Hartmann, Nicolai, *Ethics*, III, London, 1951.
Hiriyanna, M., *Outlines of Indian Philosophy*, London, 1967.
Hobhouse, L.T., *Morals in Evolution*, London, 1915.
Homes, Edmond, *The Creed of Buddha*, London, 1949.
Hopkins, E.W., *Ethics of India*, New Haven, 1924.
Horner, I.B., *The Early Buddhist Theory of Man Perfected*, A Study of the Arahan. London, 1936 reprinted, New Delhi, 1979.
Humphreys, Christmas, *Buddhism*, Hammondsworth, 1972.
Iyer, K. Balasubramania, *Hindu Ideals*, Bombay, 1969.
Jain, Hiralal, *Bhāratīya Saṁskriti men Jaina Dharma kā Yogadāna*,

Bhopal, 1975.
Jayatilleke, K.N., *Early Buddhist Theory of Knowledge*, London, 1963.
——, *Message of the Buddha*, London, 1975.
Johnson, Sharman E., *Jesus in His Own Times*, London, 1958.
Joshi, L.M., *Studies in the Buddhistic Culture of India*. Delhi, 1967.
Kane, P.V., *History of the Dharmaśāstra*, I, pt. 1, II, pt. 2, Poona.
Kaviraj, Gopinath, *Bhāratīya Saṁskriti aur Sādhanā*, pt. I, Patna, 1963.
Keith, A.B., *Buddhist Philosophy in India and Ceylon*, New Delhi, 1979.
——, & A.A. Macdonell, *Vedic Index of Names and Subjects*, 2 vols, Varanasi, 1958.
Kern, H., *Manual of Indian Buddhism*, Delhi, 1974.
Koros, Alexander Csoma, *The Life and Teachings of Buddha*, Calcutta, 1957.
Law, B.C., *Indological Studies*, II, Calcutta, 1952.
Lessing, F.D. and Alex Wayman, *Introduction to the Buddhist Tantric Systems*, Delhi, 1978.
Lewis, Clarence Irwing, *The Ground and the Nature of the Right*, New York, 1955.
Lewis, H.D., *Morals and the New Theology*, London, 1947.
Ling, Trevor, *The Buddha*, Hammondsworth, 1976.
Lubac, Henri de, *Aspects of Buddhism*, London, 1953.
McPhail, James M., *Asoka*, Calcutta, 1951.
Majumdar, R.C. and Pusalker, A.D. ed., *The History and Culture of the Indian People*, I, *The Vedic Age*, London, 1957.
Maitra, S.K., *The Ethics of the Hindus*, Calcutta, 1956.
Marshall, J., *Mohenjodaro and the Indus Civilization*, I, London, 1931.
Masuda, J., 'Origin and Outlines of Early Indian Buddhist Schools of Vasumitra's Treatise', Asia Major, pt. II, fasc. 2, 1925.
McGovern, W.M., *An Introduction to Mahayana Buddhism*, Varanasi, 1968.
McKenzie, John, *Hindu Ethics*, New Delhi, 1972.
Misra, G.S.P., *Prāchīna Bhāratīya Samāja evam Arthavyavasthā* Jaipur, 1983.
——, *The Age of Vinaya*, New Delhi, 1972.
Mookerji, R.K., *Ancient Indian Education*, London, 1940.
——, *Asoka*, sec. rev. edn., Delhi, 1955.
Moore, George Foot, *History of Religions*, II, Edinburgh, 1948.

Nakamura, Hajime, *Buddhism in Comparative Light*, Islam and the Modern Age Society, New Delhi, 1975.
——, *Ways of Thinking of Eastern Peoples, India, China, Tibet, Japan*, Honolulu, 1964.
Oldenberg, H., *Buddha*, trans. W. Hoey, London, 1904.
Pande, G.C., *Bauddha Dharma ke Vikāsa kā Itihāsa*, Lucknow, 1963.
——, *Mūlya Mīmāṁsā*, Jaipur, 1973.
——, *Śramana Tradition—Its History and Contribution to Indian Culture*, Ahmedabad, 1978.
——, *Studies in the Origins of Buddhism*, Allahabad, 1957.
Poussin, de la Vallée, *Le Boudhisme*, third edn, Paris, 1925.
——, *L'Inde jusquau 300 Avant J.C.*
——, *'Nirvāṇa', Etude sur L'Histoire de Religions*, 5, Paris, 1925.
Radhakrishnan, S., *History of Indian Philosophy*, I, London, 1941.
——, ed., *Mahatma Gandhi*, London, 1959.
Ranade, R.D., *A Constructive Survey of Upanisadic Philosophy*, Poona, 1926.
Rao, Vijai Bahadur, *Uttara-Vaidika Samāja evam Saṁskṛiti*, Varanasi, 1966.
Rapson, E.J. ed., *Cambridge History of India*, I, Ancient India, Delhi, 1955.
Rashdall, Hastings, *The Theory of Good and Evil*, sec. edn, Oxford, 1948.
Raychaudhari, Hemchandra, *Materials for the Study of the Early History of the Vaishnava Sect*, Calcutta, 1936, reprinted, New Delhi, 1975.
Rhys Davids, (Mrs.) C.A.F., *Gotama, The Man*, London, 1928.
——, *Sakya, or Buddhist Origins*, New Delhi, 1978.
——, *The Birth of Indian Psychology and its Development in Buddhism*, New Delhi, 1978.
——, *What was the Original Gospel*? London.
Rhys Davids, T.W., *Buddhism*, London, 1899.
——, *Buddhist India*, sixth edn., Calcutta, 1955.
Saddhatissa, H., *Buddhist Ethics—Essence of Buddhism*, London, 1970.
Sahakian, William S., *Systems of Ethics and Value Theory*, New York, 1963.
Samkrityāyana, Rahul, *Purātattva Nibandhāvalī*, sec. edn., Allahabad, 1958.
Sathaye, S.G., *Moral Choice and Early Hindu Thought*, Bombay, 1970.

Schopenhauer, *Studies in Pessimism*, trans. T.B. Saunders, Edinburgh, 1937.
Senart, E., *Essai sur la Legende de Buddha*, Paris, 1882.
——, *Les Inscriptions de Piyadasi*, Tome II, Paris, 1886.
Sen, Mohit and M.B. Rao, ed., *Das Kapital Centenary Volume*, New Delhi, 1968.
Sharma, R.S., *Śūdras in Ancient India*, Varanasi, 1958.
Smith, Vincent A. *Aśoka*, Oxford, 1901.
Stecherbatsky, Th., *The Central Conception of Buddhism and the Meaning of the word 'Dharma'*, third edn., Calcutta, 1961.
——, *Buddhist Logic*, 2 vols, New Delhi, 1984.
Streeter, Burnett Hillman, *The Buddha and the Christ* (The Bampon Lectures for 1932), London, 1932.
Suzuki, B.L., *Mahayana Buddhism*, third edn., London, 1959.
Suzuki, D.T., *Outlines of Mahayana Buddhism*, New York, 1973.
Takakusu, J., *Essentials of Buddhist Philosophy*, New Delhi, 1975.
Thapar, Romila, *Ancient Indian Social History*, New Delhi, 1978.
——, *Aśoka and the Decline of the Mauryas*, sec. edn., Delhi, 1973.
Thomas, E.J., *The Life of Buddha*, London, 1949.
Titus, Harold H. and Morris T. Keeton, ed., *The Range of Ethics*, New Delhi, 1972.
Toynbee, Arnold J., *A Study of History*, III, Oxford, 1948.
Troeltsch, Ernst, *Social Teaching of the Christian Churches*, trans. Olive Wyon, I, London, 1956.
Varma, Vishwanath Prasad, *Early Buddhism and its Origins*, New Delhi, 1973.
Vidyabhusan, S.C., *History of the Mediaeval School of Indian Logic*, Calcutta, 1909, reprint, New Delhi, 1977.
Wagle, Narendra, *Society at the Time of the Buddha*, Bombay, 1966.
Watters, Thomas, *On Yuan Chwang's Travels in India*, 2 vols. New Delhi, 1973.
Wayman, Alex, *The Buddhist Tantras*, New York, 1973.
Weber, Max, *The Religions of India: The Sociology of Hinduism and Buddhism*, Chicago, 1958.
Westermarck, *Origin and Development of Moral Ideas*, I, London, 1906.
Winternitz, M., *History of Indian Literature*, II, New Delhi, 1975.
Wittgenstein, Ludwig, *Tractatus logico-philosophicus*, New Delhi, 1955.

IV. Journals, Commemoration Volumes, Presentation Volumes and Dictionaries

B.C. Law Volume, I.

Buddhist Hybrid Sanskṛit Grammar and Dictionary by Franklin Edgerton, New Haven, 1953.

Buddhist Studies. A Yearly Research Journal of the Department of Buddhist Studies, University of Delhi.

Ceylon University Review.

Encyclopaedia of Religion and Ethics, ed. James Hastings, New York, 1955.

Indian Antiquary (Third Series).

Jaina Antiquary.

Jijñāsā, (A Journal of History of Ideas and Culture, Department of History and Indian Culture, University of Rajasthan, Jaipur).

Journal of the American Oriental Society.

Journal of the Asiatic Society of Bengal.

Journal of the Royal Asiatic Society of Great Britain and Ireland.

Journal of the Bihar Research Society.

Journal Asiatique.

Memoirs of the Archaeological Survey of India.

Pali-English Dictionary, ed. T.W. Rhys Davids and William, Stede New Delhi, 1975.

Poona Oriental Series.

Proceedings of the International Conference of the History, Archaeology and Culture of Central Asia in the Kushan Period, II, Moscow, 1975.

Quest.

Religion.

The Hibbert Journal.

The Journal of Asian Studies.

The Mahabodhi.

The Proceedings of the Indian History Congress.

The Visva Bharati Quarterly.

Index

Abhidhamma 58, 62, 67, 159-62, 165
Action: *Kuśala, akuśala* and *avyākata* 40, 44
Ājīvaka view of 48, 50; Brahmanical view of 51fn; Jaina view of 33-35; Buddhist view of 42-44; and moral standard 40-43; detached action, in *Gītā* 45, in Christianity 45-46, in Buddhism 44-47; determinism and freedom 48-51
Activism (*pravṛtti*) 1
Adhiccasamuppāda 40, 56, 168
Advaya 145, 149
Ahiṁsā 89
Ahirika 66
Ajita Kesakambala 33, 75
Akusala-mūla 64
Anāgāmi 67-68
Analytical and logical method 55-58, 157-58
Anattā 47, 51-52, 57, 170
Aniccatā 47, 59, 64, 170
Anottappa 66
Anurakkhaṇa 29
Arhat 25, 67-68; contrasted with *Bodhisattva* ideal 128
Aristotle 47
Ārya (*Āryajana*) 16, 68, 74, 82, 102
Asceticism: and householder's life 80-81, 83-84; and Buddhist e'hics 71-72; in Christianity 72fn.
Aśoka: the buddhist model of a ruler 112; conception of *dhamma* 113; victory by *dhamma* 116-17
Attitude, healthy and unhealthy 62-67
Āvajjana 61

Avijjā 21, 25, 66

Bhavaṅga 60
Bhavaṅga-calana 61
Bhavaṅga-citta 60
Bhavaṅga-sota 61
Bhavaṅguppaccheda 61
Bhavarāga 66
Bodhi (*Saṁbodhi*) 102, 130
Bodhicitta 145-46; conception of and cultivation of 130-33
Bodhisattva 123, 125, 127-28, 135-37; contrasted with *Arhat* ideal 128
Brahmavihāras 44, 78, 95, 139
Buddha: life of 18-19; vision of 19-27, 70; conception of, in Hīnayāna and Mahāyāna 126-27
Buddha-eyes 70

Cakravartin conception of 110, 116
Citta 59
Cittakṣana 60
Cittapasaddhi 66
Cittaviveka 139
compassion: see *Karuṇā*
conduct: code of, for house holders 104-07; for monks and nuns 97-100
Conscious existence, nature of 58-60
Consciousness, divisions of 63-64; levels of 63

Dāna 80; as *Pāramitā* 134-36
Dhamma (Dharma) 19-20, 30; notion of, in Aśokan edicts 114; *dharmas* (elements of existence) 22, 59, 61-62, 152; *kuśala* and *akuśala* 29-30

Dhammatā 53, 56, 168
Dharma-cakra-pravartana 19, 103, 142
Dhyāna (see also *Jhāna*) as *Pāramita* 139
Diṭṭhi 65-66; *diṭṭhis* 21

Existence, four planes of 63

Gandhabba 38-39

Hiri 66
Human personality, analysis of 58-60

Ideal Uttilitarianism 43
Individual, notion of 169; concept of, in Indian thought 79-80
Individualism: Charge of, against Buddhism 79; growth of the idea of, 15
Indriya-bhāvanā 29
Intuitionism 43
Issā 66

Jaina Tīrthaṅkaras 4
Javana 61
Jhāna (*Dhyāna*) 19, 30, 93; *jhānic* practice 30

Kāmarāga 65
Kammaññatā 66
Karmapathāḥ, 137
Karman: doctrin of 31-32; in *Upanisads* 31-32; Ājīvaka view 35-36; Buddhist view 37-39; in Jainism 33-35; as moral causation 39-40; three levels of 52-53; *Karmavāda* 73, and *Kriyāvāda* 33-34; determinism and freedom 48-51; and the problem of moral responsibility 47-52; *Karmic* forces 24
Karuṇā 80, 83, 89, 95, 128, 145
Kāyapasaddhi 66
Khandhas (*Skandhas*) 23, 57-59, 67, 169
Kriyā, Jaina notion of 33
Kṣānti, as *Pāramitā* 138-39
Kukuccā 66
Kusala-mūla 64

Lahutā 66
Lobha 66
Logical (and scientific) method, in early Buddhist texts 155-70; in *Abhidhamma* books, 161-67; need and concept of definition 158-59; classification of objects 159-63

Macchariya 66
Mahāyāna: emergence of 118-22; significance of 122-25; notion of *Saṁsāra* 124; notion of *Nirvāṇa* 124; notion of *Bodhisattva* 125; notion of *bhakti* 121; metaphysical base of ethics in 131; exaltation of positive virtues in 128-30; compassion, central place of 140-41
Mahāsukha 147, 149
Makkhaliputta Gosāla 33, 35, 48, 50
Māna 65
Men, Classification of 70, 81-82, 102; ethical classification of 67-69
Mental properties (*cetasika*), moral and immoral 66-67
Mettā (*Maitri*) 83, 89, 95
Mind (*Citta*): nature of 85-87; functioning of 60-81; and objects of thought (in Mahāyāna) 131; notion of in Tantra 154; psychological states, ethical classification of 61-67
Moha 66
Morality: notion of 87; nature of 28-29; importance of 27-28; psychological basis of 54-55; moral procedure 76-77; moral progress, aid to 92-97
Muditā 95
Mudutā 66
Muni 4

Nāma-rūpa 22-23, 58
Nekkhamma 44
Nibbāna (*Nirvāṇa*) 20, 38, 68, 74, 129;

nature of 25-26
Niddha 66
Niganṭhanātaputta 33
Nivṛtti (quietism) 1

Ottappa 66

Pahāṇa 29
Pakudha kaccāyana 36
Pāramitās, notion and significance of 133-34; the six *Pāramitās* 134-40
Pārśvanātha 4
Parāvṛtti, idea of 129fn.
Path (*magga*, *paṭipadā*, Way): 26-30; eight-fold path (*aṭṭhaṅgika magga*) 27, 75, 89; as Middle Way 27, 89; *dukkhanirodhagāminī paṭipadā* 44; 78; *Kammanirodhagāminī paṭipadā* 44
Paṭigha 65
Pātimokkha-saṁvara-saṁvuto 84-85
Paṭisandhi 60
Patisandhiviññāṇa 39
Political ethics, Buddhist notion of 109-12; Aśokan model 112-17
Prajñā 28, 102, 128, 145; nature of 155-56; as *Pāramitā* 140
Prajñāpāramitā 130
Praṇidhāna 132
Pratītyasamutpāda (*paṭicca-samuppāda*) 20-21, 40, 56, 75, 168-69
Pravṛtti (activism) 1
Pṛthagjana (*puthujjana*) 16, 67, 74, 82, 102
Pūraṇa Kassapa 33, 36

Rationality, nature of, in Buddhist ethics 72-74
Ṛṣabhadeva 4
Ṛta 11, 16
Rūpakṣana 60

Saddhā 66
Sādhana-bheda 122
Sahaja, conception of 146-47
Sakadāgāmi 67-68
Sakkāyadiṭṭhi 59, 64
Samādhi 28, 30
Samarasa, as *sahaja* 146
Śamatha 139
Sammappadhānas 29
Sampaṭicchanna 61
Saṁsāra 38, 64, 129
Saṁvara 29
Saṁvrtti (phenomenality) 52-53
Saṁyojanāni (fetters) 64; ten fetters 65-66
Sandhābhāsā, explanation of 143-44fn.
Saṅgha, as the basis of social order 82-84
Sañjaya Belaṭṭhaputta 36
Santīraṇa 61
Sarvamukti 123
Sassatavāda 56, 75, 168
Sati (Mindfulness) 29, 66, 94
Sekhiya rules 99
Sikkhāpadas (ten) 89-92
Sīla (Śīla), *vāritta* and *cāritta* 78; *śīla*, *samādhi* and *prajñā* 28, 136; as *Pāramitā* 136-38
Sīlabbataparāmāsa 64, 66
Social order, Buddhist conception of 107-09
Society, conception of 100-01; social change, conception of 103-04
Sotāpatti 67
Spiritual seekers, Categories of 123fn.
Śramaṇa, connotation of 3; *Śramaṇa* movement, theory of class-affiliation,, refutation of 15-16; *Śramaṇa* tradition 2-6, and the *Upaniṣads* 5; contrast with vedic-Brahmanical beliefs 3, 30-31
St. Augustine 47fn.
Suffering (*Dukkha*), Origin of 20-22, 24-25; all pervasive character of 23; explanation of 24
Śūnyatā 130, 144-45

Tadārammaṇa 61
Takka 56, 156; *takkapariyāhataṁ* 56, 156
Taṇhā 21
Tantra, Buddhist and Brahmanical

144; Tantric ethics, theory and practice of 148-52; essence of 152-53
Ta'hāgatagarbha 129
Tathatā 129-30
Tatramajjhatā 66
Thina 66
Tilakkhaṇa 21
Trikāya, notion of 129

Ucchedavāda 75
Uddhacca 66
Ujukatā 67
Upaniṣads, philosophy and metaphysics of 13-14; ethico-spiritual legacy of 15-18; influence of (on Mahāyāna) 144
Upāya 145
Upāya-Kauśalya 122
Upekkhā 95-96
Vajra, Conception of 144
Vajrasattva 145-48
Vedic age: salient features of 6-14; religion in 10-11; Brāhmaṇa—Kṣatriya relationship in 9; Vedic ethics 12, 14-15
Vicikicchā 64-66
Vijñāna 59
Vīmaṁsānucaritaṁ 56, 156
Vipaśyana 139
Vīrya, as *Pāramitā* 139
Vīthi 61
Vīthicitta 61
Vīthimutta 60
Voṭṭhappana 61

Yadṛchāvāda 40
Yājñavalkya 17
Yatis 4
Yuganaddha 145, 149